AMERICAN
VAMPIRES

AMERICAN Vampires

Fans, Victims & Practitioners

NORINE DRESSER

W · W · Norton & Company · New York · London

Published simultaneously in Canada by Penguin Books Canada Ltd,
2801 John Street,
Markham, Ontario L3R 1B4
Printed in the United States of America.

The text of this book is composed in 10/13 Bembo,
with display type set in Bradley Outline and Linotext.
Composition and Manufacturing by The Maple-Vail Book Manufacturing Group.
Book design by Antonina Krass.

First Edition
Library of Congress Cataloging-in-Publication Data
Dresser, Norine.
American vampires : fans, victims, and practitioners / Norine
Dresser.—1st ed.
p.   cm.
Bibliography: p.
Includes index.
1. Vampires.   2. Folklore—North America.   I. Title.
GR830.V3D74   1989
398′.45—dc19   88–29062

ISBN 0-393-02678-7

W. W. Norton & Company, Inc., 500 Fifth Avenue, New York, N. Y. 10110
W. W. Norton & Company Ltd., 37 Great Russell Street, London WC1B 3NU
1 2 3 4 5 6 7 8 9 0

For Harold

Contents

"Gooood Eeebening"

I am a folklorist—someone from the academic world where the universe is like a pie, divided up into strangely carved slices. But most folklorists would agree, we've got the best part of the pie. We study the ways and reasons why humans celebrate; tell stories and jokes; heal themselves and others; sing, dance, and make music; create crafts and art; cook and eat food; play games.

We are also often called upon to illuminate some aspect of our field for the public. Specifically, I refer to the common practice of media persons contacting professional folklorists for information about holidays, customs, and beliefs to fill out an empty newspaper column, to use up some radio or television time, or to add spice to an ordinary story.

Most folklorists have had this experience. Over the years I have been contacted for opinions about hangover cures, Christmas rituals, Southeast Asian birthing practices, Valentine's Day, birthday celebrations in restaurants, cults, New Year's Eve traditions, and psychic phenomena. Once I was even called by an Italian reporter belatedly covering a Thanksgiving story in December for her Rome-based newspaper. She phoned to find out if I believed that the turkey had replaced the eagle as the American national bird.

Ordinarily, when such interviews take place I don't receive

much feedback, except from faithful friends and family members excited about my momentary publicity. However, in May 1985 there was a strikingly different kind of response to what started out as a typical telephone interview—this time by Lee Siegel, an Associated Press science writer. He called for a folklorist's evaluation of a presentation that had been made at a recent meeting of the American Association for the Advancement of Science. He asked for my assessment of Professor David Dolphin's hypothesis that blood-drinking vampires were, in fact, victims of porphyria, an incurable genetic disease. Over the phone Siegel read Professor Dolphin's correlations between the folklore of vampires and the symptoms of porphyria: a need for transfusions of a blood-based substance; a necessity to avoid sunlight; negative reactions to garlic. Initially I was excited to hear about these relationships. My response was that it was "wonderful" because it validated the notion that, contrary to popular opinion, folklore is often founded on truth. I had assumed that the disease to which Dr. Dolphin referred was historical and now obsolete.

The two sentences attributed to me in the Associated Press story were transmitted internationally. By my association with this story and my response to it, I was suddenly regarded as a vampire expert and a Dolphin supporter. I received a call from a filmmaker in Germany asking me to serve as a vampire consultant on a film he was writing. An Oklahoma City radio station telephoned and asked me to appear on a half-hour talk radio segment on vampires. I was also asked to write an article on vampires for a French magazine. A psychologist on the faculty of the Medical University of South Carolina contacted me about a case study of auto-vampirism, describing a patient of his who would masturbate and simultaneously cut into his carotid artery and drink his own blood. The Associated Press media coverage had unexpectedly plunged me into an investigation of vampires and they began to invade my life.

There is something about the vampire that promptly engages people's curiosity. I quickly became aware of this when, at the

outset of discussing this research, people responded with keen
interest. Whether I was phoning a costume shop or software
company, the respondents were so immediately captivated that
I always received attention and cooperation, and sometimes even
more than this. For example, while in New York I telephoned a
famous museum and spoke, without any personal referrals, to
an unknown librarian to inquire about graphics for my research.
Within the first few minutes of our conversation she invited me
to lunch so she could learn more about it.

While standing in a cheese shop telling an acquaintance about
the project, the clientele of the entire shop became silent as they
listened intently. This caused my observant friend to comment,
"I've never had the least interest in vampires, yet I'm fascinated.
Look at everyone else, too. The attention of this entire shop is
riveted on what you're saying."

This was not an isolated incident. A number of times while
riding in the elevator at California State University, Los Angeles, where I teach, and responding to colleagues' questions about
progress on my work, I have felt like the star entertainer for
other passengers en route to the sixth floor.

I met a friend for lunch in a restaurant one afternoon, during
which we exchanged the latest information on current involve-
ments. While I was describing the vampire project I observed a
party of five at an adjacent table finishing their meal, paying the
check, and leaving the premises. A few minutes later, two of the
group reentered the restaurant, came over to our booth, apologized for eavesdropping, and asked, "Is there such a thing as
vampires?"

As a folklorist for the past fifteen years, I have enjoyed the
excitement and enterprise in researching diverse topics that have
culminated in lectures and articles about jokes told in male gay
bars, entrepreneurial disposal of ash from Mount St. Helens,
humorous repartee exchanged by Jewish shoppers and sellers
across meat and delicatessen counters, and the tracking down of
a fifty-year-old rumor about a famous navy admiral whose picture was allegedly printed on a perforated page in the Annapolis

annual *The Lucky Bag*. However, the research involved with vampires was distinct in that it began to have almost a life of its own as it unreeled and drew me more deeply into the project.

Prior to these events, I had assumed erroneously that vampire lore was a thing of the past and that any center of vampire lore was to be found primarily in Eastern Europe. I had totally over-looked the potential significance of all the Dracula films and plays I had seen. I also had completely forgotten a pilgrimage I made over twenty years ago to see a faltering Bela Lugosi in the back room of a tawdry Las Vegas nightclub reenact his famous Drac-ula-about-to-attack-the-maiden scene. However, Dr. Dolphin's correlating of vampires and porphyria symptoms and its conse-quential effect on porphyria patients led me to inquire further into vampire beliefs in the United States, and I soon came to understand the indefensibility of my long-standing assumption that vampires belonged to the past, and to recognize that, as a folklorist, I had overlooked the fact that vampires are a signifi-cant phenomenon in contemporary American culture. I came to see that the old, scary, sometimes campy movie images set in Transylvania had been transplanted, translated, and trans-formed. The vampire symbol had begun to take on a new mean-ing and interpretation—evolving into something one could call the American vampire.

Varied methods of inquiry were utilized before reaching these conclusions. I developed and circulated three different forms of questionnaires. The 574 respondents who answered the student questionnaire about the attributes and reality of vampires came from many places across the United States and from thirty-four other countries as well. I also interviewed porphyria patients by mail and by phone from fourteen different states plus England. I received lengthy responses to a third questionnaire from vam-pire fans, including those who believe that they are vampires. Physicians and scientists from four states and five countries answered other inquiries. I corresponded with twenty-two heads of organizations and editors of small independent journals. I received phone calls from Germany, France, and Canada. I drove

110 miles to meet with one physician in Santa Barbara and flew 475 miles to meet with another physician and patients in San Francisco. I journeyed cross-country to New York to visit a fan club headquarters.

As is apparent, the data recorded and analyzed came from beyond the Los Angeles area where I live, representing opinions, experiences, and interpretations from all over the world. Most important, a large portion of additional data was taken from the media, thus revealing interests representative of the entire nation. Indeed, it is the media—radio, TV, movies, newspapers, magazines—that have largely shaped our folklore about the vampire today, altering the historical and Old World roots of belief.

Some colleagues wishing to play devil's advocate have asked, "How can you tell that your vampire informants aren't putting you on?" The answer is that there is no way I can tell for sure. Unlike the now almost apocryphal story of the folklorist of the mid-1930s diligently recording the song of black workers only to discover they were singing "White man settin' on wall, white man settin' on wall, white man settin' on wall all day long, wastin' his time, wastin' his time," I haven't yet found that my informants are playing with me. Thus I must believe them.

I have always operated under the assumption that informants usually tell the truth—that is, their truth, their interpretation of their own reality. While in this situation informants' claims may seem fanciful, I cannot discount them until I have evidence to do so. My belief is that they are honest in their statements about how they perceive themselves.

And if they were putting me on? How would that affect the research? Would it invalidate it? I don't think so. It would actually dramatize the significance of the vampire symbol. The desire of my informants to identify with these creatures would be so powerful that they actually invented symptoms, behavior, and stories to convince me of their condition.

And so the research adventure described in what follows illuminates the path that, like Dorothy's yellow brick road, led me through a new territory of ideas, encounters with a wondrous assortment of new friends and acquaintances, and ultimately altered my perspective about the culture in which we live. I didn't find the wizard at the end of my journey. I discovered the vampire, instead.

AMERICAN
VAMPIRES

Vampirism Today

Melody remembers that she was wearing a low-cut, hot-pink dress the first time she met Pam, the vampire. It was 1985 and Melody's friend Brad had arranged the meeting. "Pam's always looking for someone else. Would you be interested?"

The modest apartment filled with books and plants was located in an East Coast city and seemed almost secluded because of the quiet created by the well-insulated building. Four young people—Melody, twenty-five; the others in their early thirties—had gathered to participate in a practice they were not ashamed of, but were nonetheless wary of divulging to others, as revealed by the clothespin holding closed the orange drapes.

Pretty, blue-eyed, with long wavy dark brown hair, Pam was wearing an ankle-length, dark flower-print dress with spaghetti straps, partly covered by a black cape. She carefully arranged the setting. Turning off the lights, she lit a few candles and started playing a recording of sounds of a rain forest. "Come closer and watch," she invited Melody.

Brad was stretched out on the gold upholstered sofa. Pam kneeled over him as Melody sat on the floor next to them and leaned forward to catch every detail. First Pam massaged Brad's back and then once he became relaxed she began to sensuously lick the fingertips of his left hand.

Across the room, seated next to the computer, Pam's husband, an observer only, watched in a rather detached manner. As the act began, two cats nonchalantly paraded back and forth across the room.

Pam stabbed one of Brad's fingers with a sterilized hypodermic needle of a type normally used for animals. She pierced the skin, squeezed the finger, squeezed some more; then she sucked from it. When she finished one finger, she repeated the steps with the next one, licking each finger when she was finished.

To Melody, it all seemed quite mysterious, but she wasn't afraid. "I felt pretty good. I'm an adventurous person, so I do kind of crazy, off-the-wall things," she explained.

After spending about twenty minutes stabbing Brad's fingers and then sucking them, Pam turned to Melody and said, "Okay, you're next."

Thus began Melody's initiation into the act of vampirism, playing the role of donor for Pam's belief in her need for fresh, warm human blood.

The activities just described were freely and enthusiastically reported because Pam, Melody, and Brad have a curiosity about their own behavior. Admittedly, these young people are not representative of a large population. They are but a minute fraction of modern society. Their behavior is carried out in private, of their own volition, to the harm of no one, and for the purpose of satisfying certain inner needs, sometimes understood, other times not. In spite of the reality that they are imitating behavior not publicly sanctioned, they do not think of themselves as aberrant.

If you were to meet them they would not strike you as being strange in any way. They seem like ordinary people functioning positively in the external world with family commitments and responsible jobs. One of them is employed full time in the art world. Another holds a government position requiring knowledge of the sciences and well-developed problem-solving abilities. The third works in the medical field.

Yet this raises a few questions about why they are attracted to the act of vampirism, a behavior associated primarily with horror stories and movies. If they called themselves blood fetishists, it might be easier to comprehend, but they don't. Instead, they affiliate themselves with vampires. It is curious that they have chosen to emulate the behavior of fictional, exaggerated creatures who are generally looked upon with terror, abhorrence, even mockery. Here is a situation of life imitating folklore, but why?

The behavior of these three persons makes a statement about the power and vitality of the vampire symbol in this country, which apparently is not relegated to merely being part of left-over European legends, but is actually made viable and glorified by this tiny part of American culture.

Surely Melody, Brad, and Pam must interpret the vampire differently from the old stereotyped images portrayed by Bela Lugosi and Christopher Lee. Melody and Brad are not frantically waving a cross to frighten off the blood-sucking attacker, nor are they wearing garlic. Instead they appear to welcome the giving of their own life's vital force—their blood.

Traditionally, the vampire is a mythical creature believed to be a dead human who is doomed, unable to rest in peace and forced to leave the grave and feed upon the living by taking blood or vitality. Consequently, the act of taking another person's fluid or energy is called *vampirism*. Sometimes *psychic vampirism* is the term applied when one person takes energy and/or emotions from another. The vampire differs from the werewolf, the latter being a mythical live human who transforms into a wolf to attack the living. While there has never been any scientific evidence to indicate that these creatures are real, belief in them has existed from ancient times and throughout the world. The earliest known depiction of a vampire appears on a prehistoric Assyrian bowl showing a man copulating with a vampire.

Public awareness of the vampire became widespread in the

twentieth century after the emergence of the fictional character
Count Dracula, which was created by Irish author Bram Stoker
and in part based on historical accounts of a fifteenth-century
real Romanian tyrant, Vlad Tepes, also know as Vlad the Impaler.

American vampires have their basis in the Old World, but
have developed in a particular way, shaped by our uniquely
American forms of mass communication. American vampires
differ from European, African, Latin American, and Asian antecedents. Just as the English language spoken in the United States
has taken on its own unique characteristics, so, too, have the
vampires. They have developed a style of their own, a Yankee
style. American vampires are a powerful contemporary symbol,
affecting more lives than one might anticipate. Why is the vampire so potent here? He is an all-American guy.

What follows is a documentation of ways in which Americans
identify with and imitate the vampire's behavior. The intention
is to understand the vampires' place in our culture and to examine their impact on the lives of ordinary people.

After her first experience at being a donor, Melody became a
regular visitor to Pam for this purpose, sometimes seeing her
once a month or going as often as once a week. "I do it for my
own personal enjoyment. I mean, I have a very close and enjoyable friendship with Pam. Even if we didn't have this kind of
relationship, I'd still be friends with her, so I think this just brings
us closer." Melody and Pam have maintained this association for
over three years.

Melody has never concerned herself with wondering if there
was anything physically real about Pam's being a vampire. "It's
not for me to say. If Pam drinks blood and she says she's a vampire, who am I to say she's not? I don't have any evidence that
says she's not. I don't know any other requirements for being a
vampire, except if you drink blood, and she does."

However, Melody rejects the vampire label for herself, and
has never been a donor to anyone else. She has further discovered that it is wise not to let any boyfriends know about her

activities with Pam. Melody learned this the hard way. On several occasions in the past she thought she would be honest with the men she was romantically involved with and let them know about her relationship with Pam. "I just kind of mentioned it. I mean, I didn't mention any names, but it kind of scared a couple of them off." As a result, Melody now keeps her donor life a secret from potential suitors.

She admits that the exchange of blood is a sexual act. "Oh yes, I believe so." She revealed that her donor relationship with Pam has led, like a natural step, to other erotic acts. "It wasn't that way in the beginning, but I think it just aroused some feelings in Pam and she wanted to go on."

While Melody's involvement with real vampiric activity happened accidentally, as a result of her friendship with Brad, Brad's interest in vampirism had begun as a sexual fantasy when he was a teenager. Seeing the female vampire Angelique on TV going after men in the gothic soap opera "Dark Shadows" sexually excited him.

Brad said he has engaged in considerable introspection about his unusual interest and believes that it is related to his being victimized and psychologically abused by his parents when he was young. In the past he tried to understand his fantasy while undergoing psychotherapy, but his therapist tried to discourage him by saying there weren't people who really drank blood. "You've got to realize it's just a fantasy. Nobody can drink blood," the doctor argued. He even tried to convince Brad that it would be impossible to drink this warm, red body fluid. "I'd like to see you drink a glass of it sometime," he once challenged, according to Brad.

Articulate and an avid reader, Brad tried to explain that in other parts of the world people do drink blood, citing African tribes, among them the Masai, who drink cow's blood with milk. His therapist was disgusted to hear of such things, but this did not discourage Brad. It was a fantasy he was not willing to relinquish, so when he met Pam in 1984 through a network of "Dark

Shadows" fans, he was elated because Pam revealed she had previously experimented with vampirism and was interested in trying it with him.

At first he encouraged her to bite him. It was enjoyable, but painful, too. It was pleasurable in terms of his being able to finally live the fantasy in real life, and painful in the sense that it really hurt. Brad muses that his former therapist's eyes would have bulged at the scene.

While Pam obliged his fantasy needs at first by biting him, she prefers to prick the finger as a means of obtaining the blood. Eventually that became her most-used method with Brad and others as well. In addition, she has replaced the animal hypodermic needle with an Auto-Lancet, an over-the-counter drugstore device used by diabetics to prick their fingers for measuring blood-sugar levels. Pam claims that it is safe, clean, leaves no scars, and is practically painless. Its one drawback is that only drops of blood can be extracted, but for Pam that doesn't matter. She needs just a small amount at a time—one teaspoon to one tablespoon, she said.

Asked about the sexual aspects of his giving blood in such a manner, Brad described a kind of psychic bond that grew between him and Pam. He recalled being at home and, when thinking about her, that part of his neck where Pam had bitten him would suddenly start to ache and draw. Despite the intimacy they shared, he held his erotic impulses in check because he didn't want to get involved with a married woman, especially with the wife of someone he genuinely liked and respected, a man who tolerated his wife's peculiar habits.

For several years Brad donated his blood to Pam on a monthly basis. He has always thought of this act as a gentle, harmless fantasy. He allows for the sexual aspects and believes it is better than the golden showers (a euphemism for sexual partners urinating on each other) or mud sports (coprophilia) or "any of those other disgusting things that some of the more normal people in our society pursue with great affectation and delight."

Brad sees the vampiric bite as only a couple of steps beyond the love bite, a few degrees beyond the hickey. "It's nice when it's under the proper setting, when it's controlled." Yet, he warned about some of those "crazies" who take it and turn it into a perversion, such as sadomasochism. "That's not so hot. It's something you have to be careful about."

Pam's own vampiric practices became fixed five years ago when she encountered Kristin, who lives in another state. Kristin claims her need for blood to be one cup per week during winter and three-quarters to one and one-quarter pint per week during the summer. She doesn't get "high" on blood. Rather, it makes her feel energized, full of life, satisfied. Animal blood doesn't supply what she needs. She says that without warm human blood she becomes weakened or sick. Once she even ended up in the hospital needing a transfusion.

Kristin, also in her thirties, stated that she obtains blood from donors rather than victims, whom she describes as "Those who are forced to give." On the other hand, donors give willingly with or without an exchange of something, that is, sex, money, dinner. To find donors she usually avoids bars and picking up people. Instead, her friends find other friends, or she meets them at places such as bowling alleys, arcades, or occasionally in a library or at a park.

At times it is difficult to find donors. When the "hunger gets bad," she starts pacing. Sometimes she has to go to another town to find donors. "Explaining to someone of my need happens when the time is right. I sense it." She starts out talking about movies, then the occult, and from there she broaches the subject. "There have been times at the last minute people back out. I let them go. All is done willingly and with agreement not to tell."

Unlike Pam, Kristin prefers to bite her donors on the neck with her small, "fang-like" teeth. One of her donors describes it as being a pinch-like pain where penetration of the skin has occurred. Others say it feels like an injection. One former donor revealed that Kristin lacked tenderness and growled while she was biting him. That was frightening to him, even more so later when she explained that there was a panther inside her—a black cat. She felt that she was this black cat at certain times and didn't know whether she might rip a person apart. When the donor heard this, he decided never to give blood to her again.

Rarely does the bite mark leave a scar, but according to Kristin, people don't care anyway because they're proud of the marks. "They ask for more. Sometimes for the sake of getting bit. . . . It fulfills their fantasy!" Instead of biting she would prefer using syringe needles, but she reports that people are squeamish about needles. "I've used single-edge razor blades to cut the skin, but again I'm told they'd rather be bitten."

Kristin perceives of herself as having been born that way. She says that vampirism ran in her family, with only one or two per generation. She claims that as an infant she kept biting herself until she bled. When she was growing up, other schoolchildren teased her about her pallor. Bright sunlight hurt her eyes, and today she must wear sunglasses during the daylight. Although she has inherited her condition, she believes she can pass it on to others through her bite and transmission of something she refers to as a "V" cell. She "transfuses" varying "dosages" of the "V" cell to different donors. Feedings take place day or night, but she prefers darkness and must be alone with the donor. Some donors tell her they get turned on when bitten.

Kristin asserted that she is not a satanist, does not worship the devil, does not kill people or animals, and is not with any witch coven. She works "solo."

It was through Kristin that Pam believes she received the "V" cell, transmitted when Pam was initiated into the donor role for Kristin. This subsequently created Pam's need for donors, which began to manifest itself during a full moon about six months after Pam had first given blood to Kristin.

Pam describes physical changes she believes have taken place in her as a result of this "V" cell transfusion—a kind of itching and throbbing in the gums above her canine teeth, especially during the full and new moons when she has a craving. Pam says that hot weather increases the hunger. "It feels like little pinch-like sensations or a bite or a burning sort of feeling in the veins." Kristin, too, reports the same type of sensations, describing her veins as feeling like they are on fire during hot weather.

Pam's eyes now seem to be more sensitive to light and glare, and when she has the "hunger" they take on a more animal- or cat-like look. In fact, she claims that her husband is able to detect these changes and will say, "The cat's up,"or "Hey cat!" Pam says that the cat aspect of her comes out a lot, particularly when she and her husband make love. "It's like the beast gets excited or something. There's something there," she said in a puzzled manner. "Like it's not all me. Maybe it's possession," she speculated.

Pam doesn't quite understand the changes going on within her. She reports that ever since she has been giving and taking human blood she has stopped being plagued by canker sores. She doesn't comprehend why. In addition, she wonders whether or not her condition would ever be passed on to her child, if she were to have one.

She is not certain whether or not she has passed on the "V" cell to any of her donors, although she reports that some of them have noticed changes within themselves. For example, one of her female donors reports a "pressure" feeling over her canine teeth which is stimulated by exposure to sun and heat.

Because of the potential transmission of the AIDS virus through the exchange of blood, Pam is very concerned about her donors' health and asks them numerous personal questions before taking their blood. She is reluctant to take on too many donors or unknown ones, so now when her hunger is aroused and she has no one to meet her need, she substitutes by eating raw hamburger or cows' hearts, even taking blood from her husband or herself to satisfy the craving. In contrast, Kristin is less worried about AIDS and says she can "tell" when someone has good or bad blood. She doesn't seem to be concerned about risks to her health.

Since Pam has only been drinking human blood for a few years, she believes she could stop the habit, if necessary. However, at present she finds the feeding so emotionally and physically satisfying that she has no desire to discontinue the practice. She says that a few hours following a feeding her symptoms of need stop—her eyes become normal, and she sleeps well. It has a calming effect on her.

Here are two women who appear to take pleasure—even pride—in the act of vampirism and in calling themselves vampires. Neither of them seems to have any qualms about being associated with a creature who in the past was reviled. They seem not to be dealing with the notion that they will live forever, but rather to be applying the vampire name to themselves based primarily on their habits of drinking blood. There is no association whatsoever with the undead state—not being able to rest in peace—usually associated with vampires.

Kristin's and Pam's need to be associated with vampire behavior may be one way of gaining attention or giving themselves a sense of power. Perhaps it is just another way to create a stage where they can perform and star in front of a captive audience. It would take lengthy and psychoanalytic analysis to discover their motivations for the need and rewards of this unusual behavior—something beyond the ken of this study.

Brad mentioned that he did not enjoy feeling like a slave to the vampire. Instead he preferred being the recipient of unconditional love, his term for the way Pam treats him in his role as donor. Maybe this is related to the history of abuse by his parents, particularly by his mother, which he feels always restricted him to merely superficial relationships with women later in life. He recalls the *"Sturm und Drang"* of his adolescence and the anxiety he felt about relating to other women. This he ties directly to his attraction to the female vampire relationship.

On the other hand, Melody appears to be someone who merely enjoys sampling the variety of spices that life offers—someone who is very open and experimental in everything she does.

Jeanne Youngson, Ph.D., founder and president of the Count Dracula Fan Club, has been conducting interviews for over eleven years with people who have a need to drink blood and who think of themselves as either vampires or blood fetishists. While the act of drinking blood is the same for both vampires and blood fetishists, there is a difference in the way these people think of themselves. For some, being a vampire has a more romantic and sympathetic connotation. This label sets them apart from ordinary persons, making them more exotic by virtue of their blood-drinking habits. For others, the term *blood fetishism* is more scientific and satisfactory. Almost all of these blood drinkers have revealed a traumatic childhood, being victims of either abuse, neglect, abandonment, loneliness, or molestation. While Youngson has dealt with only a small statistical sample, the regularity of reports of a disturbed childhood background has made her hypothesize that there is a definite link between the need for blood and the need for a close, warm human connection.

She makes this generalization based on life histories that her informants write as well as on information elicited from a questionnaire that asks, for example, about the first blood-drinking experience, sexual experiences, and fantasies. In addition, she asks informants if their childhoods were happy, if they were ever molested, and if they believe that sexual abuse has contributed to their vampirism.

Sometimes she receives unsolicited letters from people involved with vampire life who are heard from only once, contacts who unmask their feelings to her, never to be heard from again, so she is never able to fill in important informational gaps. One such person was Belle, a woman who wrote, "I am a self-made vampire! Due to sheer boredom I have created an exciting personality out of a drudge and have never been happier!"

Belle divulged that no one knew about her hidden self, which made it that much more exciting. She carried out her concealed life by writing herself very long, sexy letters from a secret lover, an imaginary vampire called Malcolm. Sometimes when she left the house, she slipped those letters under the door, so that when she returned home she could find them and be "surprised."

She named her lover Malcolm after an uncle who always brought her presents as a child. He was tall, and in spite of his acne scars, she always thought he was good-looking. Unfortunately he was killed in an auto accident at the age of thirty-two. Ever since she has always liked men with acne scars.

Belle wrote of her husband that he was "a good man but not very romantic." He was a high school dropout, earning a living as a long-distance trucker. Belle's parents had been against their marriage, but in spite of this they were wed as soon as she was graduated from high school. Her own children now are married and have moved away.

For Belle, "being a vampire has opened up a whole new world for me." She describes herself as having her feelings easily hurt if her children don't write or send her a birthday card or come to visit as often as she wishes. Having another life unknown to others reduces her pain and lessens her need for attention from her family.

She is astonished by the realization that her fantasy life could make such a difference in her real life, but there was a time when she worried that she was going "bonkers." Because of this concern, she consulted a psychologist whose name was posted on her dentist's bulletin board. She made an appointment, spent fifty dollars, and told him about her private thoughts.

The psychologist was reassuring, said Belle. He convinced her that as long as she was aware that it was only make-believe, there was nothing to worry about. Belle now feels at ease with her fantasy world because it has provided an escape from drudgery, loneliness, and emotional neglect. It is unlikely that she will ever be heard from again.

Then there is Donna, who as a lonely youngster was introduced to blood drinking by her next-door neighbors, a German couple who gave the child the love and attention she missed from her parents. The husband was a butcher, and he would bring home packages of steak, drain the blood into a cup, and drink it.

This couple introduced the girl to the practice, and eventually she began to enjoy it. The early death of Donna's mother, a traumatic encounter with an exhibitionist, and an unhappy childhood stood in sharp contrast to the happy moments the girl spent with her neighbors, who eventually moved away. Now, as an adult, she associates drinking blood from meat with warm, nurturing memories of her neighbors and sexual fantasies about the butcher. Even though drinking blood from meat is not uncommon, nor is it an aberration, Donna considers herself a vampire.

Why she has decided to give herself this label is curious. When Youngson asked her to explain the difference between a blood fetishist and a vampire, Donna said, "A blood fetishist is somebody who is mentally sick and gets blood by illegal means. A vampire is somebody who likes to drink blood for reasons of his own." She explained, "I'm not too sure about these things, except that blood fetishist sounds like it has to be against the law. I don't feel as if I am breaking any laws with my blood drinking, and I do consider myself a vampire."

Andrew is another person who drinks cow's blood and thinks the habit qualifies him as a vampire. He reveals a tragic background. His parents were killed by a runaway truck that crashed through a diner where they were eating. Andrew was then sent to live with his uncle and aunt and their four children, but his aunt rejected him and was particularly perturbed by his bed-wetting habits. He felt humiliated when she made him wash out his soiled linens by hand in the barnyard trough and hang them on the clothesline. Sometimes they froze and he had to sleep in the hayloft.

One day a friend told him about the men in the slaughter-house who drank cow's blood, so he tried it. He made a small slit in the neck of a cow and drank its blood. To Andrew it was warm and nourishing and he felt stronger after drinking it. Years later when he saw the film *The Killing Fields,* which in one scene shows a prisoner of war drinking cow's blood, he was shocked and nearly "fell out of my seat!" This reawakened his memories and pain.

Another young man contacted Youngson. He thought he was Dracula and for that reason tried to remain indoors as much as possible. He limited his outdoor activities to nightime hours and during the summer would visit cemeteries and lie atop graves. He claimed that this was the only time he felt content. He practiced other vampire traditions—avoiding mirrors and garlic—and delighted in sucking his loosened teeth until his gums bled; then he swallowed the blood.

What is unique about this young man is that he is one of the few who has successfully rid himself of these habits through the use of psychotherapy. Today he attends one of the top East Coast universities. In retrospect, his former vampire activities may have been related to being left alone for long periods of time because of working parents. During his unsupervised hours he imaginatively decorated his bedroom to look like a tomb. His parents, pleased with his ability to amuse himself in a constructive manner while on his own, inadvertently encouraged his unusual interests and bizarre behavior by delighting in his handiwork.

Youngson told of another case involving one of her informants, who, because of her blood-drinking habits, thought of herself as a vampire, at least during her adolescence. Now she considers herself a blood fetishist. As a youngster, Rose had attended Catholic schools and had been impressed with pictures of Christ bleeding and being whipped and tortured. These images and the nuns' repeated message that Jesus loved them so much that he bled for humanity's salvation deeply affected this young woman.

Years after, when Rose became an elementary school teacher and the children injured themselves on the playground, she cleaned their wounds and saved the bloodied cotton, later sucking the blood from it. This habit was never discovered by anyone, but eventually she quit teaching and got a job in a factory employing many women who had strong beliefs in voodoo and witchcraft.

In this setting Rose was able to obtain blood by promising to work spells for other personnel in exchange for three drops of their blood, which they put on a clean piece of paper. Fortunately for this woman, most of what her fellow employees wished for was fulfilled, so she was able to have her blood goodies regularly, while her co-workers remained content.

According to Youngson, some informants have revealed inventive ways of obtaining blood. For example, one woman acquired it by raking her lovers' backs with her fingernails, then licking off the blood from the nails. This woman, who considers herself a "glamorous vampire," claims that most men love this habit and have told her that she is the greatest lover they ever had.

Then there is Deborah, a flight attendant with a major airline who has developed a need for human blood. She uses her boy-friend as her intermediary and source. The boyfriend works in a hospital blood bank. Twice a week he siphons fifty cubic centi-meters (about two tablespoons) from the hospital supplies. He does this by using a syringe and withdrawing twenty-five to thirty cubic centimeters of blood out of a five-hundred-cubic-centimeter container, transferring it into a small bottle which he carries to her in his pocket. He has never been caught and the amount he pilfers is enough to satisfy her. However, given the AIDS scare in relation to blood, it is possible they will discon-tinue this practice until such time that accurate hospital testing can be guaranteed.

Because people are reluctant to publicly admit to the practice of ingesting another person's blood and the numbers involved with this are so small, no statistics have been gathered regarding the direct hazards of contracting AIDS in this matter. However, there is indirect medical evidence to suggest that ingesting blood might be a risky procedure.

There have been several cases where health workers were splashed with AIDS-contaminated blood on cracks or rashes on the face. This resulted in their testing positive for the AIDS virus. In addition, there has been one recorded case of AIDS in a woman who had reported only oral intercourse, where she was a recip-ient of the semen, which also carries the virus. Therefore, oral contact was the method by which she contracted the disease. Furthermore, the lining of the mouth is similar to the lining of the rectal area and it is well known that there is increased risk of transmitting AIDS through rectal intercourse.

On the other hand, if AIDS-infected blood was ingested, once it moved down into the stomach the digestive enzymes would likely destroy the virus. Thus, the danger of getting AIDS from infected blood would come more from the hazard of contact with breaks in the skin of the mouth (including cold sores) or face, rather than from the chance of it getting into the blood-stream from the stomach. Consequently, a realistic fear of AIDS has affected the habits of those who think of themselves as vampires.

Dee, an Ohio woman who calls herself a vampire, says that she has almost completely stopped taking blood from people unless she's very familiar with their life-style. Now she obtains the blood she needs from raw beef steaks, which she prefers to pork (so as to avoid parasites) and chicken blood, which she considers to be "just plain disgusting." For Dee these substitutes seem cold; she misses the intimacy she felt when taking blood from another living being.

One last self-labeled vampire from Youngson's file is a man who calls himself a "metaphoric vampire" because he engages in illegal business practices. "If the people I con are suckers (no pun intended), they deserve to be 'bled.' " He claims no conscience as far as women are concerned: "Females are such gullible dears. I date only the beautiful—flight attendants, models, showgirls. The younger the better."

He has deliberately extinguished all feeling toward his fellow human beings. He does not care if there are earthquakes and thousands die. He does not care if foreign countries blow each other to bits. He does not care if a person in the next apartment is murdered or the homeless freeze to death by the millions. He just doesn't care.

He excuses his behavior. "Allow me to point out that I am no worse than the average man. I believe we are all vampires in one way or another. Show me the person who will *really* inconvenience himself to help a stranger, and I'll show you a non-vampire."

This man's outlook is unlike most others who identify with

the vampire. He does not seek closeness or intimacy. Rather, he seeks revenge and he desires to be the cool taker of whatever advantage he can gain over others. For him, being a vampire brings power and control. He seems to hold his fellow man in contempt.

There is another group of persons who identify with the vampire in a different way, who think of themselves as outside the schema of contemporary vampire phenomena. These are members of the Order of the Vampyre, a special-interest division within the Temple of Set, which evolved from the closing of Anton Szandor LaVey's Church of Satan.

LaVey had attempted to bring respectability to the Church of Satan and at the height of his religious career was a media celebrity, appearing on the Johnny Carson show and in national magazines. His professional background included being an oboist in the San Francisco Ballet Orchestra, an assistant lion trainer in the Clyde Beatty Circus, a nightclub organist, and a police photographer. Along the way he developed an interest in the occult, and became a collector of books on the topic that led to his creation of a Magic Circle study group.

This was the genesis of his San Franciso-based Church of Satan, which he founded in 1966 and which became famous for its colorful black masses open only to Church of Satan members in good standing featuring a live naked woman posing as an altar to symbolize the pleasures of the flesh, an important tenet of the church.

LaVey's goal was to encourage the study of the black arts and repudiate what he saw as the religious hypocrisy of conventional society. However, LaVey's church closed in 1975 when many of its members resigned to form a new organization, the Temple of Set.

Setians value both individualism and self-actualization. For those who have risen to qualify for the Order of the Vampyre (OV), their goal is to become acquainted with the characteristics of the Vampyric Being. They do not use blood in any manner, nor do they identify with the undead state. Instead they look at some of the alleged powers of the vampire creature, seeking the essence behind the myth, the noble quality of the archetype—elegance, sophistication, and charm—as personified by the Count Saint-Germain vampire figure in Chelsea Quinn Yarbro's novel *Hotel Transylvania*. In Yarbro's work, the Count is loosely based on a mysterious, eighteenth-century historical figure who practices alchemy, has a passion for diamonds, and is conspicuous in his fine-quality black-and-white clothes.

Recognizing that the real Vampyre can be hideous, the OV acknowledges that it can be glamourous as well and encourages learning the skill of applying cosmetics, using their voices effectively, and acquiring methods of holding another person's gaze. One of their co-Grand Masters is Lilith Aquino (no relation to the president of the Philippines). Her attractive appearance—red dress contrasting with well-made-up fair complexion and striking black hair—during an interview on the Oprah Winfrey television show gave testimony to the skillfulness she has acquired, serving well as a role model for other members of the OV.

Development of the powers of imagination, visualization, and invisibility is encouraged in this order along with the use and study of art, music, and literature. It is clear that despite their name, these Vampyres have a different agenda from the other vampires already described. Perhaps that is one of the reasons they have chosen to spell their name differently, which also helps to maintain their sense of mystery.

Since most of the OV information is never made public, the number of members remains unknown. All they will reveal is that they have been in existence for several years, that the membership comprises roughly a little over a third of the Temple membership (also an unknown figure), and that male and female members are equal in number. The OV meets during the Temple's annual International Conclave in places like Las Vagas, New Orleans, Toronto. During these meetings, Setians from all over the world gather for a week of social and magical events. That is when the OV has its formal meeting as well as its ceremonial Ritual Workings. Outside of these yearly gatherings, church members do not congregate on a regular basis. They claim that their deliberately individualistic atmosphere is not easily conducive to group activities on a routine or programmed basis and proudly point out that they are not a congregation of docile followers—only cooperative philosophers and magicians. As a result, members of the Order of the Vampyre communicate with one another primarily through their newsletters *Nightwing* and *The Vampyre Papers.*

Ironically, the Temple of Set deplores other kinds of vampires, called psychic vampires. This idea is based upon a passage found in Anton LaVey's *The Satanic Bible,* which describes psychic vampires as persons who make you feel guilty if you don't do favors for them—those who, like leeches, drain others of their energy and emotions.

Advising that you should not waste your time with these people because they can destroy you, LaVey gives concrete advice about avoiding their clutches. In the "General Information and Admission Policies" of the Temple of Set, there is also a negative reference to psychic vampires, referred to as those who wish to partake of the Church of Satan without making a personal commitment to it, to enjoy aspects of the philosophy without contributing. They cite those persons who "continued to vampirize the Church indefinitely," ultimately contributing to its demise. In spite of his warnings and advice to others, LaVey himself was unable to control this phenomenon under his own organizational roof.

Setians are firm in their desire to prevent this from happening to them. They will not tolerate psychic vampires in their organization, promising that if they were inadvertently to become members, once identified, they would be asked to leave.

The Temple of Set is currently headed by Lilith's husband, Michael A. Aquino, Ph.D., a controversial figure by virtue of his unusual looks—inverted v-shaped eyebrows, Friar Tuck hairdo, round face, and dark robe garb—and his occupation. He is a Vietnam War–decorated lieutenant colonel in the U.S. Army, now on active reserve, working in military intelligence as a psychological warfare officer, and holding security clearance for top-secret information.

In his appearance with his wife on Oprah Winfrey's show, Aquino mentioned his military occupation, defended the Temple of Set from those who would link it with more sinister satanic groups, and agreed that his unique appearance probably served as the model for one of the actors in *The Omen* series of movies.

According to an army public affairs officer in Washington, Aquino's satanic practices are protected by his constitutional freedom of religion. Furthermore, his record shows that he is trustworthy and capable.

The term "psychic vampire" is used outside the Temple of Set but with different connotations. Stefan, another self-proclaimed vampire who volunteered information, is in his early fifties. He was born and raised in a Polish neighborhood in a small Pennsylvania town where his parents ran a mom-and-pop grocery store located across the street from their house.

As a youngster Stefan had many responsibilities—taking care of his beautiful younger sister, whom he adored; translating for his parents, who spoke little English; cooking; and performing household duties. At Catholic school the nuns made painful innuendos about his delicate looks and high-strung personality, calling him by female names—Anna and Marya. In spite of his preference to play with girls more than boys, Stefan was an avid sports fan and attended all the high school football and baseball games.

A traumatic event shook Stefan's life when his sister was four. She was hit by a car while chasing a ball into the street. At the time of the accident, Stefan was at a baseball game, so on his way home when he saw blood on the road near his home, he was unaware that it was hers.

Stefan and his family fervidly prayed for the injured child during the days she spent on the critical list. "It was a terrible time for all of us until we found out she would live," he recalls with anguish.

"The worst part was that the blood stayed on the street for days afterward," he remembers. He tells of being haunted by the accident and having recurring dreams in which she was hit over and over and over again. There was always a lot of blood in these dreams, which were in vivid color.

Stefan admits feeling guilty and responsible for the accident. He believes that if he had gone straight home from school instead of going to the baseball game, he would have been watching her and would have been able to prevent her from running into the street. To punish himself, he obtained some switches and began beating his legs until the blood ran. He did this off and on for the next several years, whenever his sister got cranky, which she often did. According to her brother, the little girl changed dramatically once she came home from the hospital. She was no longer the darling child she had been before the accident. She was touchy and flew off the handle at the slightest provocation.

The next years were equally difficult for Stefan. His mother had a heart attack, his father closed the store to be with her in the hospital, and his sister went to live with an aunt. During the time the boy was alone in the house he discovered a large jar hidden in the back of a closet. It contained a male fetus, which Stefan described.

"Its eyes were closed and its little fists were clenched tightly as if in anger. . . . I knew immediately that it was my twin brother."

No one had ever told him that he was a twin. All he knew was that he was born at home in his parents' bed, yet instinctively he had always felt that a part of him was missing.

> Sometimes when I'd be walking down the street I would feel there should be someone walking beside me. I got the same feeling when I went to the movies and there was an empty seat next to me. I had always felt the "absence of a presence."

In spite of Stefan's intuition that there was a part of him that was lacking, finding the fetus was a terrible shock. At the same time he describes the discovery as being a form of relief as well. He returned the jar to the closet and since that day, he never again had the feeling of incompleteness because "I knew where he was."

After this time he began experiencing great anxiety and decided to experiment with relaxation exercises and ESP. He read books about psychic phenomena and tried sending mental messages to people while they slept. He was quite successful with his sister.

However, Stefan was still having the "blood dreams." Now they involved his kneeling down in the street and licking up his sister's blood. He also continued to beat his legs with a switch, only now he licked the blood off after he was finished. This caused feelings of faintness and lightheadedness.

Stefan describes his first venture as a psychic vampire. One day at a bus station he noticed a blonde, sixteen-year-old girl asleep on a bench. He sat down across from her and tried his first out-of-body experiment. He concentrated on floating up and over to her and sucking blood from her neck.

After a few minutes she woke with a start and glared at him. This convinced Stefan that he had succeeded. "I was a successful psychic vampire!" Immediately he felt free of anxiety and remained that way for nearly a week.

Stefan's experience is the reverse of most psychic vampirism cases, which are usually reported from the point of view of the "victim" who feels depleted or sapped of his or her strength and emotions. In this situation there is no way to know what Stefan's "victim" experienced or thought.

Stefan continued his experiments on people napping in other public places: parks, libraries, and once in a dentist's waiting room. He claims that he always felt relaxed and somehow superior afterward. At this time in his life he worked in a diner, but still lived at home.

The turning point in Stefan's life came when he met a young hunchbacked woman at a Protestant church service. She befriended him and said she sensed a deep unhappiness within him. Eventually he told her of his "shameful secrets." Stefan believes that this friend, who as a disabled person had also known great suffering, provided him with deep understanding. With her help he managed to stop his self-destructive habits and eventually pulled himself together both mentally and physically, so that today he is able to live on his own and run his own small diner.

Stefan's story seems to have a happy ending. For him, being a psychic vampire brought relief from the gnawing feelings resulting from a lifetime accumulation of pitiable events and scars. The vampiric act provided him with a closeness which he had felt lacking all his life. From an outsider's point of view, Stefan had no physical closeness with his victims. Yet, his perceived ability to psychically extract some essence from another human being filled the void caused by the many losses he suffered—lack of attention from his overworked parents, little respect from the nuns, the death of his twin brother, and lack of comradeship from other male friends.

Stefan also regrets never having instigated a sexual relationship with his understanding woman friend, his "savior." "I'm afraid that at the time, I was not able to cope with her physical disability."

Today he is still alone and celibate, but accepting of himself.

Other individuals have taken on the identity of the vampire, but with other outcomes. For example, in Ft. Lauderdale, Florida, in 1977, a man six feet four inches tall with long hair was terrorizing children and adults at two local elementary schools, one middle school, and a high school. Wearing a cape and fangs, he would run up to the students and spread his arms wide. The children ran home crying. Reports said local officials' "blood was boiling!"

A similar prankster intermittently harassed a family in the Seattle area. According to police spokesperson JoAnn Cratty, he had a vampire scar and wore heavy makeup, a cape, and black clothes. His victims described him as being young, tall, and slender and driving a black vehicle—on one occasion, a hearse. He merely smiled and escaped into the night. Ms. Cratty said the visits came at irregular times and did not seem to coincide with symbolic occasions, such as Halloween or a full moon. But they were always at night.

Pranksters dressed as vampires are not unique to the United States. They have also been found in Yugoslavia, where vampire impersonators harassed villagers and vandalized villages many years ago. In one incident some men used vampire cloaks for love trysts with young women, while in another an inventive lover dressed as a vampire to frighten away inquisitive neighbors while he carried on a three-month affair with a widow.

Other instances in which people dress or behave as vampires have been recorded. In 1985, a self-proclaimed vampire, proposed to help the Missouri Tigers College football team beat the California Golden Bears. In painted white face highlighted with purple veins, wearing slicked-back black hair, fanged teeth, black-and-red cape, and carrying a walking stick, he handed Coach Woody Widenhofer a business card identifying himself as a "vampire for hire with five hundred and eight years' experience."

The vampire offered to put a Romanian curse on the Tigers' opposing team free of charge, in the form of a hex on the goal line so they would not be able to score. He was concerned that if the Tigers did not take up his offer the team would lose again, which Vladimir considered tragic. He boasted, "Once put hex on ship. I think they call it *Titanic*. It would not let Dracula on board." The Tigers refused the vampire's offer. They lost.

On April 2, 1981, the Associated Press ran a story datelined Mineral Point, Wisconsin, where a police officer making rounds through the Graceland Cemetery, spotted a six foot three inch tall "ugly person" with a white-painted face wearing a dark cape. After encountering Officer Pepper among the gravestones, the man disappeared. Following the filing of this report, there was a rash of creepy white-faced vampire pranksters jumping out and scaring people on the streets of the downtown area the following night.

The police were not eager to return to the cemetery either. A senior official reported, "I can't get anyone to go back to the cemetery at night. I even offered to pay [the officer] overtime to stake the place out for his vampire, but he wouldn't bite."

All examples given thus far seem to indicate that those persons who attempt to emulate the behavior of the vampire are doing so because of the power it gives—allowing one person to manipulate another both physically and/or emotionally—as exemplified by the behavior of the pranksters who terrorized unsuspecting strangers, by the metaphoric vampire who looked down on others, and by Stefan, too, who talked about feeling superior to his victims after a "successful" psychic vampire act. Power is clearly the motivating attraction for members of Order of the Vampyre as well.

Fulfilling a need for intimacy is also revealed as a reason for informants' unusual life-styles. Certainly Brad, Donna (who attached herself to her kind neighbors), orphaned Andrew, Dee, Belle, and the boy who laid on tombs all disclose a lack of closeness and a neediness for human connections. For some, like Pam, Melody, and Brad, the physically close relationship can also be an erotic act.

The taking on of the vampire persona seems to satisfy a need for exhibitionism or to serve as an attention-getting device. It makes one different from others. Certainly acting like a vampire qualifies for making a person "stand out in the crowd." Based on what these examples reveal, the vampire provides glamour and an escape from the humdrum life.

So far no one in the illustrations just given has been hurt. On the other hand, a vampire incident with a tragic consequence took place in Parma, Ohio, on November 1, 1981. A man dressed as a vampire for a Halloween party died after accidentally stabbing himself in the chest with a knife. In an attempt to make it appear that he had a stake in his heart, twenty-three-year-old Ernest A. Pecek drove a pointed, very sharp, double-edged knife into a pine board taped to his chest.

Police are uncertain about what happened, but they have labeled it an accident. Pecek either forced the knife into his chest accidentally with a hammer as he was pounding the knife into the board, or he perhaps fell with the apparatus in place. The victim's landlady said he was able to get upstairs from the basement, but collapsed before he could tell her what happened.

There have been other tragedies associated with vampiric activity. On February 12, 1988, a fourteen-year-old girl in a small southern town placed a gun in her mouth and killed herself. Stories circulated that she had been a heavy metal music fan and that she belonged to a satanic cult. When spokespersons were asked if the child also had been involved with drug use, no definitive answer was given. However, it was known that at age thirteen this girl had seen the movie *The Lost Boys* many times and had been intrigued by what she viewed as the attractive life-style of the movie's four vampire teenagers, who wore long, bleached hair, earrings, leather, and metal.

In the film, these "lost boys" roared about at night on motorbikes terrorizing their town of Santa Carla, "murder capital of the world," by kidnapping and killing the locals. (One month later, in Sauk Rapids–St. Cloud, Minnesota, *The Lost Boys* was again cited as a source of inspiration, this time for the gruesome murder of a thirty-year-old vagrant by three teenagers who licked the victim's blood off their hands after they beat and stabbed him to death. The sheriff proclaimed that one of the boys cited the *Lost Boys* video as the source of his interest in vampirism. Subsequently some videotape shops in the area removed the film from their shelves, while others reported an increase in rentals.)

Rumor had it that the girl wrote a letter to her cousin explaining her suicide motive. Verification of the contents of the note has been impossible because the police are withholding this evidence. However, as the story goes, and as it rapidly circulated through the town of 37,000 inhabitants, the girl promised to return to her school reincarnated as "Samantha the Vampire," on Monday, February 29, Leap Year's Day, to "get" some of her friends and bring them back with her as vampires. According to one person, she would be doing these friends a favor by having them join her in a better way of life. Some versions of the story claim that she had prepared a hit list of twenty-five fellow students she intended to kill. Although the police held back the letter, a report in the local paper stated that a minister had shown the alleged letter to the principal of the school which she attended, and he verified that the note did contain references to vampires.

The suicide and subsequent rumors that flew through the community caused pandemonium at the school, where some children delighted in sneaking up behind their classmates, grabbing them, and saying, "He's going to get you!" or "You're one of the ones!" or "The vampire's going to get you!"

Underlying and long-term fears of satanic cults were renewed among both parents and children. Because the town was located in the Bible Belt, where the population believes in predestination, where the teaching of Revelations occurs in local churches, and where local graffiti consist of "Satan Lives!" and "Satan Rules!" the vampire satanic cult issues immediately became intertwined.

During the time period between the girl's death and her threatened return, some students wore clothes bearing satanic symbols, such as the inverted cross and pentagrams. Other children wrote 666 (the symbol of the devil) on their hands. This behavior spread to another school where girls used their mascara brushes to paint 666 on bathroom walls.

The school started a crisis intervention program, beginning the first day of classes after the girl's death. Between sixty and seventy-five at risk students—friends of the dead girl, as well as teenagers previously identified as potential suicides—were brought in for counseling sessions with the school system's mental health professionals.

School officials contacted the parents of the at-risk students, giving advice and requesting that they watch their children carefully. The local police chief urged parents to keep their children in school on the targeted date as a way to discourage the other children's fears. Furthermore, students were warned that anyone bringing weapons to school on that day would be arrested and that the principal would personally press charges against them.

The Friday before Samantha's predicted reappearance, school administrators held an assembly to encourage attendance the next Monday. They assured students that there would be a police officer on duty all that day. By the time Monday arrived, rumors and fear had spread to other schools in the area, and police officers were stationed at all the middle schools in the school system.

What is significant and horrifying is that this girl apparently desired to be a vampire, fantasizing that she would be able to return, in the legendary fashion, to convert others to her state. It appears that she saw this behavior as being an improvement over her experiences of real life. Was ordinary life for this fourteen-year-old that hopeless, that difficult, that colorless, that she had to resort to this dramatic act? What qualities of these fictional creatures provided her with a solution to her problems?

Some mental health experts suggest that children's suicides more generally reflect family situations where great communication barriers exist.

Certainly a community health professional is in a better position to interpret the tragedy than a folklorist. However, what cannot be ignored is that on the day of her threatened return as "Samantha the Vampire" 225 children stayed home from school, representing a 25 percent absentee rate, as opposed to the normal rate of only 7 or 8 percent. The sentiment conveyed by some parents was, "Yeah, I'm taking my kid out of school. These chain-wielding, bat-carrying people at school will never hurt my baby."

While it is impossible to assess the motivation of each family's decision to keep their children at home, implicit in this act was some belief that their children's welfare was threatened. Once the word "vampire" was introduced into the community tragedy, an unpredictable wild card came into play and many parents, understandably, wished to take no chances of their children being hurt or frightened or becoming victims of some mentally unbalanced person desiring to take advantage of the situation.

It may not have been a wholehearted fear of vampires. Perhaps a "just-in-case" attitude was behind their decisions. On the other hand, we can't totally rule out the possibility that for some of the parents and children, vampires can and do exist. Beliefs in vampires as real entities might seem anachronistic in today's high-tech and scientifically aware society, but, surprisingly, there are pockets of belief in this unreal creature.

Blood Is Thicker . . .

"'**V**AMPIRE' FAILS TO MAKE APPEARANCE." This newspaper headline was the follow-up to the anticipated and dreaded return of "Samantha the Vampire." The principal tried to downplay the significant absentee rate by saying he would prefer that attention be directed to the 675 students who came to school on Monday. One student who did show up was reported as saying, "Ain't nothing gonna happen. This is just a bunch of bull mess." Another student made a more sensitive observation. She said, "Everybody was walkin' on eggshells and some dude carried a cross."

When no unusual incidents occurred, an administrator stated emphatically, "When it was over Monday, it was over." He seemed certain that worries had been put to rest. Yet the mental health official who was interviewed took a slightly different position, believing that it wasn't a completely closed issue. He also conceded the possibility that in four years, on the next Leap Year's Day, the story and fear of Samantha's threatened return could be reactivated, especially if media attention was focused on this anniversary date.

While some might scoff at the idea that anyone today could believe in vampires, this incident demonstrates that belief in supernatural entities, particularly evil ones, has the potential to affect behavior. This episode reveals that there is a possible acceptance of the idea lurking in people's minds despite the lack of scientific evidence proving that a human being can return from the dead to carry others back to the grave.

Contemporary American acceptance of the vampire has evolved over time, built upon a foundation of prior beliefs in the supernatural brought here by immigrants from all parts of the world. In their introduction to *The Occult in America,* Howard Kerr and Charles Crow point out that such beliefs have been found everywhere. They state that the early colonists brought with them fear of witchcraft and beliefs in astrology, palmistry, and magical healing. They assert that occult religion—beliefs and practices which differed from those of the world's major religions—was a part of the backgrounds of black slaves as well, with parallel ideas found among some white elites. European settlers—both the learned and common folk—believed in hags, demons, ghouls, and specters.

Almost every culture has in its stockpile of mythic characters those who return from the dead to conceivably do mischief or harm. They may be called ghosts (returning spirits of the dead who can be benign or malevolent), zombies (humans in a death-like state who are recovered from the cemetery to work among the living), or vampires (the undead who attack the living). These have been imported here, too, with the polyglot of newcomers who settled in America. In addition, the original settlers of this land, Native Americans, had analogous beliefs. There is an Ojibwa legend of a ghostly man-eater and a Cherokee belief in witches and wizards who thrive and fatten upon the livers of exhumed murder victims. These evil spirits invisibly gather around the bedside of any desperately ill tribe member to torment him or her. They sometimes go so far as to remove the person from bed, lifting him up and dashing him into the ground until dead. After burial these vicious spirits dig up the body and feed upon the liver to avoid death and to lengthen their own "lives."

In some parts of the world there is the belief that the ghosts of persons who have just died might like to take a companion with them to the world of the dead. Generally it is surviving relatives who are candidates for this trip. However, it is possible to out-wit these ghosts by creating a dummy or effigy to fool them into thinking it is the real person they have taken.

A good example of this comes from Tahiti, where in the past the priest would place pieces of leaves on the chest and under the arms of the deceased. Then he would incant:

> There are your family. There is your child. There is your wife. There is your father, and there is your mother. Be satisfied yonder [that is, in the world of spirits]. Look not towards those who are left in the world.

Through this act and with these words the ghost is tricked into a state of eternal rest and his relatives can rest easy here on earth.

In *The Serpent and the Rainbow,* Harvard-trained ethnobotanist Wade Davis writes of zombies, a different form of the living dead. He documents a number of cases in Haiti including one about a sixty-year-old woman who was killed over a land dis-pute in 1966, but was found wandering in her home village four-teen years later. He also tells of a thirty-year-old woman who was killed by her husband and declared dead by the local official, yet her mother found her alive three years afterward. These are only two of many examples he gives of individuals who were declared officially dead, were buried, and yet were discovered to be alive years later. Davis's studies, which are widely accepted, indicate that zombification is caused by a chemical substance, called "zombie poison" by the locals, administered as a part of voodoo ritual. In the case of zombies, there appears to be an explanation for these living dead. With vampires, there is no reality to their undead state.

European history is filled with events demonstrating a fascination with and an abhorrence of vampires. In 1732 fourteen books were published on the subject of vampirism in Germany alone. During the eighteenth century "outbreaks" of vampirism were said to occur periodically, with one of the best documented taking place near Belgrade in Medeugna, Yugoslavia, in 1732. Signed records by three army surgeons and two other officers sent into the area testify to the exhumation of bodies that were gorged with new blood, which according to the tradition of the time was considered "proof" of the vampire state.

This Yugoslavian incident revolved around a young man, Arnola Paole, who had confessed to his wife that as a soldier stationed in Greece he had killed a vampire. Frightened, he had resigned from the military and returned to his village but was plagued with foreboding. One day he fell from his wagon and died.

After a few weeks, a number of villagers claimed great feelings of exhaustion and declared that Paole had appeared to them. When some of these villagers died, the other town members became terrified and it was decided that Paole's body should be exhumed to find out whether or not he was a vampire.

Sure enough, when the coffin was opened the corpse was there with lips still wet with fresh blood. Local custom required that in order to terminate the vampire's activities the body had to be staked through the heart, and as the report reveals, when this was done a shriek emanated from the corpse, which simultaneously emitted jets of blood as the stake was driven through. Paole's victims were also staked as a preventive measure and all were burned.

Six years later, after more misfortune befell the village, twelve more bodies were exhumed and deemed to be vampires because their bodies were in a nondecomposed, fresh state. They, too, were staked and burned.

The vampire's presence has been with us for centuries, going back to a vampire theme contained in the legend of Gilgamesh, a Sumerian hero representing the sun who battles two lions, interpreted to be the powers of darkness. Vampire themes are also found in ancient Indian, Mexican, and Latin American writings, where vampires were thought to be women who had died in their first labor.

A Chinese vampire is found as early as the T'ang Dynasty, and in Europe vampire tales became popular in the twelfth century, affecting vampire legends of Indian, Celtic, and Arabic sources. It is possible that the vampire theme may have reached Western Europe through Turkey and the Balkans by way of India. Modern sources exist today in Malaya, Indochina, India, Africa, and South America.

Vampire descriptions, causes, kinds of misdeeds, forms of protection against them, and modes for doing away with them vary from culture to culture. Vampires often serve as a convenient explanation for crop failure and storms, death of livestock, milkless cows, or any other tragedy striking a home or village.

In Romanian villages beliefs in vampires can serve as a bond uniting and stabilizing the community. Signs of the vampire's presence mean that villagers have not been following the code for social behavior. For example, vampires provide the explanation for the occurrence of certain anomalies (children born with a tail or with a caul) thought to be avoidable if villagers had only observed religious customs more carefully, particularly those related to birth and death.

Through time there has been documentation regarding physical characteristics of persons accused of being vampires. These bodies were taken from graves, examined, and their conditions commented upon. The reports do not mention pallor; instead, the color of the bodies has been described as ruddy, red, dark, black, or purplish. Contrary to contemporary depictions, in the past the pointed tongue was more commonly considered the tool of attack, no doubt inspired by the appearance of exhumed corpses which, due to the natural process of decomposition, generally revealed bloated faces and protruding tongues rather than sharpened canine teeth. In historical accounts fangs are almost never cited. There are only two examples where teeth have been noted as part of the observation of exhumed bodies said to be vampires. This may be due to an illusion caused by the receding of the gums on a skull that has become mummified, causing the teeth to look longer.

Although characteristics and descriptions of vampires may differ according to time and place, the one aspect that has remained consistent throughout history and across cultures is that vampires are dead creatures who feed upon the living by taking blood, vitality, or energy.

The heartland of vampire beliefs over the last few centuries has been concentrated among the Slavic people of Eastern Europe. However, ideas about vampires are extensive and have spread to and developed unique characteristics in Greece, Albania, Romania, China, Malaya, Indonesia, and India.

In Indonesia the vampire is in the form of a woman with long hair and nails who has a hollow on her back. She has been cursed and her soul rejected by God because she committed suicide after being raped and impregnated by "rascals." Vengefully she floats in a long white dress searching for male victims, desiring to suck their blood. She appears at night near the *asam* tree, or on bends of the road. In traditional accounts, when she encounters a man she seduces him, bringing him to a place which appears to be beautiful at night but in the light of day turns out to be a tomb. Similarly, at night she is beautiful, but when her victim sees her in the morning she is hideous. In contemporary media–affected variations of the story, she will often seduce husbands and then impregnate their wives, who subsequently give birth to maggots or snakes.

This Javanese *sundal bolong* (hollowed bitch) figure is very reminiscent of the Mexican legend of another avenging woman, *La Llorona,* the weeping woman dressed in white who is doomed to search eternally for children as punishment for killing her own children (usually said to be by drowning). When she finds them she harms them or kills them. Sometimes she, too, plays the seductress, seeking men as her murder victims. Though the first New World stories about her were noted as far back as the sixteenth century, tales of her adventures can be found in any schoolyard today in Mexico and in the United States where children of Mexican background congregate. With *La Llorona* there is usually no reference to blood sucking.

Akin to this evil female entity is the thirteenth-century Hebrew *estrie,* a vampire who preyed on little children, sometimes eating grown-ups, too. She could fly about at night and change her form. One legend about her recounts that when she once was ill one of two women attending her fell asleep, at which time the *estrie* tried to attack her to suck her blood. However, the woman awoke and she and her companion were able to overpower the *estrie,* who was unable to obtain the desired blood. Consequently, she died, for that is the only way these creatures survive—on human blood. When one of these entities is being buried and her mouth is open, it means that she will continue her vampiristic activities for another twelve months. The only way to prevent this from happening is to fill her mouth with earth.

Vampire variations abound. In the West African country of Nigeria, among the Ibibio people, vampire ideas are intertwined with beliefs in witchcraft. Here the victim's soul is removed and transformed into a goat, sheep, or cow. The sufferer begins to slowly waste away and when the animal containing the soul is unknowingly slaughtered and eaten, the victim instantly dies.

The Togolese of West Africa also tie witches to vampires. Some of them believe that witches can ride on the backs of animals, transform themselves into animals, and make themselves invisible. Some tribes contend that witches hypnotize their victims and then suck their blood. More malicious deeds they perform are to remove children from their mothers' wombs and then put them back dead. They can withdraw the essence from food offerings and also blight crops.

Beliefs in the British West Indies reflect concepts of the supernatural from both Africa and Europe. One example is the *ligaroo,* an evil person who can transform itself into other animal shapes, flying at night, appearing as a ball of fire, sucking the blood of its animal, or human, victims. In one version the teller describes outwitting the creature by dousing a cow with kero-

sene so that the strong odor prevents the evil entity from sucking the cow's blood.

Among the Nahuatl Indians living in the southern section of
the Valley of Mexico, many of whose descendants are now part
of North American culture, there exists a tradition of vampire
witches called *tlaciques*. These creatures transform themselves into
a ball of fire or into the shape of a turkey in order to suck human
blood without discovery. They have other qualities similar to
our notion of the vampire. *Tlaciques* are cold because their trans-
formations take place at night, but they have warm bodies when
in human form.

In the seventeenth century, a sixty-year-old, highly respected
Silesian, an alderman, died after being kicked by his horse. The
moment of his death proved dramatic—a black cat rushed into
the room, jumped on the bed, and scratched the corpse's face.
Between his death and burial severe storms plagued the area;
after the burial townsfolk reported seeing the departed and hearing his voice. Unusual occurrences took place: milk was missing
from jugs and bowls; milk was transformed into blood; old men
were strangled; poultry was killed and consumed.

After six months of problems the suspicious townsfolk
exhumed the body of the alderman and discovered that fresh
blood was still in his legs and he could open and shut his eyes.
The authorities ordered the body dismembered and burned. From
then on the town rested with ease, plagued no more.

The Kashubs are a small Slavic group of people, currently living in Ontario, Canada. They have an active belief in vampires,
including the idea that the mark of the vampire can be detected
at birth through the presence either of a caul (a membrane sometimes covering the head of a child at birth) or one or more teeth.
Antidotes are available for these ominous signs.

If the caul is the portent of evil, it is dried, ground into ashes,
then fed to the child when he or she reaches the age of seven.
The person leads an otherwise normal life and it is only at the
time of death that danger arises. If proper precautions are not
taken—the placing of miniature poplar crosses and quantities of

sand in the coffin—the vampire will rise from the grave at night
and ring the church bell. Those who hear it will die, first the
vampire's close relatives and then others. The only recourse is
to exhume the body and decapitate it.

Gypsies are said to regard vampires with horror. It is thought
that the source of their beliefs in vampires comes from India,
where in the western region the *bhuta* is found. The *bhuta* has the
power to enter men's bodies, causing sickness and death. It can
animate dead bodies and then eat men alive.

There is a correspondingly vile counterpart in northern India,
the *brahmaparush,* who drinks from the skull and eats flesh from
the victim's head while wearing a wreath of intestines around
his own head. Another Indian vampire creature is embodied in
the *rakshasa,* who haunts cemeteries, animates dead bodies, and
transforms himself into different animals.

As Gypsies migrated through Europe their beliefs adapted to
reflect those of the people among whom they settled. Slavic and
German Gypsies believe that vampires have no bones in their
bodies. Some Swedish Gypsies assert that vampires can take on
the appearance of a horse or bird, while among the Slavs they
may transform into a frog, spider, or flea. Moslem Gypsies of
Yugoslavia believe that pumpkins and watermelons are capable
of becoming vampires. If these foods are kept for more than ten
days, or after Christmas, changes will occur. A trace of blood
may be seen on them; they may make sounds, and they can
harass people and cattle, but without doing too much harm.

Whatever the form, if a vampire leaves his grave, Gypsies
interpret this as a malicious act, for it may kill by sucking blood
or eating parts of bodies, commit violence or terror, destroy
property, set fires, break dishes, or cause physical illness. Sexual
desire, too, may motivate vampires to return from the grave,
their libidos so strong that excessive sexual activities with their
widows often leave these women in a state of exhaustion.

These multicultural examples illustrate the variety of vampire
beliefs held by people throughout the world. Not all the beliefs
were "imported" to this country, but it is apparent that accept-

ing ideas of fiendish supernatural entities is not unusual. People everywhere have always personified evil. Believing in supernatural troublemakers is a way to cope with the ups and downs of daily life, particularly the downs.

The harsh New England environment during colonial times—severe winters, starvation, disease, hostile Indians, and unfamiliar food, plants, and animal life—created an atmosphere in which colonists turned toward spiritual sources for interpretations of the hardships they had to endure. It is easy to understand how the people might have looked for external reasons as causes of their suffering in their struggle for daily survival. An evil entity might be the cause, or perhaps misfortune was merely retribution for their own wrongdoing.

Puritans believed in providences, those extraordinary events interpreted as divine messages from God revealing his pleasure or displeasure with the colonists' behavior. For these people, man survived only as a result of God's benevolence. An escape from a shipwreck or from starvation meant that the Almighty was rewarding those survivors. Conversely, a monstrous birth—a child born with two mouths, horns over the eyes, pricks and scales on the body, and claws on the foot—was an omen of God's disapproval. Sudden blindness, unexpected drownings, raving women, and naked bodies walking to church were seen as signs of God's displeasure. Other negative heavenly communications were recorded: hail as big as duck eggs, flaming comets and stars, a father shot in the bowels by his son, a pregnant housewife slain by an Indian, burning homes, smallpox epidemics, Indian attacks, lightning bolts, choking cows. These were holy judgments against sinners.

Early preoccupation with supernatural intervention in daily life was commonplace in the New England setting. The devil, for example, was a familiar character in the cast of evil entities that plagued man on these shores. The English folklorist Katharine Briggs observed, "Thoughtful and learned men of all shades of opinion believed, no less than the man in the street and the man behind the plough, in the constant presence of the Devil."

Puritans linked the Indians with the devil because of the unusual divination and healing rituals performed by their shamans or powaws. Despite the exotic ceremonies, the immigrants were sometimes desperate enough to try these Indian treatments. On one occasion a planter suffering from distemper submitted to an unusual Indian healing ritual. First he had to drink a mixture of herbs and roots; then the Indian tightly wound a live rattlesnake around the man's waist, ordering that he sleep in bed with the viper. When morning came, the snake was dead and the planter's illness was over—thought to have been transferred to the snake.

Indians had their own beliefs in the devil. They thought of this personification of evil as being embodied in "Cheepie," a frightening spirit who was once described as flying over the field with a long rope hanging from one of his legs and looking like an Englishman.

Satan entered into everyday life. The phrase "Devil take me!" was heard in daily speech by certain "loose talkers." There is the tale of the young Frenchman who sold his soul to the devil in exchange for money. The young man had sealed the pact with his signature signed in blood, but later repented and wanted to end his own life. Ministers interceded on behalf of this young man. They fasted and prayed with him in the field where the pact had been made. They appealed to God to exert his power over the devil to try to get the contract back. They were successful. A cloud appeared over them and a blood-signed contract floated downward. The jubilant young man seized it and tore it to shreds. He had won the battle.

This event was considered a providence and was interpreted to mean that certain powers of good could overcome evil. This tale and ones similar to it seem a likely source for Stephen Vincent Benét's story *The Devil and Daniel Webster*. Though it takes place in a later American time frame, the elements are the same. A sympathetic character, this time a poor, unlucky young farmer, Jabez Stone, is hit by hard times. His crops are blighted; he doesn't have enough food for his children. He becomes so desperate one day that he makes a pact with the devil, signing his name in blood.

After seven years pass, the devil, Scratch, comes to collect his soul. Stone turns to Daniel Webster, famed orator, to plead his case. Daniel Webster was the essence of good. According to Benét, "There were thousands that trusted in him right next to God Almighty. . . . They said, when he stood up to speak, stars and stripes came right out of the sky, and once he spoke against a river and made it sink into the ground."

Battling the devil with eloquent words, Webster succeeds in saving the soul of Jabez Stone. The story illustrates the prevalent belief that while forces of evil were common among men, equally powerful were certain select forces of good (this time embodied in a patriot and man of gifted words).

The effect of providences and beliefs in the devil and witches inspired other American authors to incorporate these themes into their writings, for authors are also influenced by the lore that surrounds them. It is not surprising that many of America's most serious and popular writers have made use of images or references to the netherworld.

Nathaniel Hawthorne's story "Young Goodman Brown" is the tale of how the devil gained control of and gathered into his congregation all the good folks of Salem, including the deacons, the catechism teacher, the devout Christians of the town, and Brown's own wife, Faith. At his sermon the devil preaches:

> Depending upon one another's hearts, ye had still hoped that virtue were not all a dream. Now are ye undeceived. Evil is the nature of mankind. Evil must be your only happiness. Welcome again, my children, to the communion of your race.

Hawthorne seems to be saying that the accusers of the witches of Salem—the respected and seemingly virtuous people of the community—were as evil as those who were accused and punished. The author's interest in these events was no doubt connected to his family's involvement in the trials. His ancestor John

Hathorn (*sic,* Hawthorne) was one of three judges who presided over the Salem witch trials.

The famed preacher Cotton Mather warned of the sinfulness alive in New England during the seventeenth century, describing the workings of the devil and his witches and warning that evil forces sought to siphon souls away from God. Evil forces to Mather, as well as to his father, Increase, included devils, ghosts, and witches.

Witchcraft was punishable by death as early as 1641. Article 94, Section 2 of the first Massachusetts code of laws reads: "If any man or woman be a witch (that is hath or consulteth with a familiar spirit) they shall be put to death." In order to harm their victims, witches had to enter their homes; consequently, procedures were developed to prevent them from doing so. A door would be hung upside down; a bag of salt would be kept under the bed in the master bedroom; a horseshoe would be hung over each entrance. One was also safe by carrying a piece of dried sassafras root, dried clove of garlic, or sprig of mistletoe.

Just as it was possible to defeat the devil with clever words, so too, was it possible to undo the effect of witches' spells. A victim could place seven drops of any vegetable oil into a dish of cold water containing a small piece of iron and rub his finger along the edge of the dish in a clockwise direction for three minutes, thus weakening the force of the spell, which could be completely broken if the procedure was repeated seven times in one day at two-hour intervals.

But Puritans were admonished not to take matters into their own hands to fight the evil forces. Increase Mather threatened to punish anyone who tried to draw blood from suspected witches or who bottled the urine of witches or nailed horseshoes over their door. As folklorist Richard Dorson relates, Increase was certain that the art of unbewitching could only have been learned from magicians and devils themselves.

It was thought that the first witches reached New England by stowing away on ships and arriving with the other colonists in order to do their unholy work in the new land. That unholy work was to cause misfortune, a skill witches had honed throughout history but had increased in power during the Middle Ages as a result of entering into a relationship with Satan.

American involvement with witches has been well documented by historians and has inspired important fiction writers as well. John Updike's *Witches of Eastwick* updates the story of witches, the devil, and New England to portray the ambiguity of women's individual power to procreate and their collective power to destroy the work of the devil, who in this story is a rich, attractive, devil-may-care playboy. The witches are three young and appealing women who succumb to his charm and his supernatural manipulations until he interferes too heavily with their female strengths and own goals. Then they use their collective supernatural powers to destroy him.

Arthur Miller's play *The Crucible* tells of the turmoil and trauma caused by the hysteria which swept seventeenth-century Salem. It is the story of Elizabeth Howe's being set up and framed as a witch by her live-in maid. Others are falsely accused as well, and innocent characters must make moral decisions—to give a false confession and be spared, or to deny trumped-up charges and be put to death.

From early on, beliefs in witches and devils were interwoven. Vampires, too, became part of the fabric, and the association has not disappeared, as exemplified today by the Order of the Vampyre. It therefore seems appropriate, and not unexpected, that during the height of this interest in witchcraft, which culminated in the Salem witch trials, the first printed reference to vampires occurs. The British reverend Montague Summers, who has written important histories about vampires and werewolves, comments that during the height of these trials (1691–1693) there were certain details that might be construed as evidence of vampirism. He recounts that many of the "afflicted children" complained that apparitions hurt and harassed them, draining their energy. In particular, he cites the cases of Abigail Williams and

Mary Walcut (*sic,* Wolcott), who decreed they had actually been bitten, with complete tooth marks (uppers and lowers) imprinted on their wrists as evidence.

The Reverend Deodat Lawson, minister at Salem Village from 1684 to 1688, wrote the first printed account of the witchcraft there, to which Summers refers. He observes that while staying at the Nathaniel Ingersoll lodging, Mary Walcott came to speak to him, but while standing near the door she suddenly cried out because she felt a bite on her wrist. The reverend took a candle and inspected the wrist to discover what appeared to be both upper and lower teeth marks in the girl's flesh. Lawson refers to the unexplained marks in his account as a full set of teeth marks rather than one or two pierce marks. There is no mention of blood loss. However, Summers claims that energy was drained.

During the nineteenth century the common Anglo-American idea about vampires was that they caused diseases within families. If someone died of consumption and a close family member fell ill, the first person to die was considered the culprit who desired to take the rest of the family along. Thus, if other family members became ill, they were thought to be under attack by the deceased.

Common practice was to open the grave and examine the corpse's heart. If it was bloodless and decaying it was assumed that the disease came from some other cause, and the heart was restored to its body. However, if the heart was fresh and contained liquid blood, it was thought that the deceased had been feeding on the life of the sick person. The only solution was to burn the heart to ashes.

It was reported, for example, that the heart of a man was burned in Woodstock Green, Vermont, sometime around 1829. He had died of consumption six months before, and his body had been buried in the ground. After his death his brother became ill; within a short time it was apparent that he, too, had consumption. When this diagnosis was confirmed the family exhumed the body of the first brother and examined his heart. Finding an undecayed heart still containing liquid blood, they were convinced that he was the cause of the disease. They removed the heart, reburied the body, and burned the heart to ashes in an iron pot.

In New England the rationale for this practice of exhuming a corpse to examine the heart came from a belief that consumption was a spiritual rather than a physical disease. There was no understanding that consumption spread through close physical contact, that family members of the consumptive patient were the most likely candidates to get the disease themselves. Because early New Englanders had no awareness of the germ theory, consumption in a person who had had a family member die of the disease recently was taken as a sign of a supernatural visit by the newly departed for the purpose of taking the relative to the grave as well. Finding blood in the disinterred person's heart signaled that the deceased was draining and stealing blood from the living, thus causing the rapid decline of the ill family member.

In Connecticut, a story from the *Norwich Courier* of May 20, 1854, reveals that a family by the name of Ray "became convinced that several dead members of the family were feeding upon the living." After Horace Ray of Griswold, Connecticut, died of consumption, two of his sons also became afflicted and died of the same disease. When a third son fell ill, the bodies of the two brothers were exhumed and burned by family and friends in Jewett City. The *Courier* commented on this "strange, and to us hitherto unheard of superstition." The *Courier*'s reporter must have been unaware that this was a practice of his time.

The story of Mercy Brown is another well-publicized example of this belief and custom. She died in January 1892 in Exeter, Rhode Island. Her father, George Brown, lost his wife to consumption, leaving him with six children to care for. Two years later the eldest daughter died of the same illness, and a few years after that the brother, Edwin, became ill and moved to Colorado Springs. While he was gone, another daughter, Mercy, passed away, and when Edwin returned to Rhode Island he became critically ill.

In desperation, Edwin's father agreed to exhume the bodies of his wife and two daughters, all of whom were buried in the Exeter Cemetery. Examination of the wife and oldest daughter revealed nothing but skeletons, but with Mercy's body, the results were different. It is claimed that blood dripped from the heart and liver. Because of this, the heart and liver had to be cremated.

Another incident from Rhode Island relates to nineteen-year-old Nellie L. Vaughn of Coventry, Rhode Island, who died in 1889. While alive and even after her death there was never any talk of her being a vampire, professes a 100-year-old man who knew Nellie personally and belonged to the same church. In spite of this, rumors began circulating that Nellie was a vampire after a teacher from Coventry High School told his 1967 class that a vampire was buried in a cemetery off Route 102.

According to a report in the *Providence Journal Bulletin,* the teacher did not mention the name of the cemetery, yet students assumed it was the cemetery affiliated with the Meeting House Church. The story was no doubt reinforced by the words on Nellie's headstone, "I am waiting and watching for you," and from a claim that no vegetation or lichen would grow on the grave.

The rumor of Nellie being a vampire persists; according to an article in 1982 by Richard Dujardin, "Hardly a day goes by without people showing up at the cemetery to look at [the] woman's grave. Tombstones have been overturned. There even appears to have been an attempt to dig up the coffin."

In a 1983 unpublished manuscript, Michael E. Bell of the Rhode Island Folklife Project reports a story from oral tradition about the village of Peace Dale, Rhode Island, where in 1874 William Rose dug up the body of his daughter and burned her heart. He, too, judged that she was "wasting away" the lives of other family members. Bell records a similar tale from oral tradition relating to a Nancy Young, who was believed to have killed off her family as well.

Bell makes a significant contribution to the literature when he recounts that a colleague of his, working with the Bram Stoker collection, recalled finding a newspaper clipping among Stoker's papers that included a reference to one of these New England incidents. Bell suggests, "If this is the case, it is likely that Rhode Island's local tradition of vampirism had an influence on the creation of the world's most famous vampire." He points to the possible irony that Rhode Island's local vampires may have helped to create the fictional Dracula, who, in turn, has returned to transform and influence the image of vampires in Rhode Island, and indeed throughout the United States.

More incidents have been recorded. In the 1890s in a village located near Newport, Rhode Island, George Stetson interviewed an "intelligent man," a mason who told of his two brothers dying of consumption. After the second brother fell ill, a wealthy friend advised the family to take out the first body and burn its heart. Considering this a sacrilege, the brother refused, and he subsequently died. Later on, when the mason himself was attacked by the disease, the same advice was given. This time the body of his most recently deceased brother was exhumed. Because "living" blood was found in the heart and in the circulatory system, the heart was cremated, and the mason immediately began to recover. At the time of the interview Stetson described the surviving brother as "standing before me a hale, hearty, and vigorous man of fifty years."

One caution that Stetson offers is that although these events and actions appear to reveal what seems to us now as obvious beliefs in vampires, New Englanders did not label this practice of burning the heart of the deceased consumptive as vampirism or as being related to vampires. Stetson writes that among the local community the vampire superstition was unknown by its proper name, yet Stetson, as a scholar, recognized what it was. The practice, moreover, was not limited to Rhode Island. In Chicago, as well, the lungs of a woman who had died from consumption were removed and burned to protect her surviving relatives.

But Stetson was concerned about Rhode Island. In an 1896 issue of the *American Anthropologist* he expressed amazement that this "barbarous superstition" had a stronger hold in Rhode Island than in any other part of the country. He was particularly struck by what he considered an incongruity—compared to other parts of the country, educational advantages and the level of literacy and culture in Rhode Island were relatively high.

In this late-nineteenth-century article Stetson expressed wonder that beliefs in vampires still retained a hold after centuries of intellectual progress. In spite of increased knowledge of natural laws and appreciation of the principles of natural, mental, and moral philosophy, he contended, there was no correlative decline in what he called "primitive and crude superstitions." Imagine how Stetson would react today, nearly 100 years later, upon learning that beliefs in vampires still thrive!

The ordinary assumption one might make is that the New England association of consumption with powers of the undead came from Europe, especially Britain. There is evidence to support that possibility because similar beliefs were also found in certain parts of England. It has been suggested that attributing the cause of the disease to a recently buried corpse might have been a means of comprehending the irony of consumption, a disease to which a healthy-looking person could suddenly fall prey and quickly die.

During the late 1890s a different kind of vampire legend circulated, centering on a house located on Green Street in Schenectady, New York. A silhouette of a human body was painted in mold on the cellar floor. In spite of constant sweeping and scrubbing, it could not be removed; the outline of a reclining man would always reappear in the form of mold. It was later discovered that the house had been built over an old Dutch burial ground. One interpretation of this phenomenon was that the recurring shape on the cellar floor was the outline of a vampire trying in vain to leave its grave, but prevented from doing so because of a "virtuous spell" that had been cast on the location.

A curious reference to vampires occurred in 1920, when Charles S. Potts, M.D., delivered his presidential address before the Philadelphia Psychiatric Society. Potts began his speech decrying the lack of justice at the Salem witch trials in the seventeenth century. Critical of the lack of progress in human rights, he charged that even twentieth-century people's rights were being trampled on and that injustice remained, often without redress. Among a variety of examples he cited was one from Newark, New Jersey, where policewomen were ordered to vigorously wash the painted cheeks of girls on the streets. As part of the punishment, the police had to have the girls photographed as vampires. Here, streetwalkers who endured their own form of persecution were forced to accept an additional social stigma. This would not have occurred unless there was a prevalent belief in vampires at that time.

Early in U.S. history, black populations also had a tradition of vampire legends and beliefs. One example is a tale recorded in 1893 from Missourians of mixed Negro and Indian ancestry. In this account Aunt Mymee, a Negro nanny, is entertaining a sick white child by telling a tale about a witch woman who had been running around with the devil. The devil's wife found out and was after her. Later, when children were born from this union of witch and devil, there were so many offspring that the witch fed them blood rather than milk. At first the blood came from deer, and then from all sorts of other creatures. Aunt Mymee makes it clear that the witch did not shoot the creatures. She describes the witch sneaking up on an unattended animal, and then etching rings in the ground around it while saying charms, casting a spell to prevent the creature from lifting a leg or hoof. Then she sends for her blood-sucking offspring, who drain all of the animal's blood until he falls down dead.

The witch keeps up the blood-draining process for a long time, at first very cautiously for fear that the devil's wife might discover her. But after a while, when the devil's wife does not catch her, the witch becomes bold as brass. She becomes more aggressive, killing and allowing all the animals to be drained of blood because her children are growing and their appetites have become greater. Her children are now so hungry that they eat from sunrise to sunset.

The few remaining animals in the area begin to worry, knowing that nothing with red blood in it is going to be left if the witch and her family keep this up. So they get together to see how they might remedy the situation.

As a solution, the wolf sends the fox and badger to find the devil's wife and tell her of their plight. She listens to their story and goes after the witch, killing her with a club of fire that burns the woman up, until not even the ashes are left.

After the devil's wife kills the witch, she goes after the children, but without success because the children were half devil and impossible to kill. So the devil's wife changes them into mosquitoes, and there they are to this day, as mean and hungry as ever, but now they're only "lil suckers."

This tale shares the common motif of a vampire's blood-sucking habit and burning as a method of destroying the vampire. But notice once again that there has been no label of vampire or vampirism applied to either the culprit or the practice. The characteristics of the witch woman qualify her as a vampire. Those persons who tell this story may not necessarily believe that it is true. Yet, in the retelling, concepts about vampires and their offspring are being communicated.

Other vampire beliefs among blacks are found in the South as well, including one about Old Sue, a 100-year-old plantation Negro who was accused of sucking children's blood while they slept, so that she could keep on living. Fellow farm workers described seeing her travel faster than a bird can fly, standing in the door with big, black, bat-like wings that lifted her into the air and out of sight. In one case, the morning after Old Sue was seen in this condition, a baby was found dead. To protect against the powers of Old Sue other plantation workers wore red pepper in their shoes.

Vampire beliefs are also found in Southern white populations. The legend of the Bell witch tells about the misfortunes of the Bell family, who moved from North Carolina to the midlands of Tennessee in the early 1800s and then to northern Mississippi about 1840.

Mr. Bell, a North Carolinian planter, hired an obstreperous overseer who was such a bully that whenever he and Mr. Bell had a row, the overseer afterward went out and beat up the slaves. The confrontations between Mr. Bell and this man became so frequent that one day Bell shot his arrogant employee. Bell was brought to trial, but the jury let him go. After this, Bell's crops began to fail miserably. His mules died; his cattle became ill. He had to sell his slaves, all but one old woman. Finally, Bell went broke, sold his land, and moved his family and the old woman to Tennessee.

As soon as he moved to Tennessee, strange things began to happen. His children were thrown out of bed mysteriously with their nightclothes removed and their hair messed. Milk was missing. The old slave woman advised the family that it was the overseer who was haunting them.

The Bell witch/ghost continued to wreak havoc and play such pranks on the family that they later moved to Mississippi. While there the overseer's ghost advised Mr. Bell that he wished to marry Bell's favored daughter, Mary. Mr. Bell was adamant in his refusal. Very shortly thereafter, Mary took sick and died. On the day she was buried a large black bird, wearing a bell, hovered over the wagon bearing her coffin to the graveyard.

This story is widely known in Tennessee and Mississippi and has been interpreted as a form of vampire tale, with the vampire not being a consumption-causing entity or blood-sucking corpse, but instead a mischievous body who has returned to torture and drain the living—milk, crops, cattle, life. In this type of vampire belief, the dead envy the living and persecute and take something from them, their friends, and their relatives.

Further implications of the Bell witch as vampire come from some of his pranks; stealing milk, for example, was a common belief. The collectors of this tale quote George Lyman Kittredge regarding German vampires, who are commonly believed to drain cows dry. In addition, the Mississippi version represents the witch as lover of the daughter and her tormentor to the death. Tormenting a lover until death is another common vampire role.

Like the New England exhumation practices which make no mention of vampirism, in the Bell witch legend the word *vampire* is not used. However, certain concepts relating to vampires are clearly implicit.

On February 6, 1981, a more clear-cut example of American belief in the phenomenon of vampires was reported from Kitzingen, West Germany. The news report was headlined "GI's Risk Necks in Vampire Watch." Apparently attracted by a nineteenth-century family grave decorated with bats and skulls in the middle of Old Testament scenes, U.S. soldiers of the 3rd Infantry Army stationed in Kitzingen regularly gathered at midnight in front of the tomb, waiting for Count Dracula to emerge in search of victims.

One soldier reported that he hadn't been down there at night, but that there were many soldiers sitting there waiting for Dracula to exit. He commented, "I don't know if they really think they'll see him, but when somebody is convinced, perhaps they can make it happen."

A spokesperson for the army division described the graveyard as scary, mysterious, old—like a shrine. Its reputation spread because it was the first thing soldiers asked about when they arrived in Kitzingen.

GIs ignored the fact that this grave is seven hundred miles from Transylvania. They also disregarded information that the mysterious grave was actually the burial site of the Herold family, whose tomb was restored a few years before, making the bats and skulls that had always been there more visible. Unable to fight the GIs' craze, the Kitzingen mayor was resigned about the situation. "You can't stop these young fellows from believing what they want."

On U.S. soil today beliefs in vampires are revealed by a handful of blood drinkers and by the behavior exhibited in Panama City. But just how widespread is the belief?

In an attempt to determine the extent of the belief in the existence of vampires, I distributed a questionnaire to 574 students from three high schools and three colleges in Los Angeles and one college classroom in Bristol, England. The age range of respondents was fifteen to sixty-three and they came from thirty-four different countries, including the United States. Nine instructors administered the questionnaires to their classes on my behalf. There was no discussion of the subject prior to filling out the forms, and students were guaranteed anonymity.

No attempt was made to correlate religion or socioeconomic levels with belief. Instead, I wished to discover only what people believed and why *they* thought they believed that way.

To the question "Do you believe it is possible that vampires exist as real entities?" 27 percent responded yes. The questions were designed for open-ended answers, and the largest number of reasons given for believing in vampires fell into an "Anything is possible" category (22 percent). Examples of this kind of explanation follow:

> No one has proved otherwise.
>
> Because there are a lot of things unknown to man that do exist.
>
> I have no conviction that life as we know it is all that there is.
>
> I have seen no evidence to disprove their existence.

Other kinds of reasons were given:

> A vampire is simply one of the undead. If people can exist, so can vampires.
>
> Because other supernatural things have occurred according to myth. Until the myth is proven false, I believe it.
>
> There have been so many documented sightings of vampires and documented proof of people who have had unexplained bites on the neck, it is hard not to believe.

Beliefs of some students were based on perception:

What one perceives exists.

All things are possible in the mind of the believer.

If you believe, then you are.

You could imagine it.

The unconscious could mimic desired effects.

A few students mentioned that there might be a biological reason—caused by disease—and there were some who believed that vampires were "disturbed":

. . . crazies out there.

. . . all in their heads.

There were some who dealt with blood-drinking characteristics:

There are those who enjoy drinking blood.

There may be certain people that drink other's blood.

It is likely some people suck blood from their associates.

Still others based their belief on the devil:

Evil forces do exist.

Because I feel that this is the work of the Devil. The Devil does exist, so I know vampires exist.

Notice that beliefs in the devil are interlaced with the vampire and that this association of different evil entities is not a new idea.

Lack of evidence was the most common reason given for those students not believing in vampires. Responses included:

Because I have never seen one.

There has been no proven evidence that I have seen to make me believe that there are, so I do not believe in them.

I'd like to [believe]—all my childhood fears jump out and say, Yes! Yes!—but everything rational tells me that "living dead" are just figments or fantasies.

It seems impossible to think that humans would not have evolved those characteristics in [and] of themselves if they were possible. Also I see no logic in the supernatural.

A cynic wrote that it was only an overpublication of a superstition. He hypothesized that if vampires did exist, "People would develop anti-vampire products and try to make money off of people's fears."

Other kinds of negative responses included the following:

No person can be undead or survive and thrive on human blood. Nor is anyone going to vaporize in sunlight and change into a bat.

I have always thought of it as just a myth, simply made up for the effect of horror.

I'm quite ignorant of the supernatural possibilities, so I'm basing this judgment on my average logic.

I just don't believe that a person would go around biting people's necks for food. It's just all rumors that people made over the years.

Religion forbids me to believe in such an entity.

Because I believe in God and the Bible. They don't mention such a beast.

They are just part of imaginations of storytellers and writers.

When a man is born as a man he lives as a man and dies as a man.

Because how can some fool live in a casket, fly around, bite people on the neck and hypnotize people.

I'm sorry, but I have a hard time believing such an entity exists. Fangs growing, Poo!

Later a different questionnaire was circulated to members of vampire fan clubs. A few revealed mixed feelings about the possibility of vampires existing as real entities.

> My standard answer to this question is to ask me twice—once at noon and once at midnight. At noon I find it very easy to be scientific and answer that vampires cannot exist, if only because of the lack of a larger causal relation. With so many people in the world there would be more vampires which would lead to more visible vampires. At midnight I tend to keep in mind the family legends. (There's a rumor that one of my forebears was dug up after his death and staked because of strange attacks that occurred after his untimely demise—but then, that's pretty common in the Slovak areas of the world.)

> I would say immediately, "Of course not! Are you a nutcase?" Still there are many many strange things in this world . . . However (and this is slightly embarrassing), there will always be that very tiny grain of uncertainty, not doubt, but rather an open-mindedness, that does not entirely dismiss the very possibilty of some things which we could term occult or supernatural.

> If someone told me that a vampire haunted a certain cemetery in a rural out-of-the-way part of the countryside, I would scoff. Yet I doubt I would want to go through that same cemetery by myself late at night (unless I had a revolver with with silver bullets).

What the foregoing quotes reveal is that there is a tradition in the United States about belief in the existence of vampires. Native Americans had such ideas, immigrants brought their own concepts, and in the new American climate these ideas adapted, flourished. Certainly there has been an active tradition documented from the nineteenth century on. The results of the high school and college survey point out that the vampire has made inroads into our contemporary consciousness. The 27 percent of students who believed in the possibility of vampires being true entities seems significant, particularly if we assume that we are more enlightened now than our forebears. Add to this the Panama City incident, and one has to wonder how this has happened. Yet it is not hard to understand young people's stretched powers of credibility given the times in which they live—where human fertilization can take place in a flat glass dish, where human hearts can be replaced by mechanical contraptions, where Mars is our next destination in space.

To know and relate a tale about vampires and their behavior is not necessarily the same as believing that vampires exist as real entities. Telling a story explaining how mosquitoes are vampire offspring does not mean one actually believes in the concept. Yet to the teller and audience, ideas, no matter how preposterous, are expressed and perhaps discussed, challenged, or reinforced.

For example, a man in Northern California described his amusement at seeing a Bela Lugosi–style vampire displayed in a print ad from a building tools and supplies company. As the man broke through the wall of his house with newly purchased materials from this company, a bat flew out. While this did not make the man believe in a vampire/bat transformation, his emotions and memories were nonetheless stirred enough to lead him to phone a friend long distance to report on this peculiar cause-and-effect event.

The episode reminded him of stories and themes experienced earlier, no doubt leading to a process of hypothesizing—perhaps even willingness to accept the ideas about vampires—and doubts. Ultimately, the possibility of such entities existing was laid to rest—at least until the next strange occurrence, perhaps, or when describing the experience after an interval of time.

It is because of this questioning process, which occurs under particular circumstances, that it is difficult to separate a story from the belief in it. Somewhere within the story or legend there is an emotion-bound connection. Most of the time it is hard to know how strong that connection may be. This seems to be expressed best by the vampire fan who tried to comprehend her ambiguity as to whether or not she believed in vampires as real entities—"ask me twice—once at noon and once at midnight." She aptly described that dichotomy of feelings that many experience.

Even if one claims not to believe in the vampire as a true entity, there may be hidden doubts which can surface under particular circumstances. On the other hand, as questionnaires revealed, over a quarter of the students surveyed did believe that this entity could exist in reality. Yet no one reported having seen a vampire as the basis of his or her belief. Those who said they believed based their affirmative response primarily on the possibility that it *might exist.*

A concept and set of associations can be learned informally, becoming deeply ingrained without conscious awareness until the appropriate moment occurs when the ideas surface, are questioned, and may become interactive. The precipitant can be a headline, a story, a news flash, or something so innocuous as an advertisement stuck under a windshield wiper.

Even if a person disbelieves the reality of a vampire, it is possible for that same person to transmit information about it, repeat past stories, and thus perpetuate the existence of the belief, whether real to the teller or not. This is done to entertain, to bolster one's own status as a storyteller, or perhaps to keep control of younger listeners. It may even occur as a way to build up a sense of bravado in order to deal with those real menaces in one's life.

Sometimes it is not just accidental that a belief in the supernatural is made operative. Nonrational beliefs can be deliberately activated by some to purposefully control another's actions. Sometimes it is for the purpose of manipulating the behavior of groups of people.

An illustration of this comes from the memoirs of Edward Geary Lansdale, retired major general of the United States Air Force. General Lansdale recalls the fall of 1950 when he was sent by the United States government to become involved with the political struggle then taking place in the Philippines.

At that time the CIA was supporting the leadership of President Elpidio Quirino and Defense Secretary Ramon Magsaysay, who in 1953 succeeded Quirino as president. The power of these leaders was being undermined by Huk *(Hukbalahap)* guerrillas, insurgents who were attempting to win over the sympathy of Filipino peasants struggling to survive during a period of great economic instability. Lansdale devised a scheme to thwart the Huks' success.

Lansdale was aware of the local belief in the *aswang,* a vampire-like entity considered to be so evil that when first buried even the ground rejected it. He had learned about this creature from his wife, a Filipina who was born on the island of Bohol, the legendary home of the *aswang.* Mrs. Lansdale's siblings, who were born on Luzon, one of the Philippines' other islands, used to tease her about her Bohol birthplace, sometimes throwing garlic at her. Because of her *aswang* connection she became the butt of all the family jokes. Her husband was keenly interested in these stories of her youth.

The *aswang* is sometimes described as having the head of an animal and the body of a human, with a protruding tongue about eight to ten feet long. It can also be characterized as being only a half body with wings, a creature who emerges to commit evil acts at midnight, when the moon is bright.

Filipino legend has it that they haunt the living in constant search of fresh blood, using their tongues to search for little openings in small bamboo houses to prey on disobedient children, pregnant women, undeserving men, the sick, and the weak. They are interpreted as an omen of death if seen under a house. Licking the shadow of a sick person is one of the ways the *aswang* can cause death, but rubbing garlic under the arms, like deodorant, can ward them off.

A Filipina related that among her people, particularly in the villages, the *aswang* are looked upon as a powerful force whose existence is not questioned. Stories about them have been learned from village elders, who are respected among these nonliterate people. Tales about the *aswang,* often told in story-spinning sessions after work and school, are valued as truths.

Knowing of the people's dread of this vampire-like creature, Lansdale and his men devised a plan to manipulate these beliefs to suit their political needs. Magsaysay wished to remove local troops who were being used to protect the villagers from the Huks, but village leaders were fearful of being left without protection.

As Lansdale relates, his solution was to get rid of the Huks and thus relieve any need for local troops. He utilized a combat psychological warfare (psywar) squad brought in to plant stories among the villagers that there was an *aswang* who lived on the hill where the Huks were based. Lansdale's men allowed two nights to give the stories time to circulate. Then they set up an ambush.

As a Huk patrol came down the trail, the psywar squad quietly kidnapped the last man in the patrol. In vampire style they punctured his neck with two holes, drained the body of blood by holding it upside down, and then replaced the corpse on the trail.

Eventually the other members of the Huk patrol realized that one of their men was missing. As anticipated and well planned, when they returned and found their bloodless comrade, the patrol members believed that he had been the prey of the *aswang* and that anyone who remained on the hill would eventually become a victim as well.

By the time daylight arrived, the entire Huk squadron had moved out of the vicinity. The villagers, too, were affected, believing that a vampire was on the rampage desperately searching for blood. When the local people were convinced that the Huks had departed, Magsaysay removed the troops to his desired location without any protest from the villagers.

The event took place in 1950. In 1988, among nine Filipino emigrants who are now migrant workers in the Central Valley of California, the story is still told. The men reminisce about how the rumors circulated that the vampire would prey on Huks and Huk sympathizers, but villagers were not convinced that these *aswang* attacks would be confined to the current political outsiders. They recall how these stories had frightened them, particularly hearing about the state of blood-drained bodies. Some even remember families who wore garlic around their necks and spread garlic in their homes.

Although these men have been living in the United States for more than twenty years, at the time of the incident they were serving in the Filipino military and were aware of CIA involvement in local politics. Some had resented the ways in which the CIA killed their enemy. They wondered why they couldn't just kill the Huks and respect the dead instead of playing with the corpses.

On the other hand, as former Filipino military men, they believed the CIA was doing them a favor because the Huks were their common enemy. However, as they recall, villagers as well as Huks left the land. Towns were emptied and the land was redistributed to the multinational companies. Lansdale's plan had worked. The villagers stopped helping the Huks with food and shelter, causing the Huks loss of strength. They were no longer a viable force.

As a postscript, in spite of their Americanization and length of time away from their homeland, five of these Filipino men still retain their belief in the *aswang*. It is difficult to shake such well-learned and emotion-laden beliefs.

Taking beliefs, especially ones rooted in fear, and reactivating them for political purposes has occurred elsewhere. It is commonly found in military situations, with historical incidents going back as far as Genghis Khan, who planted rumors before attacks to unnerve his enemies. These stories inflated the true number and strength of his troops and exaggerated the ruthlessness of his army.

The deliberate use of stories for deceitful purposes is not limited to the military, though. The corporate world has been affected as well. In 1934 two-man teams passed a rumor that a leper had been discovered working in the Chesterfield cigarette factory in Richmond, Virginia. Apparently those who passed the rumor would enter crowded subway cars at opposite ends, moving toward each other, then conversing about the leper in front of others standing nearby. Sales were sufficiently affected to cause Liggett and Myers, the Chesterfield manufacturers, to offer a reward of $25,000 to anyone submitting evidence of those responsible. No one was ever found.

Internationally, Hitler's and the Third Reich's manipulation of folklore through the revival of Nordic-Germanic folktales was used to indoctrinate Germany's youth as a vehicle for propaganda resulting in the most horrendous twentieth-century example of exploitation of beliefs to achieve political goals—the promotion of anti-Semitism and fear. In this case the repercussions were global.

In order to manipulate beliefs, there has to be a useful channel of communication. In a village situation such as in the Philippines, it was the "grapevine" method that was employed. Military intelligence promotes use of this word-of-mouth technique by first finding out who the best information channels are—those persons who are believed and respected by other community members. It is important to know where to plant the story. Sometimes it is with a driver or a traveler.

Use of the grapevine, called oral transmission by folklorists, occurs naturally in the communication of any story or belief. Here, too, there are certain credible community members who are key to passing on information or a story. It might be the father who tells a joke to his family at the dinner table and certain members pass it along to friends. It can also be the older girls on the block revealing the "facts of life" to younger children. It might be a party guest who has caught the attention of friends with his latest "news."

However, an even more effective and powerful method of transmission in the United States today is the mass media. Media can mean billboards, telephone, paperback books, movies. But it is satellite television transmission that provides the process of passing along stories and beliefs that subsequently affect hundreds of millions of people.

Power of the Media

*Even people who don't like vampires know what
one is. The vampire is as common as a Big Mac.*

—a vampire fan.

The acceptance of belief in the vampire and its pervasiveness today can be accounted for through the influence of popular culture and the media. They don't permit the vampire to die. They have become the generators of vampire lore and its transmitter and perpetuator through movies, cartoons, headlines, advertisements. Television, in particular, has become the prime mode for the vampire's resuscitations and reincarnations. From seeing old movies, reinforced by animated versions, "Sesame Street," and commercials, the public is continuously bombarded with the vampire image.

In 1978, within hours following the television broadcast of a movie showing a hero driving the vampires out of England by sprinkling pieces of holy wafers on graves, 200 consecrated Holy Communion wafers were stolen from St. Lucy's Roman Catholic Church in Altamont, New York. Given the proximity in time between the viewing of this program and the robbery, one has to assume a connection. If the act was a serious one, it reveals that the viewer/robber was taking no chances about protection from vampire attacks. If the stolen wafers were taken only as a gag, it nonetheless shows that someone was stimulated sufficiently to commit this offense against the church, inspired by the retelling of an old story.

In a questionnaire distributed to 574 students inquiring whether or not respondents believed in the possibility of the existence of vampires, 15 percent said that they learned about vampires from other people, but 49 percent of the sample reported that they first learned of vampires from television and films. The questions were "Who told you? Under what circumstances?" These are typical answers:

> I saw the movie "Dracula."

> In private discussion with my mother in preparation for a television program.

> Alone, just watching TV.

> I saw a show on TV.

> The late movie—Abbott and Costello.

Fans, those persons who are members of clubs celebrating either Dracula or other vampire characterizations, also credited the media as a major source of learning:

> I had seen some Dracula movies, but Barnabas in "Dark Shadows" had the most effect on me. This was in 1970 sometime when they first ran the show here in Columbus.

> I was an avid reader and I remember reading Bram Stoker's *Dracula*. To be honest, I wasn't overly impressed. But when I discovered "Dark Shadows" on television, they [vampires] began to have greater attraction. Barnabas Collins, ah *there* was a most elegant vampire and he never frightened me like the later vampires of "Salem's Lot" or "The Nightstalker."

"Bela Lugosi's portrayal of Dracula was my first exposure," another fan admitted. "Considering the number of years that have passed since that first encounter, it would appear that I was hooked for life. It was a Saturday afternoon matinee and in my opinion the best nickel I ever spent."

Another said:

> I was six years old and first encountered the vampire via the "Dark Shadows" TV soap opera. I clearly remember asking my step mother what it was and how it made the "marks" they were always talking about on the show. She explained the best she could at the time and then warned me not to watch the show—but it was too late. I was hooked. At the time I was visiting my father in Seattle. (He and my mother had been divorced for about four to five years.) The anxiety surrounding my visits could, I suppose, have heightened my receptivity to the fantasy of the vampire, but once I returned home, and for the remainder of my life I have been fascinated by this creature.

In many cases, students revealed that the media were responsible for their belief in vampires. "Because I have seen them in the movies." Seeing the image of these creatures projected on a screen, whether at home or in a theater, gives them credibility.

Another example of this comes from a student who said he believed in vampires because "I've seen convincing documentaries and movies." Others responded:

> Because I heard it on the news.

> Because they do [exist]. I've seen them on TV.

> Yes, because I have seen many movies and stories about vampires and they are so real. So, I believe it's possible that vampires will exist as real entities.

Indeed, the media provide the proof. Even in analyzing the answers of students who did not believe in vampires, again the media were cited as sources of truth. According to one student, the reason he did not believe in vampires was that if they did exist, he would have seen them on the evening news. Another nonbeliever said, "Because I've never seen one interviewed on TV." A third student explained, "Because I have never seen or heard on the news that someone was bitten on the neck."

Johnny Carson, an American late-night-TV tradition himself, opens his nightly shows with a series of shots of himself in the personae of various American characters—Ronald Reagan, the Lone Ranger, Ben Franklin, a baseball player, a huckster, Liberace. Often included is a shot of Carson as Count Dracula.

Sponsors feed the vampire. They spend money promoting his image because they know this symbol is a guaranteed attention grabber. The vampire is exploited by advertisers because he generates a strong reaction. He works well to sell products; he can be capitalized on in the marketplace.

A precedent for doing so goes back to the early 1970s, when two major corporations utilized vampire themes in their print ads. One was Gillette Toiletries, Inc., which ran an ad campaign for "Dracula and the Dry Look," showing Dracula with glossy, patent-leather-looking hair being sneered at by his son, who instead used Brylcreme and sported a "dry look." The other was Smirnoff Vodka, with a promotion for "The Vampire Gimlet." This print ad showed a woman in a long gown with a wide-band choker around her neck. She is anxiously waiting, peering out a window. The words "Hurry Sundown" appear above her. Printed below the picture is a recipe for "The Vampire Gimlet," mixed in the usual vodka and lime juice gimlet proportions, but this time served with a black olive.

For the future, another Dracula-related alcoholic beverage is inevitably on its way to being promoted—Alcomix Dracula Liqueur. Unveiled as a new product at the 1987 World Food Market in Cologne, West Germany, Dracula liqueur is a blood-colored drink made of "hot pepper, thunder and lightning." Its container is a black bottle topped by a dripping red cap and bottle collar that looks like a set of fangs. Racks of glass test tubes for imbibing the liqueur will be sold with the bottle.

Advertisers are well aware of the benefits of using a symbol with such instant recognition. Television and radio are obvious channels for effectively communicating their commercial messages, which abound in the Southern California area, a national media center.

In the spring of 1986 a Snarol ad aired on KNBC television in Los Angeles showing Dracula-garbed garden pests. The narrator warned, "They come at night." Then the bugs chanted in Transylvanian cadence, "I want to bite your tomatoes." Dracula as the prototypical vampire has become a ubiquitous part of the American cultural landscape, including his incarnation as a plant parasite.

A 1987 TV mouthwash ad showed a vampire character; the narrator boasted, "Any mouth will feel cleaner," assuming that the viewer knows why the vampire's mouth needs special attention, and what peculiar eating habits have caused it to be a candidate for special cleansing. Those five words and an image lasting only a few seconds cannot have impact unless the audience has prior knowledge of what a vampire is and what it does.

Transmitting the vampire symbol is not solely dependent on visual messages. Vocal signals are equally effective. For example, in 1988 the Trident Gum Company had a radio ad circulating in New York City with a vampire commenting on the positive effects of chewing "Tridentsky" gum. By just changing the name to "Tridentsky," an Eastern European accent was implied conveying the advertiser's message that chewing gum was good for teeth, even a vampire's teeth.

A cat food company sponsored a television ad showing two cats. One was wearing a blue ribbon, the other a pink one. The cat in blue, speaking with an Eastern European accent, asks his companion, "Maybe a little bite at my place?" The relationship between the male cat, his implied vampirism, and cat food is a bit confusing, but apparently the advertising agency believed that the association would be good for canned cat food sales.

Prominent adman George Lois has said that in creating advertisements his goal is to come up with such memorable ideas that the client should either faint or throw him out of the room. It would be interesting to know how the cat food ad creator had been received.

In 1988 Chiquita Banana orange juice had a TV commercial showing a Dracula-like person recoiling when handed a glass of orange fluid to drink instead of his usual red. Here not even words are necessary to convey the message. The visual image reverses the expected pattern; thus it has impact.

A TV ad shows a pretty girl in bed who has just been awakened by something mysterious. A bat is seen at her window trying unsuccessfully to get into her room. The bat is transformed into Count Dracula, but he cannot get in either because inadvertently he has just set off the maiden's Schlage Security System. The alarm goes off, and the vampire is foiled. The narrator boasts, "It won't cost you an arm and a neck." The print version of this same ad shows Count Dracula peering into a window with the caption, "Keep Out Uninvited Guests." The menacing figure lurking at the window is a powerful selling tool for crime-conscious city and suburban dwellers. It is an ad that is hard to forget because it raises anxiety levels.

In March 1987, a chain of Southern California pizza parlors cleverly utilized all the Dracula *shtick.* Numero Uno Pizza ran a television promotion called "The Bite for Two." A vampire and his date are seen sitting in a restaurant booth; the vampire is about to sink his teeth into the neck of his girlfriend when the waiter interrupts and asks, "May I help you?"

With an Eastern European accent the vampire says, "We just stepped out for a bite."

The waiter asks, "Well, how about Numero Uno's 'Bite for Two'?"

The vampire answers that one bite will do and continues to move toward his girlfriend's neck. The girlfriend protests, asking to know more about the "Bite for Two." When the waiter mentions deep-dish pizza, the vampire responds, "I could sink my teeth into that."

The waiter continues. "Choice of pasta," he says as he shows both a white sauce and a red sauce.

The vampire responds with delight, "Ahh, red, my favorite color."

The waiter continues to enumerate. "Two crisp salads, soup, and garlic puffs." Revolted by hearing the word "garlic" the vampire exclaims, "Garlic!"

Triumphant, the waiter says, "One bite and we gotcha!"

"That should have been my line," says the vampire—this time spoken without an accent.

The waiter responds, "The 'Bite for Two'—$9.95."

This ad incorporates almost every common vampire motif and joke. The humor is familiar and comfortable. These are old jokes

INEXPENSIVE HOME SECURITY SYSTEM PROTECTS YOU AGAINST UNINVITED GUESTS.

Reprinted by permission of Schlage Lock Company

in a new setting, the pizza restaurant. The agency that created this ad assumes that American viewers will enjoy the gags and both remember and purchase the product.

The owners of the Transilvania Convenient Market in the Eagle Rock section of Los Angeles explained why they had chosen that name for their establishment. Surprisingly, the proprietors, Eva and Nick Stoisor, turned out to be from Romania.

"Everybody knows when you say Transylvania, what it is, whether or not they know about the real Vlad Tepes, so it would be easy for everyone to get it in their minds," Nick explained. Although Nick is a newcomer to the United States, he has quickly picked up an understanding of American advertising techniques. His teenage son has taken the idea a step further. He had a neighborhood friend create a mural on the side of the building, painting a mountainous region with a castle on top of the mountain, bats flying around it, and in the foreground, a vampire figure with fangs. Prominently painted across the middle of the mural is the word "Transilvania" written in the neighborhood Hispanic style of graffiti lettering.

Here is an excellent example of the vampire tradition adapting to the local community. Mr. Stoisor reports that the Dracula motif has been successful in attracting customers and giving them a basis upon which to communicate about a familiar theme while they purchase their sandwiches and soft drinks.

Larry Eberle, marketing communication manager for ECAD, a company that produces a software program distributed internationally for layout verification called "Dracula," tells how valuable it has been to have this name for their product:

> If you take a look at other ads people have in trade magazines, you see a computer chip and a computer screen. You're about ready to fall asleep. Then you open our page and here's Dracula and a beautiful lady on a motorbike. It certainly catches your eye. It has been very effective and the company has had a lot of fun with it. First of all, the software's very good. Then let's face it, the people who are using our software are doing work that's very esoteric, deep,

technical, and let's face it—boring. It gets a little boring to sit and look at the computer screen all day. Dracula is a little bit of escapism and it works well in our ads.

Company legend provides the rationale for the connection between Dracula and what this software provides. Originally the software was called Design Rule Checker. Some of the men were out drinking on Halloween and they were saying, "*Design Rule* Checker. D.R.C. What kind of name can we make out of DRC?" They came up with Dracula.

When ECAD opened its office in England it was near the Hammer Studios; so company personnel went over and rented some Dracula props. "Some ladies dressed up like Vampira. Of course Dracula was there and they put on this skit and Dracula came out of his coffin," Eberle explained.

When software trade shows first started, ECAD hired an actor dressed like Dracula to walk around and show up at their hospitality suite. This, too, turned out to be valuable. Now customers say, "I want Dracula."

Particularly at Halloween, the vampire motif now flourishes on the tube, at the cinema, and in print. In 1986 a full-page advertisement appeared in the *Los Angeles Times* with words printed on top of a black cape, a vampire's head appearing just above it. It was captioned "A Halloween War to lower car prices . . . and raise your spirits. The battle of the 'Monster'ous import car dealers is on. Who will be the number one import car dealer on Van Nuys Boulevard?"

The drawings showed two vehicles facing each other in competition. One car was driven by a Frankenstein character. Opposite him a vampire was seated in a pickup truck. A crescent moon hung in the background. One caption read, "Sink your teeth into a good deal." "You can Count on it," appeared beneath the picture of the vampire. The creators of this eye-catching promotion knew they had built-in assurance that readers would pay attention.

During the trick-or-treat season, choosing to dress in a vampire costume is made all the easier by the availability of *accoutre-ments*. At one magic and costume shop in Los Angeles during a recent year, there were several brands available for each type of accessory: "Whistling Dracula teeth, fit right over your own teeth"; "Safe non-toxic Dracula Blood," in a handy plastic squeezable tube; a Count Dracula medallion ornamented with a ruby-colored stone and hung from a red velvet ribbon; and red two-inch vampire fingernails which were "slit to fit all ages," for an easy fit.

Several different Los Angeles–area costume shops were polled to determine by costume rentals the popularity of Dracula during the 1986 Halloween season. Responses varied. A nearby costume shop said that Dracula is very popular, but that rental of costumes varies from year to year. The salesperson ranked the vampire figure in the "top ten" in terms of popularity.

Six years ago another store ran out of Dracula capes even before Halloween had arrived. In 1986 they had a few capes left over. "It decreased a lot," the shopkeeper declared. This representative placed Dracula in the "top twenty" of popular costumes and speculated that the decrease in 1986 might be explained by customers putting together costumes on their own rather than renting complete outfits. She said that they sold a lot of vampire makeup kits, which cost $12.95.

At a large costume shop containing six floors of more than one million costumes they reported:

> Every Halloween we get lots of requests for Dracula. They just see something black with a cape in front of them. That's all they see. We tell them that he wore evening tails. They say, "He did?"
>
> That's wonderful because we charge $95 for the tails. Of course, it's a little less if you don't go with a top hat. He never wore a top hat. Funny, he'd look like Fred Astaire.

The salesman described the different kinds of capes, some with huge bat-wing collars. He said these were very popular and related that by the time October 31 arrives the shop always rents all of the Dracula capes "down to the dregs." He said that those customers who come in late are usually so desperate they'd take the capes even if they had green instead of a red lining. He rated the Dracula costume as being in the "top ten."

Out in Bellflower, a suburb in the southwest portion of Los Angeles County, Dracula was not very popular. In 1986 the most popular costumes were a dance-hall girl and flapper for women and a gambler and gangster for men.

In contrast, the owner of another Hollywood costume shop who has been in business for fifteen years related, "Every year, Dracula is the most popular." She said that the only time his popularity waned was when *Star Wars* first came out. Then he lost out to Darth Vader for a few years. Now, she doesn't get calls for Darth Vader anymore, and Dracula is back on top of the list again. When Darth Vader took over, she thought Dracula had finally been replaced. "But he wasn't. He came back." She giggled. "That's right. He didn't do anything very unusual for him. He came back."

Nationally, Alan Salmela, regional sales manager of Spearhead Industries of Minneapolis, Minnesota, believes that the vampire is popular because it's so easy for people to execute its character. His company, a seasonal toy distributor in business for over ten years, produces vampire teeth, makeup, cape, and a complete costume kit sold all over the country.

Salmela explains that the vampire and Halloween business is growing bigger every year, but for his company it is only since 1983 that the vampire character has become so prominent. Adults, especially, are now more involved with the holiday and Salmela attributes this to the Tylenol-tampering scare, referring to the 1982 tragedy when seven people died of cyanide which had been placed in Extra-Strength Tylenol capsules. This story broke at the end of September and in Salmela's view that year more parents began supervising children's indoor parties instead of sending them out for trick or treat. He thinks this led to the parents dressing up, too, and eventually entering more into the annual celebration. His company now supplies many more adult costumes than in the past, when the market was primarily geared for children.

For Salmela's company, costume distribution seems to be generally even across the country, with the exception of the West Coast, which has a very high volume of sales, no doubt related to fairly pleasant weather conditions during the season. This allows for broader participation in outdoor carnivals and parades.

Lou Di Marco, field sales manager of the R. M. Palmer Company in West Reading, Pennsylvania, concurs with Salmela's assessment regarding the increase in the vampire's prominence at Halloween. The Palmer Company has been manufacturing candy for over forty years, but it is only since 1985 that they have been producing vampire-themed chocolate treats for Halloween—Creepy Coffins with lift-up lids and Double Crisp Creatures, featuring Count Crunch and Vampbite.

In the 1986 Halloween season, Dracula was actively involved. Hires Root Beer and Crush Orange Drink sponsored a "Tran

Reprinted by permission of R. M. Palmer Company

sylvania Mania" contest, advertised by using words with blood dripping from the printed letters. The grand prize was round-trip airfare for two to Romania. Second prize promised round-trip airfare for two to Lexington, Kentucky, to visit Transylvania University. The information was printed on an eight-inch-square, slick, splashy, color newspaper ad featuring a castle and bats.

In Los Angeles at the same time a billboard in Spanish promoted an ice cream brand being savored by a boy in a vampire costume. Two years later, the vampire-clad child was still featured in the ice cream ad all year round. Similarly, Mayor Tom Bradley, in his 1986 bid for governor, was seen in a *Los Angeles Times* article accompanied by a photograph of him in Oakland shaking hands with a woman who held a toddler wearing fangs.

The linking of the vampire to Halloween was more strongly forged during 1987. By virtue of his popular presence at this time, it appears that he is becoming a major Halloween symbol. The arts are affected as well, as evidenced by the California Ballet premier of *Dracula,* which opened on Halloween Eve in San Diego, California. Based on Stoker's novel and choreographed by Charles Bennet, the ballet received a cool review by critic Martin Bernheimer, who wrote, "Loved the intermissions. Hated the show." What Bernheimer loved was the audience's high-spirited participation by wearing masks and costumes (Einstein, Madame Butterfly, Frankenstein, Snow White) and arriving at the theater in hearses.

The Dracula figure has appeared in numerous seasonal print ads. For example, one year Mountain Bell took a three-quarter-page ad in the *Albuquerque Tribune* showing Bela Lugosi hovering above the caption "Introducing the telephone package for those poor souls who have to work at night." A Los Angeles furniture store took a full-page ad showing two children, one dressed as a witch and another as Dracula, under the headline "A Monstrous Grand Opening That Even The Little Monsters Will Love."

Vampire chocolate treats (Count Crunch, Creepy Coffins,

Vampbites), costuming, makeup elements, party decorations, light-up pins, buttons, and flashlights are bountiful in drug and variety stores, card and party shops, and supermarkets. The marquee at an X-rated theater in Hollywood once advertised *Gayracula* during Halloween.

The quantity of Halloween vampire cards seems to multiply each year. Hallmark alone produced fourteen during 1987. One of the most humorous had Schulz's Snoopy character asking, "Where does Dracula rent hearses?" "The Boris Car Lot," was the answer. Another showed a photo of Bela Lugosi in a menacing pose on the cover. He announced, "It's Halloween." Inside the card the message read, "And you look good enough to eat." Another card was full of Dracula riddles—asking his favorite holiday (Fangsgiving), what kind of dog he has (a bloodhound), where did they put him when he was arrested (into a red blood cell).

A Hallmark national representative reports that the vampire

© Hallmark Cards, Inc. Reprinted by permission

theme has been a part of their Halloween greeting-card line for quite a few years. Generally, the vampire is presented in a humorous style and with bold graphic design geared toward the adult market. Hallmark also observes that Halloween is becoming much more of an adult holiday.

They have now expanded beyond vampire greeting cards and have produced an audiocassette, *The Sounds of Halloween*. It displays only one figure on its cover to represent the holiday—a vampire. In 1987 they also sold a black T-shirt with the emblem "Transylvania University" in letters which looked like they were dripping blood surrounding a seal, "We Go for the Throat! E Pluribus Bitum." The middle of the seal showed a bat under which was printed "Our Founder." Even the inside tag with washing instructions contained gaglines. "One size scares all . . . Avoid Silver Bullets, Wolfbane, Garlic, Stakes Through the Heart; Stay Out of Direct Sunlight."

Sales of this controversial shirt caused a problem when the real

Kentucky-based Transylvania University objected to infringement of the university's property rights. As a result Hallmark Cards Inc. offered an apology and stopped production and distribution.

General Mills, too, ran into some vampire difficulty. The company redesigned the box containing its Count Chocula cereal, replacing the cartoon depiction of the count with a reproduction of Bela Lugosi as he was filmed in *Dracula*. However, after producing four million boxes, General Mills discovered that the computer technique used to reproduce the likeness unexpectedly caused the Count's familiar medallion to look like a Star of David. Calls of protest from Jewish community representatives caused the company to alter the design and remove the medallion from television commercials and future packages. An Anti-Defamation League spokesperson lauded General Mills's prompt action and expressed gratitude for their sensitivity and quick response to rectify the mishap.

Vampires have popped up at Halloween in the military, too, particularly at Assignment Night on an air force base in Columbus, Mississippi. On this highly anticipated occasion, which takes place one month before graduation after a rigorous year of academic and physical preparation, air force pilots-in-training, their families, and their friends are told where these new pilots will be stationed and the kinds of flying they will be performing.

One year, Assignment Night fell on Halloween. The instructor pilot made a dramatic entrance lying in a coffin borne by six pilots. Dressed as a vampire and calling himself Dracula's son, the instructor pilot rose from the casket to emcee the event and reveal each new pilot's destiny to the excited and volatile audience.

At Halloween a Burbank dentist is routinely asked to make sets of fangs for aspiring vampires. "I was on a hot streak about four or five years ago when the Boy Scouts hit me up for a Spook Alley they were running." To produce the fangs he first takes an impression of the teeth, creating a wax mold which is later duplicated in acrylic. There are six teeth in the set, spanning from cuspid to cuspid; but only the cuspids are lengthened. The set is held on by friction. "You just slide them on," the dentist explained. His own six-year-old son requested a set of fangs for his 1986 vampire costume, and a few years prior to that the dentist made a pair for someone who works in law enforcement and likes to wear them to work occasionally, "as a gag."

At an early age, American children learn about vampires and Dracula figures. More than twenty-five children's books on the subject have been published, with titles such as *A Child's Garden of Vampires, Be Your Own Vampire, The Hardy Boys and Nancy Drew Meet Dracula, Bunnicula, Vampires.*

Vampires, by Colin and Jacqui Hawkins, is a lighthearted look at vampires. Interspersed with some of the traditional ideas— wooden stakes, garlic, fangs, long sharp fingernails—are some new, funny concepts. The authors write about cultural differences in vampires, claiming that British ones read the *Times* and carry black umbrellas, while Russian vampires are allergic to the clergy and American vampires use their noses to suck blood from the ears of their victims.

The drawings are delightful and witty, and the general silliness works well to reduce fear. For example, the vampire mother reads some fairy tales to her children after they request stories about their ancestors . "Tell us about Vlad the Impaler," the children implore her at bedtime, "and how Vlad the Glad got his fang out in time. Tell us how Vlad the Mad caught Vlad the Cad in Granny's casket. Tell us about Dracula the film star . . ." Instead, the mother tells them stories about *Goldifangs and the Three Bears, Little Red Riding Fangs,* and *Vampirella and the Glass Fangs.*

In addition to regular children's books, comic book vampire figures have proliferated, particularly from Marvel Comics *(Dracula, Vampire Tales, Tomb of Dracula);* DC *(I—Vampire);* and Warren Publishing, which put out the *Vampirella* adventures.

According to one comic book store proprietor in Los Angeles, interest in traditional vampire comics is affected by television and school. "Sales pick up once summer starts and the kids start watching old Dracula films on TV."

One of the biggest new vampire comic book sellers since 1987 has been a four-part series called *Blood,* written by J. M. DeMatteis and published by Marvel Comics. These comics tend to appeal more to young adults. What makes them unique and so popular is the outstanding artwork by Kent Williams. His gothic impressionism style utilizes ink drawings over water colors that work more as true illustrations rather than traditional comic book graphics. Each panel is like an individual painting.

Children learn about vampires from educational TV. "Sesame Street" has a benign Count Dracula character, who teaches the children how to count. His flower-covered figure appeared in the 1986 Pasadena Rose Parade. A California company produces a replica doll of him complete with green satin cape. Youngsters can encounter the symbol at the breakfast table with their morning portions of Count Chocula cereal. (In England there was an ice pop called "Count Dracula's Deadly Secret—Eat One Before Sunset." Its advertisement described moon-white ice cream concealed in black-as-night water ice.)

"Drac-in-a-Box," who pops out of a handcrafted maplewood box wearing traditional vampire garb, with a wooden stake hanging from his neck, is one of the best sellers in the JAX line of forty varieties of traditional jack-in-the-boxes. The idea for this toy came from the twelve-year-old niece of owners Jane and Allan Ross, when they started their Maine company in 1983. While at first they rejected the idea as being "silly," they fortunately changed their minds and now the JAX company is quite proud of the success of this character. The popularity of the figure at this one New England–based company is a reflection of the nationwide interest in and attraction to the vampire symbol.

Count Duckula is a vampire cartoon character introduced to American children in 1988 by the British film company Cosgrove Hall. Shown over the Nickelodeon cable TV channel, "Count Duckcula" is about a vampire duck who was turned into a vegetarian when his nanny mistakenly transfused him with ketchup. This causes him to have an "uncontrollable urge for broccoli" or sometimes a dire need for a grape. In addition to Nanny his other side character is Igor, the butler. Typical vampire motifs are included: bats who speak with heavy Transylvanian accents; garlic as a threatening artifact; Duckula's appearance—widow's peak and black hair. Referring to Duckula in song as the feathered Prince of Evil who "flies through the night, looking for a bite," the entire show capitalizes on the usual gags related to vampires. For example, at commercial break time the narrator says, "Count Duckula always comes back, so stay tuned for these messages."

Wilma's Word Problems, an arithmetic word problem workbook for first- through third-graders, shows a character with two fangs, dressed in black with black hair and widow's peak. Above it reads, "Sam had three bats. Then five more came to

© 1983 by Jax. Reprinted by permission

stay. How many live with Sam now?" Subsequent pages show more vampire-based word problems: "Sam had two fangs. Then he grew seven more. How many fangs does Sam have now?" Sam, the vampire, appears in one more word problem under the heading "How many pets does each monster have in all? Sam has sixteen rats and twenty-seven bats." Another related concept occurs. A vampire bat, with fangs exposed, flies under the math problem. "Forty-nine bats hung in a cave. Sixteen flew out. How many are left?"

One would assume these vampire characters are used because the author has realized that the vampire is already a familiar and recognizable figure to a six-year-old. His fangs, widow's peak, bats, and rats are an already learned and accepted part of the six-year-old American child's culture. It would appear that children need no more information about the character in the picture in order for them to understand and solve the problem.

Generally, objects used in word problems are ones familiar to children: dogs, cats, birds. While Sam, the vampire, is not the only supernatural figure in this book (there is also a ghost, a witch, and a creature from outer space), one must assume that the author decided that children would comprehend the concept.

Frank Schaffer, publisher of this workbook, said that his company is the largest publisher of supplementary materials for young children. His books are distributed all over the United States as well as in England, Canada, and Australia. Schaffer explained that they put vampires in because they're humorous and fun for the children. "They're friendly little devils, aren't they?"

A four-year-old girl was interviewed. "Do you know who Count Dracula is?"

"No. Who is he?" she wanted to know.

"What about a vampire?"

This concept was more familiar to her. "It's a scary bat," she answered, revealing that by the age of four she had already begun to absorb some of the information about vampire characteristics.

Next a six-year-old was queried to see how much information she had acquired.

"Who is Count Dracula?"

"He counts. He has these two front teeth sticking out. He has long fingernails. He wears this cape to suck people's blood. Then no one could see," she responded with authority.

"Is he real or in the imagination?"

"Imagination," she answered.

"Is he a bad guy or a good guy?"

"A bad guy, because all vampires suck people's blood."

"From where?"

She hesitated in answering. She didn't know. Then she said, "From the arm."

"What happens after the vampire sucks your blood?"

She responded, "You won't be alive anymore. You die."

"Then what happens to you?"

"You can't do nothing."

She related that vampires were boys not girls; that they looked like men, but they have two front teeth—"big ones. I mean tall ones, like women's fingernails." She also said that the vampire on "Sesame Street" was a good Dracula, "because he doesn't suck people's blood. He counts one, two, three, four, five, six." While the child's description clearly reveals her familiarity with TV's benign "Sesame Street" Count, it is apparent that she has picked up from another source the Vampire's other, more sinister habits and incorporated them into her concept of the creature.

The Topp's Chewing Gum Company is obviously aware that very young children are familiar with vampires. This is evident by their inclusion of two vampire figures in their collection of Garbage Pail Kids, the equivalent of baseball trading cards found in chewing gum packages and sold to the grammar school set, from about six years on up. The vampires on the cards, called Evil Eddie and Nasty Nick, wear high-collared black capes lined in red, have white faces and widows' peaks, and are shown about to sink their fangs into the Barbie dolls they are clutching.

From the babe in arms wearing fangs to greet the gubernatorial candidate, to the preschoolers watching "Sesame Street" and eating Count Chocula cereal, to the first-graders doing their sums, American children are indoctrinated early and learn to accept the vampire symbol as a part of their culture. By the time they reach high school level, they can be given a vampire quiz, and most can answer quite correctly about the details of the creature's dress, appearance, and behavior. It is a quiz they can pass—and without cramming.

The high school and college student survey reveals that of 389 who were able to recall a specific age when they learned about vampires, 44 percent wrote that they had first learned about them when they were between the ages of five and eight, while 40 percent said they learned about them between the ages of eight and twelve. More students wrote that they learned about vampires when they were five years old (sixty-one), followed by fifty-three students who said that they learned about them at age ten.

In answer to the question "When did you learn about vampires?" one student wrote, "Since I started watching TV."

It is through television that children seem most often to become familiar with, and conditioned to, the symbols and behavior of vampires through advertisements, the "Sesame Street" figure, and television show re-runs. For example, "Dark Shadows" now has its own afterlife, particularly on cable channels across the country. Thus, there is the opportunity to "educate" new viewers about vampires. Reruns are also being shown of "The Munsters," another successful show, which ran from 1964 to 1966 and featured two vampire characters, the 378-year-old Grandpa, played by Al Lewis, and Eddie, the vampire kid, also known as the wolf boy, played by Butch Patrick.

"The Munsters" was based on characters created by cartoonist Charles Addams and featured in the *New Yorker* magazine. One of Addams's drawn characters, who later became Morticia on "The Addams Family" TV show, was the inspiration for actress Maila Nurmi, who took the name Vampira and became a very popular television hostess on KABC-TV in Los Angeles in 1954. Wearing a campy black wig and dressed in a seductive long black dress with tight belt to accentuate her tiny waist and cleavage, she delighted audiences with her risqué patter and pet spider, Rollo.

In an article written for *Fangoria,* a magazine about monsters, aliens, and bizarre creatures, she reminisces about her popular gimmick of drinking a formaldehyde-based cocktail while singing a parody of the Pepsi commercial popular at that time.

> Here's to Zombies, the living dead;
> May you find one, beneath your bed;
> They live on blood and you should too;
> Hemoglobin is the drink for you!
> Trickle, Trickle, Trickle, Trickle.

Vampira was Elvira's precursor in tantalizing appearance and use of double entendre, but Elvira has not pursued vampire traditions, such as drinking blood.

From the first American-made Dracula sound film starring Bela Lugosi in 1931 until now, there have been more than 100 vampire films produced in the United States including a porno version called *Dracula Sucks,* featuring John Holmes, and a black version, *Blacula,* made in 1972, starring William Marshall and Charles McCauley. *Blacula* was advertised as follows: "He's Black! He's Beautiful! He's Blacula!" Furthermore, there seems to be no letup in vampire-inspired productions in spite of the assessment made by a well-established Hollywood motion picture agent, who several years ago adamantly rejected a highly creative vampire script, claiming with disdain, "Who's interested in Dracula?"

Clearly the agent had not been paying attention to the fact that the American public, like the Count, seems to have an insatiable appetite. *Once Bitten* was released in 1985 and billed as a "tasty comedy." *Transylvania 6-5000* was released in the same year. *Vamp,* starring Grace Jones, was released in 1986, as was *Little Shop of Horrors,* an updated film version that followed on the heels of its smash musical comedy version which opened in New

York on July 27, 1982, and ran for five years. In this particular variant, the vampire is a blood-drinking plant. Another variation is *Vampire Lesbians of Sodom,* a vampire comedy by Charles Busch, which has been running Off-Broadway since 1985.

The Demon Prince: Genesis of the Vampire has been made, but not yet released. According to a *Los Angeles Times* press release, it is a romantic Gothic horror story in which two women—one good, the other evil—compete for the love of the same demon of a man. Another new film not yet released is *The Vampire of Beverly Hills,* produced by Euphoria productions in Los Angeles.

Four vampire feature films were released in 1987: *Return to Salem's Lot, Monster Squad, Near Dark* (advertised with the slogan "Pray for daylight"), and *The Lost Boys.* In search of a distributor, a low-budget version, *Vampire at Midnight* ("He's dead . . . until dark"), was also screened. In this one, adapted to a contemporary Los Angeles setting, the vampire figure is embodied in the persona of Dr. Victor Radkoff, a hypnotherapist to artists looking for a way to unleash their creative powers to achieve success.

Joel Schumacher, director of *The Lost Boys,* assessed the popularity of the vampire topic in an interview that appeared in *American Film:*

> Vampires bring up a lot of stuff. In the Victorian period, when people lived such repressed lives, a lot of sexual fantasies were lived out through these stories. But I don't think our movie deals with any of those things at all. I think it says: "Hey! There are still vampires, they just dress better."

Schumacher would probably be surprised, no doubt distressed, that his heavy metal–looking "lost boys" are cited as the source of inspiration for one suicide and a murder.

Five vampire feature films were scheduled for release in 1988: *Fright Night—Part 2,* featuring Roddy McDowall; *Vampire's Kiss,* starring Nicolas Cage, who is prey to a female vampire on the loose in New York City; *Dracula's Widow,* in which the bereaved is in quest of her husband; and *Not of This Earth,* about a nurse who fights off alien vampires.

My Best Friend Is a Vampire, was released in the spring of 1988 and geared to the high school set, as clearly seen in its advertisements showing a coffin-shaped hall locker and the slogan "Vampires and teenagers are a lot alike. They're just misunderstood."

A reviewer of this film who called it "pleasingly offbeat" could not resist the opportunities for punning. "Just when you thought Dracula was down for the count. . . . indeed [the film] sinks its teeth deep into the jocular vein. To all concerned fangs a lot."

According to film critic Davie Pirie, vampirism was a minor movie theme until 1957 when at least 200 films were produced by ten different countries.

Pirie said that by the end of 1973 the popularity of the vampire had decreased so much that in 1974 international production of films was only one-sixth what it had been the year before. However, the VCR explosion and popularity of renting home videos at low cost is giving new life to the old vampire classics. A survey of video stores revealed fifteen different vampire-related titles, from the 1931 Bela Lugosi *Dracula* through its Andy Warhol version and various incarnations with Frank Langella, George Hamilton *(Love at First Bite),* and Blacula.

The print medium has exploited the vampire as well, and Charles Addams was not the only cartoonist to utilize the vampire theme. In one, *Los Angeles Times* political cartoonist Paul Conrad shows Richard Nixon exposing fangs while standing in a graveyard amid tombstones, under a full moon. There is a suggestion of a widow's peak on the former president. Nixon's arms are extended under an outstretched cape. He makes his famous two-finger "V" gesture. Beneath the figure are the words "The vampire strikes back."

Syndicated cartoonist Gary Larson regularly includes a vampire character in his "The Far Side" feature. In one particular cartoon he refers to the character without even having to depict it. He shows a man on a soapbox warning the uninterested men and women walking around him about the dangers of vampires being everywhere. At the same time two men are unloading a giant mirror in which only the orator is seen. No pedestrians are reflected in the mirror. The entire joke rests on the audience's understanding that vampires cast no reflection in a mirror, a fact the cartoonist assumes.

Another cartoon brings up a new issue for vampires. This one was printed in a university paper. A vampire is seen sitting at a bar drinking liquor, not blood, and complaining to his bar mate, ". . . And then you start worrying, 'Wait a minute, maybe they're *all* carrying the antibodies or something.' Man, you just can't be too careful anymore . . ."

This is not an isolated association of AIDS and vampires in the media. A short-lived theatrical production called *Red Tide* explored what might happen if, among a group of modern-day vampires, one might contract the AIDS virus. Playwright Justin Tanner attempted to deal with the social reality of AIDS through the portrayal of vampires as both victims and carriers. *Red Tide* depicted the ugliness of the ostracization, hysteria, and panic caused by the disease.

While there are no statistics documenting an actual link between the ingestion of contaminated blood and the disease, the possibility of the connection, the knowledge that it can be transmitted through rashes on the face or cuts in the mouth, and the aura of mystery and fear surrounding AIDS provide natural copy opportunities for national tabloids.

The *Sun,* with the headline "Gay Vampire Catches AIDS," carried a story written by Fred Sleeves that alleged, "The merry neck-biter who swished his way from town to town luring gay lovers into this world of vampirism, apparently consumed disease-infected blood along the way." While the reporter did list a physician's name in Marseilles, France, and the name of the European gay vampire, it has been impossible to verify the story. This story was also picked up on AM radio in Los Angeles and referred to in a morning feature called "Lust in the News."

Another tabloid, the *Weekly World News,* linked vampires to

AIDS, this time with a story about German physicians. According to reporter Terry Connors, East German doctors Bremen Fischer and Hofman Piehl charge that vampires in the Middle Ages were immune to the disease but spread it through sexual, perhaps even casual, contact, rather than biting or sucking the blood of victims. An Austrian virologist, Karl Sauberer, is quoted as saying, "If we accept the idea that vampires were AIDS carriers, then the connection to homosexuality is inevitable . . . and there is, after all, a vast body of centuries-old literature that shows vampires by far preferred the company of men." According to this article, the most famous vampire of them all—Count Dracula—is widely believed to have been "shockingly promiscuous and bisexual at the very least."

Postulated by the German physicians but denied by the Austrian physician is the notion that in the Middle Ages AIDS victims mistook the purplish lesions caused by Kaposi's sarcoma (the cancer that affects many AIDS victims) for the bite marks of vampires.

A more recent issue of this same tabloid quoted a Vienna-based virologist, Dr. Josef Sperl, announcing that there has been a dramatic decline in vampire attacks in Eastern Europe because of AIDS—from seventy-five to fewer than five a month. Headlined "AIDS-Wary Vampires Pull in Their Fangs!" the article quotes the doctor as stating, "Vampires are facing the most serious threat to survival in the history of their breed."

Claiming that most vampires are homosexuals, he explains, "Their sexual preference alone puts them at great risk of getting AIDS. To make matters worse they have a taste for blood. And everybody knows that the exchange of blood is one of the ways the AIDS virus is transmitted."

These tabloids, sold at supermarket check-out stands, are just another mode of reinforcing the presence of the vampire symbol, this time tied to a new public interest and obsession, fear of AIDS. Verifiable stories or not, the combination of elements— vampires, AIDS, homosexuality—is guaranteed to seize the attention of the waiting shopper. Even without the eye-catching

AIDS component, the topic of vampires is a staple for these publications—"Fang Gang! Vampires Attack Man Watching Dracula Movie on Television," "Bizarre Vampire Marriage—It Was Love at First Bite for Caped Couple."

There is no denying the fascination with the vampire in this country. According to Martin Riccardo's *The Complete Multi-Media Vampire and Dracula Bibliography,* over 100 American stage productions of Dracula have been presented annually since 1977 by both amateur and professional groups and by schools and other organizations.

In terms of individual songs, Jamaican musician Peter Tosh produced a reggae-beat "Vampire," which was released in 1988. Putting the vampire into a political context, Tosh uses it as a metaphor for blood-sucking, power-hungry, wicked governments who take and spill the blood of the nation, fighting against everything that is good for the people.

A new vampire trend may be on the horizon. England, which often exports music ideas to the United States is currently seeing the rise of a musical and life-style cult movement called "Gothic." Followers claim to be opposed to the "punk" movement and focus on old spooky places and objects. Janet Watson, a seventeen-year-old member who looks like "an escapee from a Hammer horror movie," says that an old graveyard is her favorite place to be. A group of Gothics living in England has decorated its shared home with black walls, coffin-shaped tables, red velvet curtains, and a cage full of rats.

This new life-style is an outgrowth of two popular British bands, the Cult and the Mission. Models for the members include Morticia from TV's "Addams Family," old vampire movies, and Bram Stoker's novel. When he performs, Sean Cronin a member of the rock band the Screaming Marionettes, wears fangs, a black rubber frock coat, and skin tight pants. He "takes his gothicism very seriously indeed," and predicts a new wave of "Transylvanian rock" in the next year or so.

His forecast may be accurate, for there is already an L.A. based variant of Gothic musicians, who in spite of their name, Radio

Werewolf, dress in tuxedos and have pale and unsmiling vampire countenances. James Filthcollar, Evil Wilhelm, Nikolas Schreck, and Paul Antonelli comprise this group, which claims to have been together for all ages, but in this incarnation has been playing since 1984. On special occasions, Bongo Wolf joins them for a cameo appearance with his bongo drums, wearing a noose around his neck.

They write their own tunes, among them "Charley's Girls," about Charles Manson, and have made their movie debut in *Mortuary Academy,* not yet released, in which they play themselves, are killed, then later reanimated. "We are the guardians of the gothic spirit and we have been for all time. We've returned to bring the gothic spirit onto the earth," explained Schreck.

Dracula in the Desert, a stage presentation produced by the Antenna Theater in the San Francisco Bay area, sold out to audiences during its six-week Christmas season of 1986. In this play, Dracula tries unsuccessfully to change his character. Chris Hardman, who wrote and directed the piece, tells why he chose the famous vampire figure as the centerpiece of his creation.

> . . . because he is part of our modern mythos, something that all Americans know the story of. He's one of our very strong, very elegant, very captivating, very seductive lone-wolf characters. He's one of the guys who has passed into the media world and has become part of the standard information that everybody knows. Everyone knows that he can have no reflection, is stabbed by a stake, killed with a silver bullet, all the basic makeup of his character, just like the basic makeups of past mythological characters were known by the audience before they came into the theater.

Hardman adds that since we left our Christian folklore and heritage behind, we have inherited another—something acceptable, a semi-secular folklore which is Dracula.

Hardman's assessment seems to be verified by the large numbers of Dracula / vampire publications. Riccardo's 1983 vampire bibliography cites the American publishing of over 160 vampire short stories, over 102 vampire novels, 29 vampire anthologies, 35 vampire plays, and some vampire specialized reading fare.

Jeanne Youngson has written *The Count Dracula Chicken Cookbook,* based on her realization that when Jonathan Harker went to Dracula's castle he was served a delicious chicken dinner with tossed salad. She deduces that since Dracula didn't have any servants, he must have done everything himself.

If the dinner was that good, he must have been a good cook and had his own cookbook. With tongue in cheek she recounts the accidental discovery of Dracula's recipes in a Charing Cross bookstore, which she now shares with the world—and with sequels to follow, for example, *The Count Dracula Casserole Cookbook* and *The Count Dracula Dessert Cookbook.*

There is a how-to vampire book. Madeline X has written *How to Become a Vampire in Six Easy Lessons.* The author claims to have lived longer than any other human and writes that she was a practicing vampire until the late 1970s, when she met and married a mortal. From this union she bore twin daughters, who seem not to have inherited her condition. Since the birth of her children, Madeline has given up her vampiric activities, except "for an occasional drink."

Madeline lists several qualifications that might allow one to become a vampire on one's own—for example, eating the flesh of a sheep killed by a wolf or being born with teeth. If her list of qualifications does not apply to the reader, she presents a regime and schedule that can allow anyone to become one—or so she claims.

Greenberg the Vampire was a big seller in the graphic novel genre when it first came out in 1986. Graphic novels, which are novels in picture form, have evolved out of comic books, are larger, have stiffer covers and slicker paper, and tell one complete story per volume. They have become quite popular with adults over the last ten years.

Oscar Greenberg, king of the Jewish vampires whose tale is told in *Greenberg the Vampire,* was created by J. M. DeMatteis. Mark Badger painted the exciting graphics, which illustrate the text in comic book style, that is, with panels containing characters with word balloons. Greenberg's humorous yet dramatic story is filled with both vampire and Jewish gags. It incorporates Yiddish words such as *tuchas, schmuck, shiksa, fakakta,* and *kvetching.* It also contains Jewish clichés—for example, the aggressive momma pushing food: chopped liver, stuffed cabbage, chicken soup with kreplach, chopped eggs, roast chicken, noodle pudding, cheese blintzas.

Greenberg, who lives in Brooklyn, is a struggling writer trying to overcome writer's block and desperately trying to make a movie deal with Paradise Studios. His vampire condition has come about as a result of his being attacked by the supernatural Lilith when he was an infant. Lilith (Adam's first wife who was expelled from Eden and thought to be the mother of evil spirits) keeps interfering with Greenberg's life on earth. In a final fierce battle against her wicked force, Greenberg is saved and his writing abilities are revived.

Other specialized publishing companies have incorporated vampire themes as well. The Naiad Press, which markets literary materials to a lesbian audience, includes a vampire short story in its catalogue. "O Captain, My Captain" was written by Katherine V. Forrest, one of Naiad's most successful writers. Set in the future, this erotic tale is of a female vampire, Captain Drake, commander of a space ship, who sexually preys upon her female military assistant while on a mission in outer space. In spite of the futuristic setting, classic motifs are included: the captain transforms into a bat; sleeps during the day and in total darkness; has pale hands and skin and uneven teeth; is thin with dark hair; and is never seen taking any kind of nourishment, except tomato juice dispensed from an Autoserv.

During the 1970s and 1980s, three best-selling authors of fiction utilized the vampire theme with enormous success—Chelsea Quinn Yarbro, Stephen King, and Anne Rice. Anne Rice's *Interview with the Vampire* has sold over one million copies and recently has been reissued in a new paperback version. Its sequel, *The Vampire Lestat,* in which the vampire becomes a rock star, brought $700,000 for the rights to the paperback version alone, and Paramount Studios has paid $150,000 for film rights. Rice's third volume on vampires, *Queen of the Damned,* sold 400,000 copies before publication.

Stephen King's 1975 *Salem's Lot* was bought by New American Library for a high six figures and became a Literary Guild alternate, with $50,000 allocated for an advertising budget. It immediately sold 26,000 hardcover copies and was released in paperback the following year. *Salem's Lot,* a chilling tale of a New England town destroyed by a vampire who commits evil acts, including the sacrifice of children, climbed to number one on the *New York Times* best-seller list, and to number two on the *Publisher's Weekly* list. In 1980 a CBS television film version was made with James Mason and David Soul.

Chelsea Quinn Yarbro has published a highly popular series of novels about the vampire Ragoczy, Count Saint-Germain, who is in love with Madelaine de Montalia, an eighteenth-century aristocrat. The Saint-Germain series begins with *Hotel Transylvania,* first published in 1978. Yarbro has a coterie of followers. An "I ♥ Saint-Germain" bumper sticker has been spotted around the L.A. freeway system.

In addition to fictionalized versions of the vampire theme, there is a continuous stream of academic articles and books documenting either the exploits of the real Vlad Tepes, the film versions of the legendary Dracula, or the folklore of the phenomenon from particular time periods or different geographical locations. There are all kinds of analyses as well—psychoanalytic (*On the Nightmare* by Ernest Jones), literary (*The Living Dead* by James B. Twitchell), and historical (*Vampires, Burial, and Death* by Paul Barber).

A British hotel chain understands American popular culture and its fascination with the vampire. They conduct "Hunt-a-Vampire" weekends at their Crown Hotel in Scarborough, England, particularly aimed at U.S. tourists. "Dare you spend a weekend in Dracula country?" the brochure asks.

Upon arrival guests are given garlic, a wooden stake, and a

crucifix, to be carried at all times. The weekend begins with a "Bloody" Cocktail Reception (Bloody Mary's and Bull's Bloods), followed by a Vampire Dinner topped of by a Dracula quiz "for those with a thirst for knowledge." At 10:30 P.M. a documentary film, *In Search of Dracula,* is shown, after which horror and suspense films are presented. Before bedtime, Horlicks, a hot malted milk drink like Ovaltine, is served to calm the guests and help them sleep. But can they? During the night the hotel groans and creaks, vampire bats beat against windows, doors unexpectedly open, and mysterious screams emanate from the hallways, where apparitions of monsters appear. All this adds to the eerie and expected, yet unsettling, effects.

On Saturday, coaches take guests to Whitby, the place where Stoker spent his holidays high above the North Sea writing his famous work, and where he set the major part of the action in his novel. In Whitby tourists follow Bram Stoker's Dracula Trail with a guided tour. This includes the Bram Stoker Dracula Experience Museum featuring ten animated scenes from Stoker's tale, where visitors wander through darkened passageways seeing red-eyed bats hovering, and hearing howling wolves.

Saturday evening features a Fancy Dress Ball (fangs are available for those in need) and a four-course dinner, "Banquet Castle Dracula," served on coffin-shaped tables. A treasure hunt with Dracula in his coffin as prize is part of the after-dinner entertainment.

Sunday there is a guided tour of one of Scarborough's most haunted places, winding up with a traditional Sunday lunch and "At last—your chance to escape from Dracula's curse. Have a safe journey home."

In contrast, Romanian tourist officials were, at first, resistant to Americans' love of the Dracula myth. There are approximately 20,000 U.S. tourists who annually trek to this country. Eventually about 80 percent of them ask about Dracula.

"It's hard to tell them it isn't true," one tourist guide states. Most Americans are not aware that Bram Stoker's "Dracula" is banned in Romania, or that the real Dracula, Vlad Tepes, is thought of by Romanians as a hero, though tyrant, and considered to be the founder of Bucharest, Romania's capital city.

But the financial rewards of increased tourism caused authorities to make some changes when they noticed that some American tourists brought strings of garlic and crucifixes with them. Instead of playing down the folklore, they eventually began to incorporate more. Attesting to this is the Hotel Tihuta, a seventy-room, three-story, two-million-dollar hotel which was recently built in the Carpathian Mountains on a road linking Transylvania and Bukovina. Visitors can spend the night in a coffin. There is a torture chamber in the basement. Bats and wolves adorn the walls. "Elixir Dracula," a plum brandy, is served.

The popular American image of the vampire appears to have had its roots in Bram Stoker's mind. Stoker was inspired by Celtic tales told by his mother; historical knowledge of Vlad the Impaler learned from a Hungarian historian; stories spun for him by the fascinating traveler Sir Richard Burton (who also had very prominent canine teeth); and knowledge about Jack the Ripper, who terrorized London during 1888. If Michael E. Bell's speculation referred to earlier is correct, the author may also have been influenced by nineteenth-century New England customs of exhumation and burning of vital organs of recently buried, disease-causing suspects. Stoker took elements, combined and transformed these ideas, then embellished and personified them in Count Dracula. He made changes which have had long-lasting effects. He changed the vampire's color, making him pale. He confined the vampire's activities to nocturnal hours, and turned him into a creature who erotically preys upon virtuous, beautiful maidens. Gone are the traditional motifs of bloatedness and milkless cows.

Stoker's book *Dracula* has never been out of print since first published in 1897. His influence has been so great that when the 574 students in my study were asked where vampires originated, half answered "Transylvania."

Stoker selected the Transylvania locale for the setting of his story, but Transylvania was not a center—and certainly not *the* place—where vampires originated, for vampire tales have been collected from all over the world. Dracula scholars Raymond McNally and Radu Florescu suggest that Stoker chose Transylvania because, to persons from the British Isles, this seemed like an exotic place. Further, McNally has discovered that Stoker had been affected by and used parts of a book called *The Land Beyond* by Emily Gerard, particularly the chapter titled "Superstitions from Transylvania." This, too, possibly influenced his choice of setting for the novel.

Stoker's book has been so influential that, of the 574 students surveyed, almost everyone knew what they were and could accurately describe their characteristics as delineated by Stoker and reinforced by the movies, particularly the Bela Lugosi version.

Student surveys were completely open-ended, and informants often wrote "I don't know" as their answer. The least number of "Don't know" answers related to this question: "How are they [vampires] dressed?" Only forty-three students, or 7 percent did not know how vampires are attired. Of those who did know, the most common response was either "black cape" or "cape" (277, or 48 percent). This was followed by 183 who wrote that vampires were dressed in black and 69 who mentioned white shirts. Other items of clothing mentioned were black pants, black suit, black tuxedo, red lining on cape, black shoes, and tuxedos.

Reference to the cape by 48 percent of the students is significant. The cape was not part of the Bram Stoker creation of Dracula, but was added by Actor Hamilton Deane in 1924, when he adapted the book for the London stage. It was worn by Bela Lugosi in the 1931 film version and since then has become standard dress for vampires. The cape was significant for Lugosi offscreen as well. He was buried in it in 1956.

Actor Christopher Lee, who played Dracula in the British film version, was opposed to the outfit popularized by Lugosi, because it deviated from the book. He told writer Leonard Wolf, "Surely it is the height of ridiculous for a vampire to step out of the shadows wearing white tie, tails, patent leather shoes and full cloak." Yet, for Americans, this outfit has become the archetype for attire.

In describing the physical characteristics of a vampire, 249 students wrote "fangs," and 228 mentioned that he/she is "pale." The next most common features named, in descending order, were "dark/black hair" (92); "tall" (86); "like a normal person" (75); "slick, combed-back or greased-back hair" (60); and "thin / slender" (50). Again, this is a perfect description of the Bela Lugosi characterization, later emulated by Christopher Lee, Frank Langella, and even by George Hamilton in the spoof *Love at First Bite*.

How does one become a vampire? Eighty-seven (15 percent) of these students didn't know. Of those who did, 238 said one had to be bitten by one; 42 said one had to be bitten on the neck by one; 31 said one had to be bitten three times; and 21 specified that one had to be bitten on the neck three times. Add to this the three students who said one becomes a vampire by being infected by the bite of one and the two students who said one has to be bitten a couple of times, and the total is 337, or 59 percent, who understood, according to tradition, that being bitten was the way to become a vampire. (There were also 21 students who claimed that one had to be bitten by a bat or a vampire bat.) Thus, the vampire bite, a characteristic emphasized by Stoker and reenacted in film versions of his novel, though not necessarily found in traditional vampire folklore, is the concept that is most significant in the minds of the survey respondents.

When asked, "Under what circumstances does a vampire appear?" the most popular answer was "night," by 268 students, or 47 percent. This was a big leap from the next most quoted answer, "full moon," by 73 students. When it's "dark" (62) or when it "needs / wants / is hungry for blood" (55) came next. This again is consistent with Stoker's portrayal.

"What does a vampire do?" Thirty-three percent, or 192 people, answered, "Sucks blood." "Bites necks," said 74 students. "Drinks blood," wrote 64 of them.

"How can you protect yourself from a vampire?" Fifty-nine percent of the students (338) wrote either that one had to have a cross or crucifix or that one had to wear one. The next most significant prevention cited was garlic (200).

As to how to kill a vampire, 44 percent (252) answered with "a stake through the heart" or "a wooden stick in the heart." Exposure to sunlight / daylight was mentioned by 69 respondents.

The influence of media was also seen in the way students responded in the survey, attaching heavily advertised brand names to their answers. A vampire dresses in a "Pierre Cardin tux." He is fashionable, "like GQ." He wears "Sergio Valente jeans" or "black C&R [an L.A. low-cost men's shop heavily advertised on TV] pants." He wears "trendy/black Reeboks." The way to destroy him is to "Shine a light on him—Duracell."

The media version of Bram Stoker's Count Dracula became personified by Bela Lugosi, not only to the public, but to the actor himself. A co-worker in the *Dracula* film recalls a costumed Lugosi standing on the set each day before a full-length mirror repeating, "I *am* Dracula. I *am* Dracula." While it is not uncommon for actors to "psych" themselves up this way before a performance, Lugosi's fellow cast member commented that there was something different and significant about the way Lugosi carried out this act.

Hollywood writer Lisa Mitchell confirms the idea of Lugosi's strong identification with the Dracula character, suggesting that toward the end of his life, "Not only had Bela reconciled himself to having his personality blended forever with that of Dracula, he had actually grown to love it."

In compliance with his request, he was buried in his Dracula cape. His grave marker is inscribed "Bella Lugosi, 1882–1956, Beloved Father." Lugosi biographer Arthur Lennig states, "It is not as father to a child that he will generally be remembered; rather as father to a great myth and legend, the embodiment of Dracula."

The popularity of the Dracula figure in the United States can be credited in great part to the impact of Bela Lugosi and his pronounced speaking style. Even though he has been dead for over thirty years, Lugosi's accent and portrayal of Count Dracula will be forever perpetuated in popular culture—through the huckstering of such products as cat food, pizza, and snail repellents; through the teaching of numbers to youngsters; in greeting cards ("I vant to suck your blood") and on buttons ("Gooood Eeevening"); through media reruns and future productions; and also through oral transmission.

In the study of folklore, the term *oral transmission* is used to describe a process which has been considered as the primary mode of communication of concepts, stories, customs, games, riddles, jokes, and proverbs. This refers to the act of one person directly telling or demonstrating something to one or more persons in an informal setting: two children confiding secrets to each other while walking to school; a mother reminiscing about dress standards while her daughter tries on prom gowns; a father showing his children how to check the oil in the car. It is a method based on interpersonal relations and is a vital part of American culture today, exemplified by the jump-rope and hand-clapping games that children play, by the jokes that flourish after every disaster, and by the singing of the birthday song and blowing out of candle flames atop decorated cakes at birthday celebrations.

In recent years the term *xerography* has been added to the folklorist's lexicon. This word describes the process of folklore transmission that occurs in office settings where the presence of the photocopying machine facilitates quick, cheap (at the company's expense), and accessible means of copying and circulating jokes, which may be in the form of cartoons, narratives, or parodies.

This process of transmitting folklore flourishes in bureaucratic settings, such as utility companies, insurance companies, and government offices, where memos, forms, and other contributions to the "paperwork empire" are added to (and sometimes take the place of) face-to-face communication. Although one person may show the humorous sheet of paper to another, who may ask to make a copy, often the photocopied lore is anonymously left on empty desks or posted on bulletin boards.

There is probably another term which could be added to the folklorist's glossary—*tubal transmission*. The television tube has become the tribal storyteller. The study detailed here has dramatically revealed its impact. Even if respondents talked about seeing motion pictures, it was rare that they referred to seeing them in movie theaters. Most students and fans mentioned seeing films on television. One student wrote, "I have answered your questions to the best of television's ability."

When a movie is viewed from a location outside the home, as in a cinema setting, there is more of a separation between what is and is not real. The viewer has escaped to a new milieu. She is watching the celluloid in a context quite different from her living room—with strangers, in a formal seating arrangement. The time organization is structured; the viewer dresses more conventionally; outsiders are in control.

In contrast, watching a film in the living room or bedroom makes it become part of one's immediate, familiar, and therefore "real" environment. Here the viewer is alone or in the presence of family or friends. He may stretch out on the sofa, lie on the floor, or pedal an exercise bike. He can even be in his own bed in pajamas or without any clothes at all. The program may have been recorded earlier on a VCR and can be played back at a time convenient to the owner.

Viewers can be engaged in other activities while watching—adults may be making love, something occasionally alluded to by Johnny Carson in his late-hour program. One is reminded of this important feature by Chance Gardener's now-classic line from the film *Being There*—"I like to watch, Eve."

Children may be eating a meal while watching. In Los Angeles during the 1950s and 1960s, Engineer Bill, the host of a popular daily children's TV show, used to guide the children in drinking their milk by playing Red Light, Green Light with them. All this points to an informal environment which is most conducive to the learning of concepts and tradition.

Unlike face-to-face interaction, during which the audience interacts directly with the teller or performer, with tubal transmission the communication is one way only—from tube to the viewer. With the exception of call-in shows, such as Dr. Ruth Westheimer's, and those limited programs from which viewers order merchandise, current technology does not yet permit direct and immediate feedback from the audience to the screen. Yet there can be communication between viewers who are watching the tube at the same time. Viewers who watch alone can, at a later time, share what they have seen or heard when they rehash the previous day's soap or the previous night's news with fellow employees, friends, or family members. This delayed mode of interpersonal communication does not lessen the influence of what has been seen. It may very well enhance it because of the repetition of information. This process creates waves of redundancy.

If not for the power of the television tube, there would not be so many Americans who are aware and knowledgeable about vampires, especially since seven hours and forty-eight minutes is now estimated to be the average daily TV viewing time of Americans. Given the amount of time people watch television and its powerful impact on them, one is immediately aware that the medium has the potential to distend the credibility of viewers. Television can make anything possible. After all, it can make an elephant fly.

In a California reading test, first-grade children were asked to mark one out of three pictures that "goes best" with words printed in an arrow. In one question the word "fly" was printed in an arrow pointing to pictures of an elephant, a bird, and a dog. Test designers assumed that "bird" was the correct and "best" answer, so they were surprised when many of the first-graders marked "elephant" as their answer. Upon querying these children as to why they had selected "elephant" as their answer, the children responded, "That's Dumbo." The test designers had not considered the possibility that to children indoctrinated by TV, Dumbo the elephant can fly. The children see this phenomenon on television and incorporate it into their perceptions of reality. Such is the power of tubal transmission.

This stretching of believability through television watching can also be interpreted as the reason that 27 percent of the students polled thought it was possible for vampires to exist as real entities. They have seen so much fantasy on TV that they have difficulty separating real from unreal entities.

Even though the majority of students did not believe in the possibility of the vampire's existence, they do accept his presence in this culture. Media bombardment starts out at a very early age, with TV commercials, films, and shows, supported by chewing gum trading cards, cereal. The vampire lurks in math workbooks. Further reminders of its presence occur especially at Halloween, a time when Bram Stoker's brainchild rises to a new position as primary holiday character. Whether in the top ten or top twenty in popularity at costume shops, the vampire is on top.

The vampire today has become a stock American character. He is an everyday phenomenon. A yellow, diamond-shaped sign saying "DRACULA ON BOARD" attached to the rear window of an old Ford Fairlane parked on a Los Angeles street exemplified the view that Dracula has become an American icon. He is as ubiquitous as the Big Mac.

Vamp Followers

VAMPIRES AND BLOOD

I am,
In your subconscious,
Ever present, often ignored,
But there.

As surely as That which is the carrier,
Of Life, nea Immortality,
Flows through your body:
I am.

I am,
The he/she who Feeds,
On the warm, red, elixir of Life,
I drink.
I, that dread nosferatu:
I come to you, knowing your need.
I am Energy,
I am Sex, lust, desire:
I, Carnality,
Bite the flesh, drink the Sacred liquid.

When the great globe of burning, aging,
Ultraviolet radiation has gone,
Leaving behind the teeming millions to rest.
I arise.

My day is your night,
I stalk,
Those who will satisfy my need.
They scream, they beg, for mercy:
I must survive.
I drink.

I am Power.

Know that this treatise be true,
I am watching you, even now.
I see your eyes reading this page,
I look, and see the blood pulsing through your jugular,
Waiting for my hot breath on your neck,
The sharp, momentary pain, as my fang pierces,
The Joy, in giving yourself to me.
Know that this be true, for I am,
And Vampires Are . . .

This poem, "Vampires and Blood," is an example of the vampire-inspired creativity that proliferates among members of fan clubs devoted to either vampires in general or Count Dracula in particular; fan clubs for movie stars who played Count Dracula; or fan clubs dedicated to giving eternal life to "Dark Shadows"—a gothic television soap opera which ran from 1966 until 1971, and is still shown in syndication throughout the country. These fans demonstrate some of the ways in which a particular segment of American society enjoys and pays tribute to the vampire. This chapter will describe some of their activities and characterize their productivity.

The editors of newsletters and magazines, "fanzines," devoted to vampires agreed to contribute to this research by placing a questionnaire in their publications. Fifty-four fans responded in great length and detail. Editors also donated sample copies for examination. As expected, these fanzines and newsletters were filled with graphics related to vampire motifs: corpses in coffins, reprints of vampire movie posters, skeletons, bats, and photos of actors who have played vampire characters. Even greater was the creativity expressed in narrative and prose forms.

As with Patrick Garrison's, most of the poems are dramatic, serious. However, running throughout these publications is a rich vein of humor, particularly in the use of cartoons, comic strips, riddles, jokes, and puns.

"A Fangtastic job!" the editor of the *Vampire Journal* comments. The same journal has a column called "Gravely Speaking." The following line is typical of the kind of punning attempted: "The play *Dracula* first sank its teeth into the Big Apple over fifty years ago—but since then bloody vampire realities have also pierced the lives of New Yorkers." A request for subscribers in the *Journal of Vampirism* jests, "We're not putting the bite on you, but a little blood money wouldn't hurt." Another membership appeal shows a vampire figure standing amid tombstones. One of the markers has "Vacancy" inscribed on it, and the caption is "The Vampire Studies Society still has a lot of openings." Beneath it is a further pitch: "By subscribing, you are automatically considered a member of the Vampire Studies Society, an organization determined to unearth the truth about the undead. Why not subscribe? You never know what we may dig up!"

"Lifestyles of the Undead and Infamous," found in the *Vampire Journal,* is the comic strip satire on the television show "Lifestyles of the Rich and Famous."

There are riddles found throughout the various publications, such as the following:

What does a vampire do at the circus?
  He goes for the Juggler.

How does a vampire rest when he can't reach his coffin?
  He lies on a blood cot.

How can you tell when a vampire has a cold?
  By his coughin'.

What are the only ships vampires will ride on?
  Blood vessels.

Why don't vampires believe in divorce?
  They prefer to bury their problems.

There are cartoons: children standing in line waiting to talk to Santa; Santa has a surprised look on his face as he listens to the child on his lap requesting "a coffin."

Fan-created music also exists.

SONG OF THE HAPPY VAMPIRES

by Donald O. Halgren

(Sung to the Tune: *The Daring Young Man on the Flying Trapeze*)

Oh, his hands on her neck, they were clammy and cold,
And his incisors sank to the bone.
His evil eye gave her a whammy, I'm told,
And she giggled while trying to groan, OHH . . .

He flies through the air in the still of the night,
The shadowy figure that comes for a bite.
His touch on the neck fills the girls with delight,
And my love he has guzzled away.

Oh, he came to her bedside quite often, to eat,
And he sampled her blood for a while,
Till she found herself empty clear down to her feet,
With an appetite equally vile, OHH . . .

She flies through the air in the still of the night,
A shadowy figure that comes for a bite.
Her touch on the neck fills the boys with delight,
And my love, she keeps guzzling away.

Oh, what did I hear by the window, just now?
Oh, hi, dear! I thought you were dead!
(What is it that causes this sweat on my brow,
When really it's cold in this bed?) OHH . . .

She flies through the air in the still of the night,
A shadowy figure that comes for a bite.
Her touch on the neck fills the boys with delight,
And my love, she keeps guzzling away.

Oh, your face is so thin, and your cheeks are so pale,
But otherwise, you're looking fine.
May I give you some sherry? (I got it on sale.)
What's that? You never drink—wine? OHH . . .

I fly through the air in the still of the night.
I creep to your bedside and take a small bite.
My touch on your neck, it will give you delight,
And I love to just guzzle away!

© 1978 by *Journal of Vampirism.* Reprinted by permission.

There are other song parodies found in other fanzines. "I Left My Fangs in San Francisco," and "Ol' Devil Fangs."
A "Dark Shadows" fan commented,

The unusual thing about the "Dark Shadows" fans is their creativity. I think anything that inspires you to do a story or a poem or draw a picture or something that's at least part originally yours, not just writing down or copying or taking shorthand notes of the dialogue, but writing dialogue and story situations of your own, it's got to be good. It's got to stretch your mind. To make somebody creative in any way is a good thing. People who go to see "Rambo" don't come home and immediately write a story. They don't want to write a story or draw a picture. They don't do any poetry. It doesn't inspire them to anything creative, but this particular TV series did.

Her observation applies not only to "Dark Shadows" fans, but to vampire fans in general.

Hundreds of "Dark Shadows" fans across the country communicate through "Dark Shadows" events and fanzines and through other vampire publications. They serve as the creators and the audience for their vampire-inspired creativity. They write to each other directly and get together at conventions. According to one fan, the appeal of "Dark Shadows" was due in part to the unique format, in which half the characters were supernatural and the other half were human:

> The humans were never very bright. They hardly ever realized that the town in which they lived, Collinsport, Maine, was filled with supernatural characters, that is, werewolves, witches, warlocks, ghosts, a phoenix.

However, the key figure of the "Dark Shadows" series was Barnabas Collins, a tragic and compassionate vampire played by Jonathan Frid, a Canadian-born actor with Shakespearean training and a master of fine arts degree in directing from the Yale Drama School. The series was believed to be in trouble with cancellation pending until the vampire character, Barnabas, was introduced in 1967. Then ratings soared, and Collins became the central personality of the series. One fan described how Barnabas was portrayed.

> Frid played this character in a sympathetic manner, making viewers pity him rather than feel disgusted by him. In some cases female viewers went beyond pity to a sort of motherly or protective "love" for him. They didn't want him to harm anyone, but they couldn't stand to see him in pain (being thirsty), so they would (sometimes literally) offer him their own necks.

Other players in the series were Joan Bennett as the mistress of Collinwood, Kathryn Leigh Scott as Maggie Evans and Josette, David Selby as Quentin Collins, Thayer David as Professor Timothy Elliott Stokes, Lara Parker as Angelique, and John Karlen as Willie Loomis.

As one fan relates, "The show was done quite camp. It wasn't done seriously. It was done tongue-in-cheek. If you're going to believe in vampires, you'd be more likely to pick it up from reading."

In some years there have been as many as four to six "Dark Shadows" conventions taking place in different locations during the year: New Orleans, Los Angeles, Manhattan, San Jose, Newark, Dallas. Convention activities generally include the showing of "Dark Shadows" videotapes and bloopers, panel discussions of plots and characters, trivia and costume contests, and the selling of memorabilia and fan art (for example, bats made out of ribbons, paintings of the "Dark Shadows" players, pictures of the stars mounted in jewelry forms). "Some of the art is almost like the things that the kid brings home for the mother to put on the refrigerator with magnets. There's so much love in it," a fan commented.

These conventions often feature guests speakers—such as Jonathan Frid with his one-man show "Fools and Fiends," or vampire lecturer/performer Thomas "Dracula Man" Schellenberger. Dressed in black and white with a few accents of red, and a few ribbons, Schellenberger makes a very impressive appearance in his costume. He gives slide presentations and speeches and runs question-and-answer sessions about vampires. Much of this is based on his own research and a 1974 trip to Romania, where he visited the tomb, castle, and birthplace of Prince Vlad Tepes, the fifteenth-century monarch who served as the prototype for Stoker's Dracula.

Schellenberger is founder and president of Dracula and Company, a national association devoted to the study of horror, fantasy, and science fiction in all forms of entertainment. In addition to appearing at conventions, he has lectured on Dracula and vampires at schools and libraries, and has appeared as "Dracula Man" on numerous television programs.

Over one thousand fans attended a "Dark Shadows" convention held in Newark, New Jersey, in October 1986. Former production crew members were there as well as cast members Jonathan Frid, Diana Millay, Donna Wandrey, Lara Parker, and Kathryn Leigh Scott, the latter selling her book, *My Scrapbook Memories of Dark Shadows.*

At this event the program participants auctioned off a pair of fangs, photographs, a few kinescopes of "Dark Shadows," and some suits that Jonathan Frid wore in 1969 while playing Barnabas. Other events included a poster caption contest, skits, a presentation of the soundtrack *The Original Music from Dark Shadows,* celebrity interviews, a raffle, and filmed and taped "Twentieth Anniversary Greetings" from "Dark Shadows" regulars unable to attend—for example, John Karlen, Emmy award winner from the "Cagney and Lacey" show. Fans participated in a field trip to the Lyndhurst estate in Tarrytown, New York, location site for the films *House of Dark Shadows* and *Night of Dark Shadows.*

During the 1987 Halloween weekend, Los Angeles hosted a "Dark Shadows" convention attended by approximately seven hundred enthusiastic fans, most of whom were in their thirties. They were a highly attentive and responsive audience, one that readily laughed almost on cue, during video reruns of "Dark Shadows" episodes, for the live presentations by former production personnel, and particularly for a panel featuring nine stars of the show. When these former cast members made their entrance, the fans jumped to their feet, wildly applauding and cheering while dozens laden with camera equipment illuminated the one-hour discussion with continually bursting flashbulb lights.

It was an informal session, with nostalgic fans adoring these cast members, who in return enjoyed and relished the fans' appreciation and questions. "Did you really enjoy playing the part of the hag?" "How were you written out of the cast?" "Which costumes did you like and dislike?"

Each member contributed an anecdote or two. They joked among themselves and with the audience. Meanwhile, in another room, memorabilia hucksters did well with their specialized market and committed purchasers. "Dark Shadows" fans are avid buyers of glossy stills of the stars, lobby cards, records and cassettes, jewelry, slides, movie posters, T-shirts. Laurence Lande, a free-lance photographer and former ballroom dance teacher, was the only dealer who seemed to display any creativity in his merchandise. Lande sold "Dark Shadows" notepads and humorous business cards for the "Dark Shadows" characters—"Barnabas Collins, vampire, available for blood drives. Night hours only." "Quentin Collins, werewolf. A howl at parties."

Three women from St. Louis were taking a break outside one of the several meeting halls. One of them held a stack of just-purchased publications for which she had paid over $80. These fans—a dental hygienist, an accountant, and a director of membership services for a trade organization—had also attended both the Newark and Dallas conventions in 1986. Different convention sites offered unique tourist attractions, they explained, claiming that this Southern California meeting made it possible to visit Disneyland and Rockwell International.

"Different locations also attract different stars. Here in L.A. we're going to have more stars that are currently working, as opposed to those who have gotten into restaurants or real estate," one fan remarked.

These fans were also ambitious, making plans to write and publish their own "vampire-zine" and sell it at future conventions by either renting a space in the dealers' room, advertising it through flyers at conventions, or selling it through the mail. They also revealed why the vampire appealed to them. One of them said,

It's the romance. I guess I was born one hundred years too late, because the courtliness, the gentleman vampire really appeals to me. Vampires are sexy. I think a lot of people get a charge out of coupling the eroticism with the danger. It's incredibly erotic.

The other fan said,

> I'm attracted to sort of a lonely figure, isolated in a different time,
> trying to keep that romantic era alive and really that is sort of the
> soul of it for me—being true to a code of chivalry.

The third one related,

> Well, that's almost the lure of Ashley in *Gone With the Wind* because
> his life has died. The life he was used to is gone and he is still trying
> to struggle alone with those values. And there's something really
> sad but very . . . something you have to admire in a way.

The dental hygienist added,

> It's so sad in "Dark Shadows" with Barnabas. He doesn't want to
> be what he is. When he isn't being totally driven by the need for
> blood, he's sorry sometimes. And it's pathetic. He remembers the
> way life was and he can't ever have it again. They keep curing him,
> but he keeps getting bitten or enchanted or whatever and turned
> right back into a vampire, so he loses it over and over again. It's so
> sad. You think, if he could only find the right woman. And it feels
> like you're the right woman and you can change him and I think
> that's part of the allure too.

Asked if there was any other comment they would like to
make about "Dark Shadows," one woman answered, "I think
we've driven the subject into the ground."

A passerby added, "And buried it about four times, tromped
on it, and driven a stake through its heart!"

Shadowcon, an older "Dark Shadows" Los Angeles convention, ran for ten years and had its last gathering in 1986. Shadowcon was created by Barbara Fister-Liltz, who now has moved
on to the larger world of Illumicon, "A gathering for the many
worlds of Media Fandom." Recognized as one of the best creators of fan art, Fister-Liltz has also produced a broad range of
"Dark Shadows" and vampire publications under the name Pan-

Reprinted by permission of Jayne A. Largent

dora Publications. These include screenplays; a jokebook; a cookbook; and a series of other fan-created anthologies of stories, puzzles, poetry, interviews, and song parodies.

In addition to attending large annual conventions, those who are attracted to the vampire have also banded together in smaller groups allowing them to communicate with one another more frequently, thus stimulating and nourishing their interest. Most clubs produce regularly circulating documents. There are also periodicals unattached to groups. What follows is an itemized sampling of organizations and publications. Each periodical has a point of distinction. Some of them deal with the more contemporary aspects of vampire interests (AIDS, video reviews). Others focus on the more traditional aspects of the horrific. What is learned by perusing these documents is that each has a specific, implied readership. What they all do, however, is require tremendous dedication from the editors and an equal commitment from readers who feed these publications and keep them alive.

Founders of Alternate Shadows, Patrick and Josette Garrison believe that what distinguishes their organization from others is that they take the vampire more seriously. One of the unique features of their group is a Red Cross blood drive, which began in 1983. Patrick, a regular donor since the age of seventeen, has personally donated four gallons of blood since the drive began. To promote blood donations from their members, the Garrisons sponsored blood donor contests in 1983, 1985, and 1986. Using members' blood donation receipts, they had drawings with selected donors being awarded complimentary luncheons at a fashionable New York City restaurant with Jonathan Frid.

An analysis of several issues of the Garrison-published *Parallel Times* reveals an emphasis on "Dark Shadows" original story-lines created by subscribers, a character study of Barnabas Collins, related poetry, comic strips, updates on television stations about to cancel or begin showing reruns of the series, interviews

Reprinted by permission of Jayne A. Largent

with stars, and stories about "Dark Shadows" characters.

Subscription costs, membership requirements, and mailing addresses for Alternate Shadows and all other organizations mentioned in this book can be found in Appendix 2.

Kathleen Resch publishes *The World of Dark Shadows,* and in 1987 (two years later than planned) she put out a 172-page Tenth Anniversary Edition for her 600 subscribers. She recalled that when she first circulated her twenty-page fanzine to thirty people in 1975, she had no idea that it would last so long, particularly since at that time most fan clubs lasted less than ten issues. When she began, "Dark Shadows" had been off the air for several years. At that time, no one had any idea the series would return in syndication form, nor did they ever dream that in the 1980s there would be thousands of active fans. Today it stands as the oldest "Dark Shadows" fanzine and the one with the widest circulation.

Shadowgram, created in 1979 by Maria Barbosa, is now edited and published by Marcy Robin and has over 1,000 subscribers. Their purpose is to provide a more condensed news bulletin featuring information about the "Dark Shadows" syndication, conventions, and the lives of cast and crew, attempting to answer the perennial question, "What ever happened to . . . ?"

Sharida Rizzuto is the ambitious editor of the *Vampire Journal.* She started in the early 1980s with a "Dark Shadows" fan club (the New Orleans chapter of the International Dark Shadows Society) and less than one year later decided to go independent. She changed the name of her publication to *The Collinsport Record,* and expanded it to a full-size fanzine. Since then, she has also started *The Collinwood Journal.*

Rizzuto now puts out eight publications in addition to the *Vampire Journal.* She is frequently involved with fandom conventions. Subscribers number several hundred, and are growing constantly. As with other fanzines, the classified section is one of the most important parts of her publication, for it is here that free exchange listings are traded between cooperating organizations. It is here that fans can communicate person-to-person, expanding their network of association with other vampire followers.

One edition of the *Vampire Journal* is ninety pages long. Within it, "Gravely Speaking," inscribed on the tombstone, is a section containing random comments from both readers and editor. Highlighted in one issue was a reprint of an interview with Ann Rice, best-selling author of *The Vampire Lestat*. Fan-created original music, both words and notation, such as, "Night: Ode to a Vampire," was also offered.

The traditional study of vampires is not dead despite the new seeds sowed by "Dark Shadows." The Count Dracula Society in Los Angeles, founded in 1962 by Dr. Donald A. Reed, began as an organization devoted to the serious study of horror films and Gothic literature. At one time there were 1,000 members, who have now dwindled to a quarter of that number. But Reed was confident that the organization is "still alive; it rises from the coffin every year."

In the past the Count Dracula Society regularly presented the Reverend R. Montague Summers Memorial Award for the advancement of Gothic literature or vampire research. Now that award is only given out occasionally. Reed, who became fascinated with Dracula when he was in junior high school, is a pioneer in Dracula fan clubs. Two hundred and fifty people attended the organization's twenty-fifth-year anniversary, all-day Dracula and horror film festival and awards ceremony on October 18, 1987, at the University of Southern California. Ray Bradbury was the featured speaker at the event supported by vampire film fans, some of whom were dressed for the occasion—an Irish vampire wearing a green sequined cape.

On the East Coast, Eric Held co-founded the Vampire Information Exchange in 1978 with Dorothy Nixon. Held, who now runs the organization alone, is a high school teacher who became interested in the subject after a fellow teacher introduced him to Stoker's *Dracula*. He edits the *Vampire Information Exchange Newsletter*.

This newsletter solicits articles, book and movie reviews,

newspaper and magazine clippings, artwork, and other "vampiric tidbits" for persons interested in all aspects of vampirism. For example, they reprinted an undated story from the *Journal-Courier,* a New Haven, Connecticut, newspaper, about John Brennan Crutchley, who was sentenced to twenty-five years in prison and fifty years' probation for kidnapping a woman and draining or drinking nearly half of her blood during a twenty-two-hour "sexula" assault. Other reprints have dealt with psychic vampires, who consciously or unconsciously drain the energy of others.

There are about seventy-five members of the Vampire Information Exchange Network, but members keep joining all the time, hearing about it mostly through word of mouth or through exchange listings with other newsletters. Eric was very pleased about his newest overseas member from Yugoslavia.

Vampire is a concise, clearly organized newsletter published by a Special Interest Group of American Mensa, Ltd., "to explore vampire lore, the werewolf, gothic horror, spine-chilling 'spooky stuff' and 'creepy things' in movies, TV and literature." Terry Cottrell's publication, averaging twelve pages, circulates to seventy members and contains pleasing layout and graphics, original and reprinted articles, book reviews, contests, poetry, commentaries, letters, and comic strips.

Vampire Quarterly, circulation 100, is written and edited by Susan M. Garrett, of Toms River, New Jersey. Started in August 1985, her publication is a lighthearted vampire reference that gives complete book report summaries of current fiction with commentary on the quality of writing so that readers can decide whether or not they want to bother with the book. Garrett believes in printing as many viewpoints as possible about as many books as possible. For the future, Susan would like to expand with a fiction supplement.

> What I'd like to compile is some good, old-fashioned horror stories that have more of a plot to them than creature meets girl; creature and girl have sex; creature is killed by or runs off with girl. Perhaps

I'm an optimist, but I really do think there's some interesting *good* fiction out there.

New Jersey has its own Dracula society, the Quincey P. Morris Dracula Society, named for the one American character in Bram Stoker's *Dracula*. In spite of Morris's omission from most stage and film adaptations, this organization considers him its hero because in the original story he gave his blood to Lucy; he possessed an American charm, wit, and courage; and he had a Texan drawl. His Bowie knife helped to destroy Count Dracula at the Borgo Pass, where he, too, lost his life. In the novel, Mina and Jonathan Harker name their first child after Quincey P. Morris in tribute to his heroism. This New Jersey–based group of 150 members decided to perpetuate his name as well, when they broke away from the London Dracula Society in 1979.

The organization has traveled to Transylvania, following in the footsteps of Jonathan Harker's pursuit. For five years they have sponsored an annual short horror story contest to encourage amateur writers. In November 1986 they held a Bram Stoker Commemorative Banquet to celebrate their tenth anniversary, with authors of vampire books as honored guests: Radu Florescu and Raymond McNalley, authors of *In Search of Dracula,* and Michael Talbot, author of *The Delicate Dependency*. According to president Charlotte L. Simsen, mother of seven, other group activities include gravestone rubbings, hunts for the Jersey Devil, book swaps, and covered dish-suppers, which require everyone to bring edible, RED dishes. Red wine or rosy-hued soft drinks are always on hand. In *Coast* magazine Mrs. Simsen wrote,

> I think the most important ingredient necessary to enjoy a hobby such as mine is a sense of humor. Many members own fangs and red satin-lined black capes, which may be worn to a theater party to see a Dracula play. Some of us wear our spider and bat jewelry all year 'round. We publish a quarterly newsletter called *The Transfusion*—once we even served red wine in blood vials.

The Count Ken Fan Club of Salem, Massachusetts, is another lighthearted organization for horror fans, started in 1984 by Ken Gilbert. Inspired to start a fan club after masquerading as Dracula at a Halloween party, he writes and edits a monthly publication featuring news items from Salem ("Local 'Witch' Runs for Mayor"), horror poetry and artwork, movie and video reviews, and reprints from tabloids. There are about forty members, including honorary members Peter Cushing, Forrest Ackerman, and Elvira.

In contrast, John L. Vellutini of San Francisco publishes the serious and scholarly *Journal of Vampirology*, specializing in vampirism and hemophilism. Based in San Francisco, Vellutini generally devotes an entire issue to a single topic which he carefully researches and writes. For example, one twenty-eight-page edition is about "The Use and Abuse of the Dead for Felonious, Judicial and Therapeutic Purposes."

One of the largest fan organizations is the Court Dracula Fan Club, which, according to its founder and president, Jeanne Keyes Youngson, Ph.D., has more than 5,000 members from twelve different countries, ranging in age from twelve to eighty-three. Among the several goals are "to maintain the image of, interest in, the memory of Bram Stoker's *Dracula,* and aid and assist members in as many ways, with as many means, as possible. The intentions and aims of The Count Dracula Fan Club are ethical, social, moral, and educational, combined with a sense of good fun."

The organization has its headquarters in a Fifth Avenue apartment building near Washington Square in New York City, where local members celebrate Christmas around a Dracutree strung with brightly colored little coffins and topped with a mask of the "Sesame Street" Count. Horror film and television screenings are regularly scheduled at the headquarters, which also houses an eclectic collection of vampire memorabilia, including masks, posters, jewelry (such as Spooky Kooky Jewelry), games (Vincent Van Vampire), toys, candy (Drac Snax, Count Crunch), figurines, models, makeup kits, buttons (I Wanna Neck), a vampire kite from England, cocktail napkins, greeting cards, and do-it-yourself vampire kits (red-tipped stake, wooden cross, wooden mallet).

The Bram Stoker Wall displays copies of Stoker's baptismal and death certificates; a 1902 signature; an autographed photo of Hamilton Deane, who adapted the book for the stage and produced, directed, and starred in it in England in 1924; a photo of Stoker's Whitby residence; and copies of the Bram Stoker Medal. Youngson eventually hopes to turn this space into a Count Dracula / vampire museum.

This fan club has several divisions, including the Count Dracula Research Library of over 25,000 volumes in hardcover and paperback; a special research division, which produces a monograph series—for example, *Vampirism in the Philippines: A Brief Description and Survey,* by Halford E. Jones; a picture file; a clipping collection; an archive of vampire and horror memorabilia; the Vampire Bookshop, containing the largest collection of Dracula and vampire books for sale in the world; the Moldavian Marketplace, selling lapel pins—for example, Am I Your Type? A, O, AB, X, RH—Dracula stationery, pins, mobiles, blood and fangs kits, and other vampire memorabilia. There is also a Pen Pal Network allowing member / collectors to buy, trade, or sell their collections.

Membership entitles the new member to a "Drakpak" of items, like a "Dracu-Buck" bookmark, and to sustain their interest in vampires, members regularly receive "freebies," such as a black-and-white wallet photo of Poenar, Dracula's *real* castle, and a monthly newsletter which keeps them informed of activities and allows them to publish their own poetry, stories, and letters. For example, in one newsletter M. L. Carter wrote an article suggesting a Vampire Liberation Movement to enable these creatures to come "out of the closet—or the coffin." The writer then speculated how this would affect many aspects of American culture, such as the job market (they would take over as night-shift workers), and how mandatory retirement policies and social security regulations might be affected. It is an amusing and delightful essay.

Youngson enthusiastically supports projects of legitimate researchers and conducts many projects of her own. For example, recently she polled forty to fifty of the organization's more knowledgeable members to discover if they believed in the existence of vampires. The results of this poll will eventually be published.

These fan organizations and publications are primarily created to weave together a wide network of fans. They serve as an important communications web of persons drawn to the vampire figure. Belonging and subscribing put fans in touch with one another and allow them an outlet for their own productivity. They may identify with the vampire loner, but by becoming affiliated, their own aloneness is lessened and they can feel at home with others who have similar interests. They talk the same language. Clubs and publications can also be seen as expressions of love for the subject.

Several fans describe their first awakening to the phenomenon:

> My first vivid recollection of actually acknowledging the existence of vampires was at the age of four years old, when "Dark Shadows" premiered on TV in 1966. I'm sure I had exposure to vampirism before that with television, but that is the first thing I really remember clearly. I know that four may sound too young to really remember and understand things, but I have memories of events, very clear memories, dating back to three years of age.

> I don't know who first told me about vampires, but when I was about five or so, me and my brother used to jump around as Dracula and his assistant. (I was the assistant, being younger.)

> I am sure that the movies were my first introduction to Dracula; however, I have an older sister who was very good at spinning tales to young ears, and she may have had some input.

I had seen some Dracula movies but Barnabas in "Dark Shadows" had the most effect on me. This was in 1970 when they first ran the show here in Columbus.

I am not sure who told me about vampires, but I suspect it was the older sister of my best friend. My friend was the same age as I was and her sister perhaps eight. The end result was that instead of taking my nap, I would watch "Dark Shadows" alone or with my friend. Sometimes her sisters would watch it with us.

There was a screening of "Dracula" on television which prompted me to study both fictional and true accounts of vampires. I devoured books, and was fascinated by a story *Pillar of Fire*. After that, I read everything I could get my hands on, on vampires.

One fan wrote that while she was growing up in Texas, her mother employed a young French / black woman from Louisiana as a housekeeper / governess. The young woman was a cult fan of Barnabas Collins and told the child about vampirism and other supernatural beliefs. They used to watch "Dark Shadows" together. The fan recalled, "I had a great deal of respect and confidence in this young woman. I remember being terrified and enthralled at the same time with Barnabas Collins."

A woman writes that she learned about vampirism from a girl a year or two older than herself who "seemed to me incredibly grown-up and sophisticated."

Another fan recollects learning about vampires from the "weird kid next door." The neighbor kid was five years older than the fan, and he collected all kinds of "spook" books, such as *Famous Monsters of Filmland*. "And I looked on him as an authority."

I learned about vampires with my cousins. We'd be sitting in my parents' back yard in a circle telling "scary stories!" The television supplied me with Bela Lugosi and Christopher Lee movies at night, which I watched with my mother, and with "Dark Shadows" in the afternoon.

A California fan wrote that he first found out about vampires when he was in the fifth grade listening to his classmates "telling movies" during rainy day sessions when children ate lunch in class and discipline was "in limbo." He first heard about *Frankenstein Meets the Wolfman,* then *Dracula.* These descriptions fed his desire to see the movies and learn more.

This fifth-grader had been influenced by anecdotes, first-person accounts of experiences his friends had in the movie theater. This is typical of the way in which folklore operates—a narrator giving an account of an incident stirs up the interest of the audience. The audience can act on the information, repeat it to someone else, or store it away for later recall. In the above example the fifth-grader was inspired to repeat his friend's experiences.

One fan knew how she learned about vampires. She said that she absorbed it naturally, in the same way she learned the English language and acquired food prejudices.

Another wrote:

> I'm twenty-six and have always been interested in the supernatural and the occult, and read tarot cards on a semi-regular basis. I've done quite a bit of research on vampires starting in 1977 for a high school term paper, and even had a small amulet made with "Sanvi, Sansanvi & Semangelar" on it for protection against vampires in my more fearful days! I realize now that most of the stories were ways for primitive peoples to rationalize what they could not fully understand, but I *do* believe there are biological vampires. After all, there are still things about the human body that science doesn't understand so why can't this phenomenon be one of them?

A different fan recorded that even though she considers her interest in vampirism to be shared by very few, she has made her interest known to friends over the years, and no one has thought of her as being "kooky or strange." She says, "Maybe everyone secretly shares the same desire to learn more about them."

Someone else wrote that he discovered vampires from the

movies when he was about eight years old. Being one of the youngest of his group of friends, he was targeted for "boogeyman type" pranks that nearly "scared the pants off me on several occasions." He said that at first he believed in their existence, and recalled one nightmare, of which there were many, in which vampires were predominant. Years later the nightmare was so vivid he made a pen-and-ink sketch to characterize it, and he included a copy with his questionnaire responses. Standard vampire motifs are found in it: the hammer and stake as a fixed mode of death and the emphasis on the sharp teeth. These motifs are also combined and associated with other cultural supernatural motifs, such as the Malaysian vampire.

A young woman wrote about the five bats she had tattooed on the outside of her left calf and the bite marks she had tattooed on the left side of her neck.

Most people think her bites are "really cool." However, her mother didn't know about them, and when she came to visit she asked what was on her daughter's neck. The daughter simply answered that it was a tattoo, and her mother never spoke of it again. On the other hand, she has observed people stop in the middle of a conversation as she walks by in her short skirt, revealing the artwork. She's overheard such comments as, "Look at that! I can't believe she's got bats on her legs."

This vampire follower said the tattoos worked to her advantage when she was once arrested.

> You know how they have to take your description and if you have noticeable marks or things like that. . . . So they said, "Why did you get bats?" And I said, "To go with these," and I showed them my neck. I had a great time. If I had to get arrested, I'm glad I got arrested by these guys. . . . They were really cool. They took me to my Versateller machine so I could bail myself out. They were really nice.

This young woman explained that her interest in vampires had been sparked ten years earlier when, in her late teens, she first read Anne Rice's *Interview with the Vampire*. Prior to that time she had been interested in the occult, but after reading Rice's book she focused her interest on vampires, and she counts as one of her most prized possessions an autographed photo of the author. Unlike most other fans, she does not like to see vampire movies because she finds them too violent. Besides, "The movies usually depict the vampire as the ugly, gory type."

Vampire fans disclose that they got "hooked" on the subject when they were young, generally with the media as their spark of interest, which has now drawn them to specialized activities, friends, and ways of spending their time and money. By the time they become members of fan clubs, most have been involved at least twenty years, which may indicate that the vampire habit is a hard one to break.

Fans are the beneficiaries of the popularity of the vampire. For them this symbol seems to function as a source of creativity, as an object of pleasure, as a toy for their play, and as a common ground for communication—face-to-face, by mail, or through their specialized publications. The vampire stimulates some to become collectors, others to become writers and publishers. It motivates many to participate in social events, to travel, to read, to research, to become experts, to reflect on themes and emotions which might not ordinarily be aired other than in a classroom or a psychotherapeutic setting. The vampire is like a thread that holds a wide band of people together.

The Lure

How can one explain the popularity of the vampire in contemporary America? There must be a reason vampires have captured the interest of the public to a large enough extent that it supports such a continuous stream of films, ads, products, books, conventions, newsletters, and fanzines. Literary scholar James Twitchell aptly describes the issue in his article "The Vampire Myth":

> It is one thing to explain why even "modern" writers such as Henry James, Oscar Wilde or D. H. Lawrence used the analogy of the vampire to describe the inner and outer lives of their characters; it is quite another to explain why there is a vampire puppet on Sesame Street, "Count Count," who teaches numbers to our children, or why vampire comics are one of the most popular genres in that medium, or even why any child would want to eat a "vitamin enriched" breakfast cereal named "Count Chocula."

Twitchell also claims that any twelve-year-old boy (why does he limit the gender?) can accurately describe the vampire's characteristics, which is confirmed for both genders, by the student survey I conducted. Although older than twelve, the respondents could clearly delineate the behavior and physical characteristics of the phenomenon.

Twitchell suggests that Dracula (along with Frankenstein) has been the most important archetype inherited from past traditions and that its contemporary presence is significant. He concludes, from a psychoanalytical perspective, that the vampire's popularity exists because it represents the most complete condensation of the problems and resolutions of preadolescence.

This may explain why children are drawn to the character. When youngsters enter the preadolescent stage of their development, they must deal with first-time feelings of sexual energy and hostility, products of normal hormonal activity that bombard children of this age. The vampire character, carrying through on his impulses of sexuality and aggression, may serve as a satisfactory fantasy figure for children in this age category, whose bodies and temperaments are potentially explosive. This is but one explanation as to why this age group may be attracted to the vampire, yet satisfying needs of sexuality and aggression is not necessarily limited to preadolescents.

From a psychiatric point of view, Paul King, M.D., medical director of the Adolescent Program at Charter Lakeside Hospital in Memphis, Tennessee, states that if youths grow up with anger, hatred, and resentment because of psychological and family problems, they cannot handle these feelings in a socially appropriate way. If they are also using mood-altering chemicals, violence can ensue. King asserts, "Then they find inspiration for it in Satan or heavy metal or in the neo-Nazi punk culture or in some of these other types of negative inspirational things that are out in society that you can buy in bookstores, see on TV or in the movies and that becomes their religion—the inspiration for their hate—and it ends up in ax murders and desecration of cemeteries or in a seventeen-year-old kid on death row in Oklahoma for murdering his family."

This is how misdirected aggression and sexual energy affect disturbed teenagers, and is a possible explanation King gives for what happened to the fourteen-year-old girl, discussed in chapter 1, who committed suicide. King, who specializes in treating troubled adolescents, analyzes that case this way: "Well, to me it sounds like someone who was into hatred and resentment, into some sort of inspiration, whether it be from horror stories or the occult or satanism or heavy metal."

From Dr. King's point of view, the *Lost Boys* movie was not the reason she killed herself, but merely the negative inspiration. "To me, the real problem is alcohol and drugs. Whether it's the kids using chemicals or the kind of destructiveness of chemical use by their parents and lack of upbringing, that's why they're full of hate," he explained.

One would expect to find similar dysfunctional backgrounds for the young men in Minnesota who killed the vagrant and licked his blood off their hands, professing that their interest was stimulated by *The Lost Boys*.

For those persons not filled with hate, the vampire's story provides a positive fantasy outlet for these same new feelings of aggression and sexuality. The vampire represents power; his sexual aspects are also apparent. He is able to do what most young people cannot do yet, and that seems to be part of his attraction for the novice. For the adult, too, he fills a similar need as a fantasy role model.

This is not just speculation, but rather what fans revealed when interpreting the vampire's lure. They were asked, "What do you believe accounts for the appeal of the vampire—for yourself and for others?" Admittedly, the informants who took time to write and share ideas are self-selected, a core group of people who communicated about an interest that compelled them in some way. They appear to be people who wish to continue to explore and write about the vampire.

They are not a random sample and the purpose of this open-ended anecdotal mode of inquiry was to raise questions and allow this knowledgeable and articulate group of vampire followers to voice their concerns. Their responses reveal that they have spent a great deal of time investigating, discussing, reading about, and engaging in introspection about the phenomenon, as well as using it as a theme for their own creative endeavors, both written and pictorial.

On some points they were in total agreement with the scholars, and, as noted before, they were well read about the subject and therefore well acquainted with current theories. Nonetheless, from their responses it is clear that they critically evaluated what they read and were able to accept or reject concepts they encountered.

For example, one of the fans responded with an interpretation similar to Twitchell's. She, too, believed that the vampire had particular appeal to the male adolescent. She declared that teenagers find the vampire fascinating because the vampire is usually an unwilling victim of a bodily change he cannot control, a change that brings on frightening new desires and cravings, a change that sets him apart from the society he has known and makes him an outsider. This makes it easy for the adolescent to identify with the vampire, since he, too, is in the grip of bodily changes beyond his control—new sexual desires which are strange and frightening to him and may seem as evil as the vampire's craving for blood.

Prof. Norine Dresser
Dept. of English
Cal. State Univ.
5151 State Univ. Drive
Lost Angels, CA.
90032

Reprinted by permission

The connection between the adolescent's bodily and emotional changes clearly alludes to the process of nocturnal emission as described by psychoanalyst Ernest Jones, who characterized the vampire as a night visitor—one who first tires the sleeper with "passionate embraces" then later withdraws a "vital fluid." To Jones this is interpreted as a way to account for erotic dreams and nightly emissions.

The aforementioned fan revealed that her ideas were not original, but were in part suggested by Stephen King, top author of contemporary horror novels. King states that fourteen-year old boys are frightened of their new sexuality. He also brings up another scary aspect of being a teenage boy—the new role of dominating women. He embellishes upon this notion when he describes how the vampire can sexually overpower a woman without having to have an erection—thus avoiding concern about performance failure.

Another fan comes to the same realization regarding sexual prowess. He writes that perhaps the vampire serves as a necessary defense mechanism against impotence. He observes that most male vampires are not portrayed as having normal intercourse.

A different respondent makes a similar observation, saying that while the attack of the vampire is always sexual, "I have sometimes wondered whether vampires were physically capable of having normal sex; insofar as I can tell, none of the legends have ever addressed this issue."

Because the questionnaire was open-end, fans discussed the vampire's qualities of attraction in a complex way, yet different categories seemed to be implied. Fans wrote about sexuality / eroticism, immortality, power, victimization by one's own body, beauty and elegance, romanticism, appeal of the forbidden, the supernatural, mystery, horror, and the unknown. However, it was quite difficult to separate the categories completely. Their discussion of the sexual appeal of the vampire was often intertwined with concepts of power and domination. For example, two people wrote the following:

Maybe the erotic, romantic possession answers our desire to fully belong to a man / woman of our dreams.

There is also the very strong sexual fantasy of the oh-so-dominant male. It is sex without guilt, for if he is in complete control, then the responsibility is also his. . . . He can compel whomever he wishes. Add the great advantages of eternal youth, beauty, health, superhuman strength and not having to get up in the morning and you have quite a list.

In this last response, in addition to power and domination, the writer refers to immortality, beauty, physical prowess, and well-being.

Herschel Prins has supplied five reasons the belief in vampires has such a hold on people all over the world. Writing in the British journal *Medicine, Science, Law,* he compiled data from the fields of anthropology, folklore, mythology, and demonology, as well as forensic medicine and forensic pathology. He summarized from the literature, stating, first, that the desire for reunion with deceased loved ones is an important motivation underlying the belief. The symbolism of blood as a life force is the second reason he listed. He labeled blood ingestion as a parasitic, "leech-like" process, and included it as the third consideration. The fourth cause listed is the sexual aspect as symbolized by the vampire's bite. As a final motive for the popularity of vampire lore, he wrote that Dracula is the symbol of the perpetuation of life.

Fans definitely agree with the notion of sexual attraction. Sexuality and erotic aspects of the vampire were the most frequently mentioned reasons for this creature's appeal. Thirty-six out of fifty-four persons addressed this issue, and it was without doubt the predominant explanation cited.

The sexual angle of the vampire legend intrigues me. The vampire coming to his / her victim and taking his / her blood has strong connotations of rape. (The idea of actually drinking someone's blood or having it drunk always struck me as being sick.)

Being bitten on the neck and under the spell of a vampire has strong sexual symbolism attached to it, certainly on a subconscious level, especially years ago when sexuality could not be talked about openly. Vampires, at some level, represent a form of sexuality—forbidden, mysterious, exciting, strong, powerful, inviting, frightening, pleasure, pain.

Another fan said that the vampire has particular appeal to women. "Our commonest complaint about mortal man (if sex manuals are to be believed) is lack of foreplay, and a vampire's lovemaking is *all* foreplay." She says that for her the idea of a tireless, insatiable lover is a very appealing fantasy.

A different person acknowledged that it was vicariously exciting to fantasize about being the object of love for a superior being, but she had some reservations. "The thought of simply being dinner is appalling." Note this person's humorous reference to cannibalism.

One fan wrote that the sexual attractiveness of the vampire was so powerful that she had always fallen in love with this type of man—"mature, worldly, articulate, gentlemanly, powerful, hypnotic, and tragically unattainable for more than a short period of time." To her, he was personified by Jonathan Frid in his TV role as Barnabas Collins, and she was attracted to men with the same physical characteristics. She described her most intense love affair as being with a man who greatly resembled Barnabas both physically and mentally, and she bemoaned the demise of that relationship, in spite of her current happy marriage to someone else.

The sexual appeal of the vampire is further recognized by Dr. Youngson of the Count Dracula Fan Club, who reports that she receives two to three letters a year from teenage girls who say they would do anything if she would just introduce them to a vampire. She equates this behavior with similar requests she received when she used to answer mail for a popular rock group during the 1960s. Bob Greene, an editor for *Esquire,* tells about a like experience involving a high school girl who contacted him after reading his article on vampires; she wished to be "drained" by one.

Many scholars from the fields of psychiatry and psychology have discussed the sexual aspect of the vampire. One view is that if myths and legends of the past are the manifestation of psychological needs, then the vampire legend must be significant because of its universality. The biting and sucking of blood is the essential element. As an example, a case study is given of a girl who enjoyed watching dog fights as a child, particularly when there was a lot of bloodshed. When she was older, the girl deliberately cut or scratched herself in order to see and suck the blood, which she considered delicious.

This act aroused strong sexual feelings, even orgasm, particularly when fantasizing about sucking the blood of some attractive male while she was sucking her own blood. On occasion during intercourse with her husband she carried out these fantasies by biting him until he bled and then sucking the blood (an act labeled oral sadism).

Another psychoanalytic perspective on the possible genesis and purpose of the vampire is based on a study of the fantasies of schizophrenic patients who identify with the attacker's fantasy of holding, controlling, and biting a victim. This same attack correlates with the fears of the patient, who can also identify with the victim. From this view the vampire legend dramatically mirrors the world of the schizophrenic.

In addition, the vampire has the ability to allow us to sympathize with the creature's unfortunate state. Here is one who wishes to love and be loved, an idea we can all relate to. On the other hand, this creature is plagued by the demands of his oral needs, another problem which can arouse our compassion. In this interpretation, if we can understand the vampire's dilemma, it is possible to also understand equivalent components of schizophrenia.

Although one fan was not referring to the schizophrenic dimensions of the vampire legend, she did comment on the aspect of empathy. "In my case I have always felt that the vampire appeals to me because I felt sympathy for him / her. The vampire has been forced to lead this dreadful half-life."

Another fan revealed understanding and sympathy as well. She was attracted by his despair because she saw this ingredient as something the vampire has in common with all intelligent beings. "It makes me empathize. It makes me want to comfort and care for the one who hurts."

Ernest Jones, a student and disciple of Freud, considers that the blood-sucking act of the vampire reveals the sexual origin of the belief. He believes that in the unconscious mind, blood is an equivalent of semen. He states, "The simple idea of the vital fluid being withdrawn through an exhausting love embrace is complicated by more perverse forms of sexuality, as well as by the admixture of sadism and hate." Jones, too, labels the blood-sucking act as oral sadism. He also ties the vampire belief to incest.

A related psychoanalytic hypothesis reinforces the notion of incest, claiming that the bite on the neck represents sexual intercourse and that the long teeth of Dracula symbolize that body part of the father that is the object of projected hate. The female is allowed "a vicarious gratification of a daughter-father incest wish." It is believed that the incest taboo works to an advantage because the female victim then pays the price—death. By carrying out the fantasy of a sexual relationship with her father, the daughter must die. Bizarre as these interpretations may seem, they are seriously entertained by Freudian-based analysts.

The sucking aspect of the vampire may be interpreted in a slightly different way, as suggested by Harry Stone, a literary scholar who has analyzed the writings of Charles Dickens. He points out that in a number of his works, such as *Great Expectations* and *David Cooperfield,* Dickens uses vampire imagery. Stone relates the vampiric act, in part, to deprivation of the breast. In *David Cooperfield,* David is shocked upon seeing his mother first suckling his half-brother. This was a profound event for David. At that moment he recognized that he would, from then on, be deprived of the warmth of his own nurturing relationship with his mother. Furthermore, he envied the pleasure that this intruder now enjoyed.

Rather than labeling the vampire's bite on the neck as oral sadism, can it be possible that the vampire's sucking at the neck as depicted in film and literature is merely a substitute for insufficient suckling at the breast? Can it be that those persons who engage in vampiric activities of taking blood from others are reenacting their own period of infancy, when they were weaned before they were ready to give up closeness and nourishment from the mother? Are these persons symbolically asking to become children again, forever resting on their mothers' bosoms, eternally safe and satisfied?

This alternative Freudian interpretation might also seem questionable, but in looking at the information provided by persons who engage in voluntary blood-drinking activities, it may not seem such an unacceptable explanation after all, for as the data in Chapter 1 suggest, many real-life "vampires" are seeking to replace feelings of warmth, closeness, and intimacy. Certainly Brad expressed this the most explicitly when he talked about receiving Pam's unconditional love.

A few fans addressed the sexual deviations of the vampire.

> All forbidden sexual practices come into play—oral, necrophiliac, incestual, homosexual.
>
> . . . blood sucking is a sexual deviation.
>
> . . . the psychopathological interferences or needs or deviations.

Calling it an "infantile retentive attitude toward sex," Stephen King says that Stoker's version of the vampire legend translates as, "I will rape you with my mouth and you will love it; instead of contributing potent fluid to your body, I will remove it."

Fans indicated that, to them, immortality is the second most important source of appeal. Twenty-six persons mentioned that this was why they believed the vampire was attractive, which correlates with Prins's summary.

> Even though I don't believe vampires exist, I very much enjoy the idea of living forever and not aging. So if there were such things as vampires, I'd probably want to be one, even though according to legend, I'd have to give up daytime life.

> Immortality, for most of us would wish to live ageless in perpetual youth, vigor and vitality.

> To never grow old, to have the strength of ten, to be able to change your form at will, to be able to make women / men bend to your will and have them enjoy it. Many mortals would think seriously about losing their life to have such abilities.

> Everyone basically wants to live forever. The world has so much to offer and no one can see it all in a lifetime; but a vampire can go beyond that . . . and can experience things that the rest of us can only dream or read about.

> Like most people with a sense of natural curiosity, I fear that my seventy-five to eighty years on this "plane" will not be enough to satisfy. To that end (eternal life, I mean) the vampire represents my desire to know the future, and to experience it myself, despite the drawbacks that might be all too apparent to anyone who stops to contemplate "eternity." How wonderful it would be to check the internal clock—stop it, in order to watch the resulting growth form the "seeds" we have planted in this lifetime. To amass knowledge from this infant life, and then to use it creatively during that extended lifespan. This aspect of the vampire existence is my first interest . . . Perhaps the idea of release from the ties of mortal life—the deadlines, the pressures, bills, and the psychic chatter of the crowd—is the other, less definable, lure.

Another fan wrote that eternal youth had particular appeal for her, especially now "as I age and watch older family members lose their physicial and mental abilities. Sometimes I think it would be worth anything to be able to stay thirty-five and healthy forever." Thus, the fans reaffirmed that one of our great desires is embodied in the vampire, the dream of eternal life.

The fans' explanations of their own attraction to the vampire differ from the reason given by one writer over a decade ago who observed that World War I, because of its bloodiness, enormous death toll, and destruction of dreams and ideals, became the turning point for the vampire's popularity. The rationale for this idea is that the public, unable to deal with wholesale killing, was able to identify with the Count as a personalized blood taker, thus allowing them to handle their real horror—the "Great War."

Emphasizing that the vampire demonstrates that death can bring peace, vampire films are interpreted as akin to medieval morality plays that attempted to reconcile the viewer to death, supposedly encouraging the audience to look forward to death as a return to order and peace.

That is not what contemporary fans revealed. Most of them see living forever as a positive value. Of course, they fantasize that this living forever would take place in a state of perfect physical condition, not as the prolongation of natural life with its attendant physical and mental deterioration. It is not eternal youth, but perfect and eternal adulthood with all faculties at their highest performance levels that they fantasize about.

The perspective of living forever being a cursed fate was overlooked by fans. No reference to immortality contained any of the wisdom commonly found in folktales, such as the one in which death is tied up in a tree. The old decrepit woman rattling down the country road complains that she's been living, "it seems, like a million years. I can't die. Some blame rascal has Death tied up in a sack and we can't die." This seems like a more realistic appraisal of living forever.

Anthropologist Ernest Becker agrees, asserting that the truth of the vampire is that our bodies are our doom. The corporeal aspects of our beings are regulated by the "earthly laws of blood and animality." Becker believes that only the spiritual aspects of man can transcend his lower materialistic self. To him the vampire story "is a perennial horror-passion play reflecting the entire truth of the human condition and the hope beyond it."

If Becker's view is valid—that the message of the vampire is that man's spirituality triumphs over his body—then it is not difficult to understand its popularity, providing satisfaction to viewers and readers on, probably, an unconscious level. Its audience gains fulfillment as they voyeuristically participate in the triumph of the spirit. Yet this view was never articulated by the fans.

Twenty-two persons said that power was the basis of the appeal of the vampire. Curiously, this quality was not specifically mentioned in Prins's review of the literature. Perhaps, this is because power is implicit in the act of the vampire's attack on his victim. Yet one fan separated this quality and discussed the appeal of power in a more general way.

> Power, because I wish I had more control over my life. I don't want to be afraid of everything; vampires have very little to fear unless they attract too much attention.

Most of the other fans referred to power more in relation to domination of others, particularly sexual domination. Feminists will certainly bemoan some of these views.

> . . . perhaps women are attracted to the sexual side of a woman being enslaved by the vampire, coming to him whenever he needs her, and submitting to him.

> He can control any woman's soul and entire being and she could be totally his if he commanded it. It's a fantasy for me and I'm sure for many women all over.

> For me, the idea of a personalized powerful demonic force that yet cannot harm you unless you invite it into your life is an aspect which gives the twin contradictory thrills of helplessness and power.

> They are creatures of power, able to drain life from their victims, or bestow eternal youth on those they favor. The hypnotic stare of

a vampire is legend, as is the enslavement of mere mortals to serve their unique needs. Power is attractive.

Who among us hasn't wondered what it would be like to bend others to our will, and move silently in the night, taking whatever we wanted?

That last description of power is perhaps the fantasy that many people have—to be able to take (or have) whatever one needs, to be able to get whatever one wants, to be in charge and do things "my way." These desires are easy to relate to.

Where Prins's summary and the respondents' answers differ is that none of the fans mentioned rejoining a dead loved one as an aspect of the appeal. It is understandable because if they became vampires after their loved ones' death, they would be "living," but the relatives would be dead. They could only make living relations immortal. Approaching this issue differently, Ernest Jones declares that the belief that the dead can visit their loved ones, particularly at night, is universal, because it is related to the desire that the dead should not forget us. He also claims that it stems from children's fears and memories of being left alone by their parents.

Why this motivation, so prominent in analyses by experts, is lacking among fans is curious. It is difficult to believe that none of them has ever lost someone close to them. Yet no one referred to this aspect of the symbol as having overt meaning for them. More acceptable is the possibility that this element is not viable for them, at least not on a conscious level. It may be another indication that perceptions about the vampire are undergoing some changes, at least for American fans.

The parasitic aspects of the blood sucking, as mentioned by Prins, are alluded to in fans' responses, but certainly do not receive major emphasis. In addition, surprisingly few persons referred to the symbolism of blood as the essence of life, to its magical properties, or to its unique quality of being able to reveal what goes on inside the body. These characteristics have been univer-

sally documented, yet with the exception of two related comments, are glaringly absent in fans' discussions. So this, too, is
an area where fan responses do not correlate with Prins's summary, Prins giving the mystic quality of blood as one of the five
major reasons extrapolated from the literature.

One of the exceptions was a person who said that the following was one of the attractions of the vampire: "the basic underlying theme of blood and all its associated mysteries." The other
exception wrote about Old Testament taboos against the drinking of blood.

In direct answer to the question "What do you think accounts
for the appeal of the vampire—for yourself and others?" the word
blood was used in answers only thirteen times, all related to sexual concerns.

> The physical closeness while drinking the blood, plus the act itself
> is considered erotic.
>
> Drinking the blood of others is a severely prohibited intimacy.
>
> For most people, I think the appeal of a vampire is his lust for
> blood as a symbol of a sexual urge that can be excused because he
> needs blood to continue his existence.
>
> The sexuality of course—bloodsucking is a sexual deviation, but
> it's also a fascination.
>
> I am attracted to vampires because of the romanticism and sexual-
> ity. I think it has something to do with sucking the blood out of
> one's body.

The act of drinking blood has both its sacred and its profane
manifestations in everyday life. The symbolic drinking of Christ's
blood in the Roman Catholic Mass is regularly engaged in by
hundreds of millions of the faithful throughout the world. In
addition, the act of blood exchange as a symbol of union can be
observed in normal children's play, an excellent example of which
can be seen in the Swedish film *My Life as a Dog*. In one scene a
twelve-year-old boy deliberately cuts his finger with a knife and

asks his female playmate to suck his finger. She complies and he announces, "Now we are married." In this country as well, it is not uncommon for children to deliberately prick their fingers, mix the blood by rubbing their fingers together, and thus become blood sisters or brothers and everlasting friends. The blood becomes the symbol of kinship.

In their book *The Wise Wound,* authors Penelope Shuttle and Peter Redgrove relate the significance of blood in vampire legends to the menstrual cycle. They go back to the creator of the modern vampire prototype, Bram Stoker, and hypothesize that his wife was frigid. They then suggest that women with unsatisfactory sex lives often have menstrual disturbances as well. They ask, "Was it some image of these [menstrual disturbances] that gave Stoker's subliminal mind the hint that formulated a myth of formidable power, out of the ferocity of the frustrated bleeding woman, crackling with energy and unacknowledged sexuality?"

Modern-day physicians do not accept this assumption. Women who have sexual dysfunctions, as well as women who have rejected sexual activity and chosen a celibate life, can have perfectly normal menstrual periods.

To support their provocative correlations between vampirism and menstruation, Shuttle and Redgrove point out that Dracula's title of Count could refer to the idea of a woman's keeping measure of her menstrual cycle—counting her days. They also suggest that the female victim's loss of blood from the neck might be an allusion to the neck of the womb—the cervix.

While these correspondences may seem a bit farfetched, the relating of a bite to menstruation occurs in a work of Claude Lévi-Strauss. Citing a belief of the Kogi tribe of Sierra de Santa Marta, Colombia, he says that the expression used to find out if a woman has her menstrual period is, "Has the bat bitten you?" This verbal expression is used as well by young men when a young woman has just begun to menstruate; they say she does so because she has been bitten by the bat. The symbolism of the bite being related to menstruation is made all the more fascinat-

ing in this instance because of the use of the bat—another symbol from the Dracula syndrome.

Other sides of the vampire's appeal were mentioned, ones not
included in Prins's summary. One fan stated that revenge was
an aspect of the vampire's appeal. Others revealed interest in the
occult and the unknown.

> They are creatures of the night, and I have always found the night
> a fascinating time. I am interested, to a degree, in the occult, and
> any supernatural idea or happening has always interested me.

> The appeal is for me at any rate, that I am terribly interested in the
> unknown and would make almost any effort to have some com-
> munication with the other world if it were at all possible and reli-
> able.

> The dark unknown. They [vampires] come to life in a world of
> darkness where shadows play tricks on one's vision and you're never
> quite sure what a dark room holds. Their powers are so great that
> almost anything seems possible, so you never know what to expect.

Some wrote about the horror as well as the thrill of fear:

> Everyone enjoys being frightened once in a while.

> I think they have a universal horror appeal. Vampires are the extreme
> opposite of saints. They have eternal life but reside in graveyards,
> coffins, wear gothic clothes and attack the living for their blood.
> They are sinister characters that people like to watch and be scared
> by in movies and TV.

To this next fan, the symbol of the vampire is multifaceted
and conjures up vivid images. This was further evidenced by the
number of well-executed drawings he sent—all inspired by the
vampire.

> They are the epitome of the secretive darkness and lurking, sinister
> menace one would most likely encounter in the pages of a good

horror book . . . the fangs, black-cloaked garments like a bat's wings, the white joker's face peering into a window at night, the fear of silver, resting in coffins under graveyard soil: all these things serve to produce a creation that is more satisfyingly chilling than any run-of-the-mill ghost story could ever do. Even the very name, vampire—Vammmm-pire!—conjures up such contrasting things as ruined castles, gothic atmosphere . . . the nocturnal existence, the very danger of it like a deadly poisonous rat hiding somewhere in your house which you can never find but can hear at night and are afraid of.

In great contrast, several fans cited the beauty, elegance, and sophistication of the vampire as being part of his appeal. "Stunning beauty" was cited by one. Others addressed his "aristocratic sophistication," "hypnotic eyes," and "old world gothic elegant side."

Many vampire characters are handsome, elegant, cultured (Lee, Langella, Hamilton, Frid) and this is very appealing to me. They seem to have old-world elegance and sophistication that I just love.

Another mentioned the value of the vampire as a scapegoat. "It's sort of handy to have a horrible person around to hate and blame things on. Having them become a vampire after they're dead would be convenient." This same view can certainly be extrapolated from the centuries-old explanations that vampires were responsible for unsuccessful harvests, spoiled milk, calamity.

A few respondents identified with the vampire as someone different, as an outsider persecuted for that difference. One fan wrote that as a child she identified with the vampire as an outsider. "The feeling that society as a whole always attempts to destroy whatever it cannot understand remains very strong for me, even today after a lapse of many years."

Another fan concurs.

I believe my interest in the vampire has partly to do with the fact that within those unearthly realms I feel more comfortable than I do in the real world. I have always considered myself an "outsider" to society also. I feel more comfortable alone most of the time than I do around people. Perhaps part of the appeal of the vampire is it gives us the belief that there are beings who can live outside the problems of society that we, as mortals, must face everyday. Beings who don't have to concern themselves with the petty problems of day-to-day existence, as we must, but instead rise above all that, with grace and dignity, and who will be walking this earth far past the time our mortal bodies have turned to dust and have been long forgotten.

Author Anne Rice feels similarly. She interprets the vampire as a metaphor for the outsider, the alienated "who feel like monsters deep inside," who can be in the middle of everything yet totally detached. Explaining that she sees the vampire as an elegant yet doomed person, she describes his beautiful appearance, his sensitivity, and his plight of being a prisoner.

An anthropological analysis interprets Dracula as an outsider who arouses hate and fear rather than sympathy, representing a "foreigner" whose appearance and behavior contrast with those of ordinary people. His peculiar habits—the food he eats, the way he obtains it, where and when he sleeps, his burial customs—arouse feelings of xenophobia.

Moreover, Dracula poses a danger and a threat because he seeks to sexually conquer the women who belong to other men. He also violates boundaries, for in order to survive, he must have foreign blood.

As a further example of anthropological perspective, it is noted that once Dracula "sexualizes" a relationship with a virgin, she immediately takes on the role of daughter and he takes from her no more, thus preserving the incest taboo.

R. W. Johnson analyzes what the vampire represents to him. Writing in "The Myth of the Twentieth Century," he concludes:

> He is human anti-matter. He lives only by killing. He doesn't eat and he hates garlic (taken with food). Water, crucial to human life,

is anathema to him, as is the Cross, the symbol of life for Christian man. He has no identity—he can't even be seen in a mirror. He cannot stand daylight, crucial to all life. He doesn't have sex, strictly speaking, or rather, for him the sexual act is always a violent rape which brings forth not another life but another death. He is immune to bullets, cannot stand Holy Water, and can pass through solid objects. He does not even die, as a man does: he is un-dead.

He is, in other words, a pure inversion. There is no anomie, no alienation, as great as the vampire's: he is *the* alienation of man, and that alienation is potentially immortal. He is ultimately exploitative—a spreading centre of alienation, despoiling others of their very lives and identities too.

Playwright Chris Hardman brings up a point of view not previously discussed when he says that Dracula's essential attraction is to find out that mystical reason why people are driven so strongly to be what they are. "We're always intrigued by people who are particularly driven by unfathomable cause," Hardman says.

He also says that Dracula reveals what is inside humans. How deep does it go? He addresses the issue of the darker side of the symbol. "Dracula is a discussion of the depths of human behavior, the epitome of what is the depth of darkness that a human can pass into."

Surprisingly, only two fans referred to the evil side of the vampire. One fan said that the vampire is appealing because of a combination of immortality and complete evil. "Life without end and evil without guilt." Yet this was the only strong negative statement made about the vampire.

Hardman contrasts Dracula with Frankenstein, whom he calls "the ecological monster—what humans create can destroy them." According to Hardman, Frankenstein is the exterior issue and Dracula is the interior one. "Dracula is cold, cool, like Mack the Knife. He's that midnight slicer, the essence of coldness and non-feeling."

Vampire fans do not interpret Dracula in such a cold, sinister way. They recognize the dark side of his sexual deviance and domination, yet vicariously enjoy his exploits. "They provide a fantasy outlet for impulses we're taught not to acknowledge," a fan wrote.

A published interview with a fan from the Count Dracula Fan Club offers a different insight.

> For one thing, I think we gain security when we meet our nightmares halfway. By being able to discuss and even see our most horrible ideas, we learn to control and transcend the physical and mental symptoms of fright and panic. We become more comfortable with ourselves. (Gee, if you can watch a partially decomposed corpse suck the life out of someone while calmly munching on french fries, surely you can stand up to your boss!)

In other words, she believes that the vampire can serve as a means of coping with our fears, giving us strength to confront our personal monsters.

Over ten years ago Louis and Carol Winkler wrote "A Reappraisal of the Vampire." In this essay they suggest that if there were such a thing as a hierarchy of evil entities, the vampire would be in a superior position over all other creatures. They elaborate that the vampire is a more formidable figure than the others,

> plus the fact that he must cause harm to mankind if he is to survive. In view of the fact that the vampire is so interesting, has been prominent so long and is specifically involved in so many important aspects pertinent to mankind, a separate position in evil hierarchy should be created for him.

According to fans, the vampire does occupy a special place. Yet most fans today seem to downplay his evil aspects when they describe him. The meaning of his symbol seems to be changing. He is perceived as less a villain and more a tragic hero. They feel sorry for him.

Fans excuse his actions because he is forced to behave this way in order to survive. They are sympathetic to his plight as a loner. Delighting in his beauty, elegance, and Old World charm, some fans revealed that they enjoyed being dominated by him, that they liked the idea of being in his power—being his victim. They relished his eroticism—and as the one person commented, his "foreplay."

Fans expressed no desire to join the dead. Rather, they would enjoy continuing to be with the living. Although they envied the vampire's ability to live forever, fans appear to be more oriented toward living in the present and ensuring that the future never ends.

One significant aspect not mentioned by any respondents, yet engaged in by almost everyone and everything attached to the vampire, is humor. Does the humor exist because it allows us to deal with the taboo topics of sex and death? Is the vampire so appealing a figure because he provides automatic opportunities for joking, punning, and playfulness?

Humor is so built in to the vampire concept that it was completely overlooked as an appealing and separate aspect of the vampire's characteristics. Fans, students, everyone contacted for this research could not resist the opportunity to make humorous asides. For example, one correspondent said "I have put a notice in our newsletter asking any of our initiates who know (or are) Undead to contact you—via a letter or phone call, not a nocturnal chomp on the neck."

Much of the humor attached to the vampire is filled with double entendres. A close look at a variety of greeting cards and Halloween buttons showed that the puns and riddles revolved primarily around the teeth and biting, such as "Fangs for the memories," or "You're somebody I could really sink my teeth into." The relationship to sex was very clear cut: "You look good enough to eat"; "You suck"; "I won't bite—at least where it shows." One company's product shows a vampire locked outside a window holding a birthday cake with lit candles. The cover is captioned, "Lock your windows and bolt your doors lest you fall prey to Armand the birthday vampire." Inside the card reads,

"He'll suck the frosting right off your cake." There were a few cards with more innocent themes: "Eat, drink and be scary"; "Do I wish you a happy Halloween? You bat I do"; "Please don't be cross with me."

That joking and punning are such a significant part of the vampire's attraction became very obvious when embarking upon this research. It was almost impossible for people not to respond with humor—something not witnessed or experienced in discussions of other malevolent supernatural entities. The subject matter evokes such an emotional response that there appears to be a great need to use humor.

A colleague in the English Department at Cal State warned, "This undertaking is a grave mistake." Yet another co-worker commented, "The whole subject sucks." Someone else commented, "Gee, megabyte takes on a whole new dimension for you." A librarian gave this greeting: "Shalom. Let me see your neck!"

During one dental appointment my dentist apologized for running late and not being able to carry out his planned performance of ushering me into his "chamber" with a Transylvanian accent. Later, while drilling, he inquired in a confidential, almost seductive tone, "Would you like me to extend your cuspids?"

A close friend, recently diagnosed with a rare disease, was quite apprehensive about the required treatment of a series of phlebotomies—a process of removing blood by opening a vein. After the first treatment he phoned and reported eagerly, "It was okay. No big deal. The only weird thing was the guy who did it to me was wearing a cape!"

Concerned over the unusual mail that began flowing into the English Department, the chairman asked, "What's going on here? Are you turning this into the Cal State Blood Studies Center?" Another faculty member exclaimed, "I think you've hit the popular jugular vein!"

I was affected as well. After reading a stack of mail from aficionados, I heard myself saying to my daughter, "This subject is so all consuming, I can hardly wait to dig in," to which she replied, "Something to sink your teeth into?"

In sum, joking remarks made to me used such words as *sucks, extend cuspids, sink your teeth, megabyte, grave, undertaking, dig in, all consuming, blood, jugular vein*. The primary allusions were to sex, then death, and finally blood, which can be equated with life, death, *and* sex.

Understandably, thinking about these basic elements of life stirs deep emotions, causing discomfort at most and ambivalence at least. We are afraid of death. Sometimes we are afraid of life. The emotional response to sex, in particular, strikes a chord which may be harmonious or dissonant. Regardless of which, reactions are rarely passive. No wonder, then, that when it comes to vampires, jokes are made. Humor becomes a convenient means for dealing with anxiety-producing topics.

"I always thought it was just kind of fun. I don't know. Maybe there is something to do with libido. It's just always funny to me. The guy is funny and scary," an informant said, attempting to figure out why he was so attracted to the symbol. This same person elaborated on the impact of the visuals. "To me those teeth are so funny. I even got a pair of plastic teeth. I couldn't wait to get a pair of those teeth with those fangs sticking out. IT WAS JUST FUN!"

In spite of the comment by folklorist Alan Dundes that there is no such thing as harmless wit, there seems to be something else behind the vampire humor. The playfulness attached to the American concept of the vampire is very much connected with the Bela Lugosi portrayal of the Count speaking with a Hungarian accent. If Dundes is correct, then people are making fun of Lugosi when imitating his speech. At one level this may be true. On the other hand, imitating that accent allows the opportunity to play with dialect. It is fun to talk that way. As an informant stated, "It always has amused me because I loved Bela Lugosi's voice. I was always fascinated by his voice."

The cadence and tonality of Lugosi's speech are exotic to the

average American. One of his biographers, Arthur Lennig, analyzed the accent in this manner:

> Yes, it is Hungarian, but it is also Lugosian as well. In the inflec-
> tions, the certain turn of the word, the odd way his lips and jaw
> muscles function, he seems to speak with great effort, as if he were
> forcing a mouth long dead to move again. His consonants are
> stressed, and the vowels are heavier and more drawn out. The above
> phrase, "forcing a mouth long dead," becomes "forse-sink a
> mauith longk deadt." The overall effect is guttural, strong, mas-
> culine, somehow the very personification of evil.

Lennig also dissects Lugosi's style of delivery, particularly his
frequent pauses.

> As Dracula he says, "I bid you—welcome." The pause before as
> well as the inflection of the word "welcome" provide a certain
> ambivalency, a combination of greeting and foreboding, cordiality
> and superiority, sincerity and irony . . . but no one, I submit, has
> ever succeeded in delivering absurd lines with such dramatic power
> and, indeed, dignity.

Lugosi's unique style of speech provides a basis of parody which
possibly lies outside the Freudian interpretation of release of hostility, to which Dundes refers. To imitate a foreign accent by
manipulating familiar words gives pleasure. Human beings like
to play with language. It is fun to talk in different ways. This is
readily observable when children make up languages, for example,
that have "op" in every word or when adults imitate the speaking styles of personalities, for example, James Cagney, Talullah
Bankhead, or Mae West.

To fall into a pseudo-Hungarian accent is almost irresistible.
When an associate was asked if he would be willing to circulate
the vampire survey among his students, he pulled himself up
into an erect posture and dramatically enunciated, "Stuuu-dents,
I vish to ask you something . . ."

When I was explaining that a German filmmaker wanted my vampire research sent to him right away, a relative responded in heavy accent, "By night letter, of course!"

While the aforementioned vampire pizza commercial script is funny in itself, the exaggerated Hungarian accent adds to the zaniness of the Count's presence in a fast-food restaurant. Note, too, that the Count on "Sesame Street" also uses the accent. The creators must have decided to retain this element of the Lugosi portrayal because it ameliorates some of the more sinister connotations of the shadowy Count. A fan described the actor's characterization as follows: "The way Bela did it, you always knew that you could get a good laugh and that you were not in the presence of Satan."

One wonders how today's vampire would be characterized by the American public and if the vampire would be so popular if, instead of Lugosi, an accentless John Barrymore had been cast in the first sound version of this film.

The appeal of the vampire is multifaceted. He has many sides and shades and seems to fill in·the blanks in the varied needs of his viewers' backgrounds. Although the vampire takes from his victim to feed his hunger, it is as if he is satisfying a hunger in his audience—a hunger for sexuality and sensuality, a desire to live forever (schizophrenic or not), a yearning to be both empowered and powerless and thus completely without any responsibility for one's own actions. This is an almost juvenile, non-adult role and might tie in to Harry Stone's notion of remaining at the breast, snug, secure, well fed, and taken care of.

There is another side, too. Perhaps the vampire is the personification of an evil force—taking something from another against their will. Maybe in this role of the empowered he provides a voyeuristic experience which then reduces the necessity for others to commit such acts. Conversely, in his media form, his elegance, accent, and exaggerated appearance in tuxedo make evil seem less scary and, for the audience identifying with the vampire's victim, allow laughter and thus some sort of control over the fear.

According to the fans, the vampire appeals to cravings about the mystery of the unknown. He brings out tenderness in some, romantic qualities in others. He may be the last link to a romantic past—literally tied to the earth as it moves outward toward space, and perhaps to technological disaster.

American vampires do not seem to be such bad fellows. They are a basis for creativity in art, narrative, films, and poetry. They satisfy a need for playfulness. It is easy to have a good laugh over them by telling riddles, punning, imitating their speech, dressing up like them, and acting silly while mimicking their antics, even wearing tattoos related to them and enjoying people's shocked responses.

Americans can enjoy the vampire's sexual exploits, and have some vicarious experiences through the suggestions of sex made in jokes and found on Halloween buttons and in cards. Fans envy the vampire's ability to live forever. Those who wrote that they perceive of themselves as vampires do not consider themselves evil; rather, they claim a "need" associated with sexuality and sensuality. In a way, vampires have become sanitized and romanticized.

As we've seen by looking at the responses of the many kinds of folk (fans, students, emulators), including the joking and kidding, ritualizing and storytelling, the vampire appears to be an appropriate symbol for comtemporary American life—he is lonely, secular, glorifies (sometimes abuses) power, and enjoys sexual freedom. And now must he, too, worry about AIDS because of his "sexual" promiscuity? L. J. Beal, Ph.D., consultant to the Count Dracula Fan Club, doesn't think so. In his view, vampires are immune to *all* diseases and must be disposed of through traditional methods. In spite of tabloid reports to the contrary, he advises that the vampire population is not in danger of dying out because of this disease.

However, a fan commenting on this issue has accepted the

idea that if a vampire is immortal, then he will not die from AIDS, only carry it. Therefore, his victims will be infected. This fan asks, "At what point does immortality enter into the victim's existence in relation to the fatal AIDS virus? A head-on between science and folklore?" For better and for worse, the ancient vampire has adapted to our time and place.

Vampire Victims

I hate to be an outcast
—a porphyria patient

Promoted by the media, the American vampire image is everywhere. Some children and adults believe that he is real—or that it is possible for him to exist in reality. The vampire has become so influential that even in some instances it appears that scientists, those whose reality is rooted in quantifiable verifiable evidence, validate his presence.

On May 30, 1985, David Dolphin, Ph.D., professor of chemistry at the University of British Columbia, gave a startling presentation to the American Association for the Advancement of Science. He hypothesized that blood-drinking vampires were, in fact, victims of porphyria, an incurable genetic disease affecting at least 50,000 patients in the United States that causes sudden symptoms of severe pain, respiratory problems, skin lesions, and sometimes death. He suggested that some of the symptoms could be alleviated by an injection of heme (the pigmented component of hemoglobin and related substances, found in largest amounts in the bone marrow, red blood cells, and the liver). Dolphin announced, "Since in the Middle Ages an injection of the red pigment of blood would not be possible, what else might take its place? If a large amount of blood were to be drunk then the heme in it, if it passes through the stomach wall to the blood-stream, would serve the same purpose." He declared, "It is our contention that blood drinking vampires were in fact victims of porphyria trying to alleviate the symptoms of their dreadful dis-ease."

Dolphin described the photosensitivity of porphyria victims, stating that the effects of exposure to even mild sunlight could be devastating. To him this would be consistent with the folk-lore concerning the nocturnal behavior of vampires. He spoke of "lesions of the skin being so severe that the nose and fingers could be destroyed." He discussed hairiness, pigmentation, and depigmentation. He indicated that while the teeth became no larger, lips and gums became taut so that the teeth appeared to be much more prominent.

Building upon an earlier hypothesis of British theorist L. Illis, Dolphin also linked these patients to werewolves, because they could become very hairy. "Imagine if you will," Dr. Dolphin stated,

> the manner in which an individual in the Middle Ages would have been received if they only went out at night and when they were seen that they would have an animal look about them being hairy, large of tooth and badly disfigured. It has been suggested, and it seems more than likely that such people might well have been con-sidered werewolves.

Dr. Dolphin expanded on his hypothesis, suggesting that chemical reactions to garlic by porphyria patients were such that garlic might increase the severity of a porphyria attack, and thus might well act to keep vampires away because they would want to avoid any substance that aggravated their condition. Accord-ing to his view, this negative effect of garlic occurs because its principal constituent is dialkyl disulfide, which destroys heme.

This can set off a reaction increasing the severity of a porphyria attack.

Dolphin also addressed the issue of the incidence of the disease. He tried to correlate the folklore of the vampire's bite, causing the victim to become a vampire, with the genetic pattern of porphyria. He explained that while siblings may share the same defective gene from this generally autosomal dominant trait (inherited from one parent), sometimes only one sibling will display symptoms. However, he noted that a strain on the system from an excess of drugs, alcohol, or sudden loss of a large quantity of blood could trigger the disease in a person genetically predisposed.

> Since the porphyrias are genetic it seems likely, in early times when travel was rare and inbreeding was not, that local pockets of the disease might be rampant (Transylvania). The likelihood then of one porphyria victim biting another, and initiating the disease, could have been high.

Professional societies like the American Association for the Advancement of Science annually hold meetings where scholars, like Dr. Dolphin, present new theoretical concepts for peers to debate and criticize. Professional meetings are created as a forum for the examination and evaluation of new concepts, as well as for reconsideration of older, well-accepted theories. Often fresh ideas are not immediately accepted. For example, when today's widely held theories of Darwin and Pasteur were initially presented to their respective societies in the nineteenth century, they were not received with general approval. The scholarly process moves very slowly.

On the other hand, the media have different objectives. Their goal is to grab the attention of the public with eye- and ear-catching topics in order to transmit information as quickly and widely as possible. So it is that newspaper and wire services across the country seized upon Dolphin's presentation. The result was front-page feature stories, often accompanied by pictures of Lon

Chaney or Bela Lugosi about to sink his teeth into the neck of a beautiful young female victim. The *Washington Post* trumpeted its story with "Dracula Wolf Man Legends May Contain a Drop of Truth: Genetic Disorder May Trigger Thirst for Blood." *Newsweek* proclaimed, "Vampire Diagnosis: Real Sick." The *Sacramento Bee* heralded, "Bad Blood Takes Bite Out of Vampire Myth." As far away as Poland, headlines announced, "Did Vampires Exist in Reality?—They Are Simply Porphyria Patients"; "Did Vampires and Werewolves Exist in the Real World?"; and "Vampires Are Simply People Sick on Porphyria."

In Providence, Rhode Island, the vampire story pushed coverage of the sensational Claus von Bulow murder trial from its prominent position on page one. Even the well-known children's publication *Weekly Reader* ran two versions of the story with photos of Bela Lugosi. One was headlined, "Did Disease Trigger Vampires' Blood Thirst?" This lead followed:

> Do you shudder at a movie when Count Dracula bares his fangs?
> Do you get goose bumps when you read about bloodsucking vampires or weird werewolves?
> Naturally your fright doesn't last long because you know vampires and werewolves are merely legendary characters, right? Well, maybe

There was sustained national and local television coverage. Tom Brokaw featured a segment on "NBC Nightly News." "PM Magazine" presented a hypothesis-as-truth version of the report, and the "Today" show also reported on Dolphin's porphyria hypothesis.

On Halloween, station KPIX-TV in San Francisco gave a titillating account of the story on its "Evening Magazine" program. Professor Dolphin was interviewed wearing his lab smock, and there was an interview with a Colorado porphyria sufferer, but as one offended viewer described it, the interviewers stopped just short of giggling as they talked about the vampire / porphyria connection.

Two TV medical series, "Trapper John" and "St. Elsewhere," created segments based on the idea. Over a year later "Divorce Court" produced an episode dealing with this same concept. From these television dramatizations and the extensive news-like television and print coverage it was clear that the media knew that the American public would love another good story about vampires and werewolves.

What the media failed to consider was how the 50,000 incurable porphyria patients would be affected when they promoted Professor Dolphin's hypothesis of a biochemical basis to ancient and feared beliefs about legendary entities.

According to the American Porphyria Foundation, whose board is composed of physicians with fifteen to twenty years' experience in the field, porphyria is not one disease, but a constellation of seven different inheritable diseases, some of which are life threatening. It is so rare as to be classified an "orphan disease"— a label applied to any disorder that affects fewer than 200,000 people. It is often a silent disease, meaning that the gene for it can be carried and passed on to others without ever causing any problems.

Porphyria is a metabolic disorder caused by a deficiency in an enzyme involved with the synthesis of heme. Each of the forms has its own symptomatology and treatment. For example, patients with acute intermittent porphyria (AIP) have no photosensitivity problems, but require injections of heme during severe bouts of pain. It is particularly dangerous if the diagnosis has not been made and if harmful drugs are administered. Although symptoms generally resolve following an attack, some patients develop chronic pain.

The symptoms often seem mysterious, appearing suddenly. They can include rapid onset of muscle paralysis in arms and legs, seizures, confusion, headaches, agitation, blindness, tachycardia (rapid heartbeat), and constant vomiting. Chemical imbalances can cause mental problems, such as hallucinations. In acute cases, respiratory failure and death result.

In contrast, patients with porphyria cutania tarda (PCT), the most common form, have skin problems, typically fragility and blistering of areas exposed to sunlight. There may be an over-abundance or lack of pigmentation and excess facial hair.

In erythropoietic protoporphyria (EPP), another form, pho-tosensitivity causes burning, itching, and thickening of the skin. One patient told how grieved she felt when people commented that she looked as if she had leprosy.

While most types of porphyria are genetically based, PCT can be either inherited or acquired. For example, as long as twenty-five years after eating grain contaminated by fungicides contain-ing hexachlorobenzene, patients in Turkey were still exhibiting PCT symptoms; some female patients needed to use hair depil-atory creams two to three times per month to remove excessive facial hair.

The blood of PCT patients has an excess of iron, which is best removed by withdrawing blood, along with the excess iron sometimes as often as twice a month, in a process called phle-botomy, which is similar to donating blood for a transfusion or to a blood bank.

The most extreme and rare form is congenital erythropoietic porphyria (CEP), also known as Gunther's disease. It usually manifests during childhood. Skin photosensitivity may be extreme and lead to blistering, severe scarring, and increased hair growth. Removal of the spleen and blood transfusions are treatment pos-sibilities.

Blood transfusions are used to suppress the patient's own marrow because it is here that the porphyrins are produced. Por-phyrins are a natural product of the body, pumped out by the bone marrow, but if they are produced at excessive rates, then symptoms of porphyria occur. Blood transfusions can shut down the body's abnormal porphyrin production.

CEP is the only form of the disease with even a remote pos-sibility of correlation with the vampire's supposed physical char-acteristics, for here there may be hairiness, mutilation affecting the nose, shortened fingers or loss of the ends of the fingers and possibly pointed teeth. However, the hypothesis could not apply even here because blood taken by mouth supposedly to counter the heme deficiency, cannot reach the blood in the circulation system. It would be broken down in the gut to iron and amino acids, which have no effect on any form of porphyria.

One CEP patient described how she carried a coat over her scarred hands to hide the mutilated fingers. She told of clerks being afraid to accept money from her and throwing change down on counters to avoid physical contact. She tearfully recounted tales of doctors who wore rubber gloves while examining her.

With CEP the teeth can become pointed and red stained because of the excessive porphyrins in the system. A patient recounted that she grew a large, orange-colored, fang-like tooth in her lower jaw and was very self-conscious about it, for she was not able to eat naturally or close her mouth over it. With the exception of CEP, porphyria develops after puberty, and frequently symptoms appear only as a result of certain environmental conditions.

The history of variegate porphyria (VP) offers an excellent example of how environmental conditions can have an impact on the disease, causing it to be expressed. Variegate porphyria is also known as South African genetic porphyria because almost all patients are descendants of an early Dutch settler who spread the trait when he married an orphan girl just after the Cape Colony was founded in 1688. While VP is considered primarily limited to South Africa (3 per 1,000 in the white population carry the gene), some cases have also been found outside that country.

For almost 300 years no symptoms of the disease were manifested. What triggered its appearance was the introduction of barbituates for the induction of anesthesia. When physicians began using these drugs to put people to sleep for surgery, they discovered an epidemic of porphyria. As a result, today in South Africa patients are routinely tested for porphyria before being given an anesthetic.

Substances known to set off the different porphyria varieties are fungicides (hexachlorobenzene), alcohol, and certain medications (birth control pills; the sulfa drugs; anti-epilepsy drugs)

Low intake of carbohydrates and calories through dieting can also precipitate an attack in patients with AIP. Garlic cannot trigger an attack or have any effect whatsoever on this disease.

One patient described how, at the age of thirty, she had to undergo routine surgery. Unaware that she had porphyria, which had been dormant up to that time, she entered the hospital as a healthy person, but came out thirty days later "a vegetable," the result of being given phenobarbital after surgery. The phenobarbital caused more pain, and because the doctors were unaware of the cause of the pain she was subsequently given further injections of the drug to alleviate it. Unfortunately, this activated her porphyria. Excruciating pain in the abdomen—"like bulldozers inside"—inability to speak, and jaws so uncontrollable that saliva dripped from her mouth caused this woman's condition to worsen until she was near death. Unable to speak, she wrote to her family, "Enough is enough. I'm going home to die." Finally, her urine turned purple. Only then was porphyria correctly diagnosed.

Purple urine is the startling and significant characteristic of this disease. In fact, the name *porphyria* is built upon the Greek root word for purple. Urine taken from patients with high levels of porphyrin in their systems darkens after standing in the light, turning the color of port wine. This same urine becomes florescent under ultraviolet light. Depending on the form of porphyria, ultraviolet light can also reveal fluorescence in gallstones, the liver, and red blood cells.

Although doctors can make an unequivocal diagnosis from appropriate laboratory tests, porphyria is called the "Little Imitator" because it is difficult to diagnose only from its symptoms, which simulate so many other illnesses: headaches like migraines, aches and pains like arthritis, agonizing abdominal pains, and tiredness. One patient reported being subjected to nine major surgeries (three of them exploratory) and "treated" by thirty different doctors before an internist finally thought of one of the porphyrias and tested her for it. Another patient described the frustration caused by the ignorance of her doctors, relating that when she was seventeen one doctor insisted that she be sterilized as a method of treatment. She refused. Today she has two children but complained, "I have seen doctors that relish the fact that I have porphyria—overhearing them discuss me like I'm a freak."

Still another patient disclosed that what she assumed to be an accepted medical recommendation by her physician was instead later defended as being based on his "professional hunch." Unhappily she discovered this only after she had agreed to have all her teeth pulled. She lamented, "And my teeth were so perfect." At an earlier time a dental professor had asked her to appear in his dental class as an example of a person with perfect teeth.

Because of the vagueness of the symptoms, patients are sometimes given a psychiatric diagnosis. As an example, one patient reported that doctors who could see that she was ill and had initially been concerned gradually turned cold, even insulting, toward her when tests continued to show nothing. When her feet swelled like footballs, her legs became as taut as wooden boards, and her throat swelled beyond her ears, they said she was "nervous," "imagined it," and "needed a hobby."

Another patient declared, "When we tell doctors that we have porphyria, they think we're Twinkies and negate everything we say. They exaggerate the mental aspects and ignore the physical."

As is apparent, to have porphyria is no laughing matter. Yet porphyria patients immediately became the targets of jokes and victims of avoidance, fear, and derision as a result of the publicity blitz ignited by the hypothesis. The association of the relatively unknown porphyria with the very well known vampire set off a chain reaction of unexpected and unpleasant events because the allure of the vampire is so strong in this country.

Desiree (Dee) Dodson, director of the American Porphyria Foundation, reported that phone and mail contacts increased 500 percent. She described it as a "nightmare" because she could not keep up with all the mail and was barraged with phone calls from incensed patients all over the country.

The distraught wife of one patient feared that her husband would begin sucking her blood. Later, she was convinced that he was actually carrying out this act during her sleeping hours and she tried unsuccessfully to convince a priest to have him exorcised.

Some patients contacted the foundation with worries about turning into vampires. Others expressed concern about growing body hair. One patient said that as soon as the media bombardment occurred, her phone rang constantly. Some friends now avoided her, but she was mainly disturbed at being the butt of jokes, many of them having to do with drinking blood in the middle of the night. She was bitter. "Nobody makes fun of leukemia and MS."

They did make fun of porphyria. Some comments to her were "I just can't take you anywhere—sniffing around trying to bite people's necks and "We all know how you vampires are." When conversing over the phone with a friend, she heard the friend's child say, "Is that one of the ladies with the werewolf disease?" Worst of all, as a result of the publicity, this patient lost weight and came out of remission, which adversely affected the course of her disease.

A porphyria patient who runs a hotline for sufferers in New England complained that she was very angry with her local paper's headline about the "Vampire Disease." She wanted to get a retraction printed and considered using as her headline "The Vampire Strikes Back." But then she realized that her answering headline would have kept the matter a joke. Referring to the severity of her disease she said, "It's just not a joke. Believe me, it's no joke."

This woman described two panic-stricken couples, each of whom was being driven apart by the publicity. In both cases the wives had the disease and the husbands could not deal with it. According to this informant, both women were newly diagnosed. Before the publicity, porphyria had been an unknown, but afterward the attitude of each of the husbands was "I don't know if I can handle this or if I want to live with this person. I don't know if I even want to talk to you" [the person running the hotline]. These husbands were horrified by the notion that they might be married to vampires. Their emotional responses blurred their logic. They began to consider that maybe the vampire was something real.

While at first this might seem preposterous, remember that 27 percent of college and high school students answering the questionnaire admitted that they thought the vampire's existence might be a possibility. The media's exaggeration of the vampire connection intensified the men's fears and raised doubts, to the detriment of their relationships with their wives.

Another patient reported that he had received a phone call from a friend who asked, "You know, I've been watching television today, and there was this program about people with porphyria being vampires, and needing blood, eating blood. Do you do that?" Others would make jokes about the full moon and howling. "We want to keep an eye on you. We want to know where you're going to be on the full moon." He said three of his best friends began to avoid him after the publicity.

Because the community in which he lived knew about his condition and had seen the sensationalized coverage in the *San Francisco Chronicle,* the man was afraid to go out for a walk alone after sundown, or to be seen near any schoolground, fearing that if something were to happen to a child he would be the first one to be suspected. He and his mother, also a porphyria patient, were so distressed by the media coverage that they planned to leave their town and establish new identities elsewhere. This is a dramatic illustration of how the hyped-up presence of the vampire in American culture had negative effects on patients.

If it had not been for the irate response to the Dolphin hypothesis by Dr. Jerome Marmorstein, a Santa Barbara, California, physician, this mother and son would have been forced to move. However, Dr. Marmorstein convinced a writer on the *Los Angeles Times* to run a follow-up story on the impact of the Dolphin hypothesis. As a result, the community rallied to support the family and convinced them that they should not move.

When David Dolphin was contacted for a statement regarding this occurrence he said his hypothesis referred to the past, stating, "Maybe this is what happened in the Middle Ages." He defended this position by insisting that it was not his intention to say "Guess what your neighbor is doing tonight?" He said he had not anticipated the surprising aftershocks of his hypothesis.

As part of my research, I placed a request for information in the American Porphyria Foundation Newsletter. It asked, "How were you affected by the publicizing of the theory regarding the association between porphyria and vampires?" Nineteen patients answered from a mailing list that went out to approximately two thousand, which included patients, physicians, researchers, and supporters.

Obviously those persons motivated enough to write were the ones who felt most strongly about the incident and who had had the most negative experiences. Here are some excerpts from their letters.

> The effect of the publicity was devastating to my family. Many phone calls were made [by family members] to TV and radio stations in order to complain.

> I received many phone calls from friends who heard and read this information. For several days I felt depressed and uptight. Then I rose above those feelings and went about my usual routine.

> It was very disturbing to me to learn that I could be a vampire. When I was a child I watched TV movies about vampires and was most frightened. I thought back to these times and to the reality that such things existed, and was upset even more. My husband said he didn't believe it but made sly jokes as to there being a "full moon tonight" and he began howling. This upset me greatly even though he said he was only joking.

> The hardest part to take was when my daughter, ten at the time, came home from school the week of Halloween with her *Senior Weekly Reader*. She said she got very upset at school and told her teacher her mother had porphyria. Her teacher didn't believe her, and her classmates made fun of her. At this time I believed

the articles to be true and didn't know how to handle the situation.

A patient described how she had cried for half a day after receiving a letter from her twenty-five-year-old, newly married daughter, who also had the disease. The daughter had been humiliated by the newspaper headline "VAMPIRES HAVE THEIR ROOTS IN RARE ILLNESS," as well as by the accompanying large, ugly picture of Dracula. That same day the young woman heard a radio announcer making a joke of it, and following that, there were many jokes told at her expense. She was asked, "Are you really bloodthirsty?" People said to her husband, "Boy, you had better not ever go to sleep first!" The use of the words *vampire* and *illness* alongside a picture of Dracula clearly underscores how readily the media trust that the public will automatically connect the three. No more need be said. It is accepted uncritically.

One woman wrote that the news coverage was hateful because she was sure that people loved believing a "TRUE story of monsters."

It was so forceful, so blatant and one was so helpless in the face of it—powerless. It's rotten to just swallow anything so insulting and false.

A different patient wrote, " I was uneasy and unhappy for a couple of weeks. I think of it with pain and horror even now." This sentiment was echoed by another, who wrote, "It was a terrible time of heavy mental anguish added to the constant physical pain."

Labeling the publicity as "spotlighting a witch's tale," a patient complained that it could easily have undone her medical progress. "I hated it and squirmed, but remained firm to the thought that truths will out. It was just so undignified."

Porphyria patients felt as if they had been singled out for attack because of all the attention to the vampirism hypothesis. It was hard on their families as well.

> My husband and son were indignant because I was subjected to anything so unprofessional and ugly and untrue. They could scarcely meet my eyes. My brothers simply didn't mention anything on the phone. They were very self-conscious, uneasy and avoided me. My other family members were the same.

Another patient sadly revealed that she had known people and even relatives who avoided her "like the plague." She was further upset by a "Marcus Welby" episode featuring a patient with porphyria who had schizophrenia and died. She wrote to porphyria specialist Dr. Donald Tschudy at the National Institutes of Health, who calmed her fears by disclaiming the television misinformation.

"It's all demoralizing and depressing," wrote another patient, particularly after seeing the "Evening Magazine" TV program making reference to the hypothesis. This patient protested by writing a letter to the station, but the damage had already been done.

As late as two years after the initial publicity "PM Magazine" featured the hypothesis, which resulted in phone calls of protest to the American Porphyria Foundation and a letter calling the television program "deplorable." The patient added, "I'm ashamed already to mention what I have."

A young woman said that some of her friends and acquaintances gave her very strange glances as if to look her over. A few even told her they would not let her near their necks because they wanted no hickey marks where she would bite. They teased her, but she felt uncomfortable with their teasing. She tried to brush it aside and change the subject.

It was only after a long recuperation period following a five-week, porphyria-related hospital stay that another patient first heard of the theory.

To be honest, it did upset me. As I told my doctor, nobody wants to be different. If it had not been for his reassurance, I think I would have been a nervous wreck.

After the initial news-type publicity associating porphyria with vampires had settled, the television dramatizations of the concept began. In a "St. Elsewhere" episode, a new patient seeks medical assistance because there is a full moon and he fears that he may turn into a vampire or werewolf. During the course of the show he bays at the moon, goes berserk in the hospital cafeteria because there is garlic in his food, and attacks and attempts to draw blood from the neck of an innocent and terrified female patient who describes her attacker as crying like a wolf. Ultimately the doctor diagnoses porphyria as the cause of the patient's behavior.

Imagine the impact on porphyria patients following this show, both at first viewing and later as a rerun. Many patients felt that the show inadvertently performed a great disservice to them not only because of the misinformation conveyed, but also because it was presented in a medical / scientific, albeit dramatic, context.

What this TV episode succeeded in doing was to perpetuate the old vampire beliefs and motifs: baying at the moon, crying like a wolf, attacking a maiden, looking insane, being influenced by the full moon, biting the neck for blood, being affected negatively by garlic. These characteristics have nothing to do with real porphyria symptoms or patient behavior. They merely reflect and reinforce media characterizations of vampires.

Yes, there was a disclaimer at the end of the teleplay by another TV doctor who explained that the victim's behavior was due to conditioned response. In other words, people made him think he was strange, and he fulfilled their prophecy. He was acting on cue. In spite of this, for the major part of the hour, the script still highlighted bizarre behavior which does not accurately or fairly describe porphyria patients.

Perpetuation of such beliefs, in spite of medical evidence to the contrary, indicates the power of contemporary folklore about the vampire. As one newspaper reporter admitted. "People are interested in werewolves and vampires. That's an eyecatching title, but they are not interested in a disease."

Even more absurd was a porphyria / vampire-based episode appearing on the television program "Divorce Court." In this story a female vocalist sues her husband for divorce. The woman's attorney claims that the husband believes he is a vampire and has thus become dangerous, resulting in the wife's recent need for emergency medical treatment.

According to the wife, her husband's behavior has changed so radically that he eats only animal organ meat, sleeps and makes love in a coffin, wears a cape, and avoids going out in the sunlight.

Later the man's behavior is accounted for by a physician who reveals that the husband is suffering from porphyria. Armed with this new information, both parties decide to seek medical treatment and try to reconcile their relationship.

The impact of this show caused one patient to write the American Porphyria Foundation stating that her husband had previously thought she was merely a hypochondriac, but after watching this episode, "He left me flat," she lamented. Other patients were better able to cope with the general media exploitation through the exchange of humor.

> Someone said, "I always knew you were odd. Now we know you're the local vampire." My response was, "I never denied being different." In one particular nasty ribbing I said, "Don't *you* wish you could fly with just a cape?"

One patient told how some friends howled for her and acted as Hollywood vamps to entertain her, but she just laughed at their madness and fun. Still another reported that her husband joked about her intolerance to garlic and his love of it, which probably helped him survive twenty years of marriage. The wife reported that she was not hurt by his comments. In contrast, her relatives were upset by the publicity, but she tried to assuage them, pointing out that just because it was written down did not mean it was true. Then she quipped, "Let me see your neck!"

Another patient wrote that she and her friends and family found it all amusing, claiming that humor was the best way to handle such a situation.

The humor sometimes concealed true feelings as well, as the following comments attest:

> I have never discussed the theory with anyone except my immediate family. We all sort of laugh and joke about it, but underneath I have an underlying fear because I believe the average person believes, at least, a little bit of everything he reads.

> I have been kidded quite a bit about being a werewolf or vampire, so I just promise not to bite them on the neck. You have to keep a sense of humor, even though at times when it was so bad, I cried a lot, alone.

Not every patient who wrote was unhappy with the attention. There were those who expressed their appreciation, even relief, that the media publicized his hypothesis because they felt the publicity might ultimately make more persons aware of the disorder and perhaps lead to further research. One reported that because there was so much ignorance about the disease, "More sensational news about it might help everywhere."

Someone else remarked, "It is hard to be alone, the only person anyone knows of like this. It helps to have it identified as a rare disease that has a long history and has afflicted many others." Other positive assessments include the following:

> I am unhappy about my disease and the last sixteen years, as it has raped me of my person. Now let's not decry "anyone" who is looking for answers, no matter what!!

> I feel better and more positive about my porphyria knowing [about] the "news" storm. I know it will create more interest by the publicity it has generated in my disease. Hopefully, it will make doc-

tors dig harder for answers and draw the public's attention where it is needed.

Media attention to Dolphin's hypothesis was long lasting. As late as 1987, two years after it was first presented, it hit the papers again when a porphyria patient, Charles W. Brownell, a forty-three-year-old brick mason of Newport News, Virginia, was implicated in a bizarre murder involving human organs found in his bloodied living room. It was not known whether Brownell, now missing, was the murderer or the victim.

George Clifford III, carrying out a routine assignment as police reporter for the *Daily Press,* discovered that Brownell had porphyria and had confided to a few of his friends that he was also a vampire.

Clifford held the story one week while checking out the theoretical relation between vampires and porphyria. "I wanted to make sure the story was solid before we went with it. I didn't want to rush it into print just because it was interesting," he explained. When he finally used the material, the word "vampire" did not appear until the third paragraph and after he had carefully detailed criticism of the hypothesis. However, the story's headline was " 'Vampire' Illness Could Provide Clue in Killing."

Ironically, later it was discovered that Brownell himself was the murder victim, but not before the wire services had used the story, exploiting once again the vampire / porphyria connection, made explicit in the UPI headline, " 'Vampire' Disease Linked to Body Parts in Newport News Case."

Unfortunately, the press could not sever the connection between vampires and the disease. The link, however, dissolved naturally when twenty-year-old Jeffrey William Wainwright, an acquaintance with whom Brownell had been sexually involved, was arrested, found guilty of second-degree murder, and sentenced to twenty years in prison.

After the first round of publicity in 1985, porphyria specialists in the United States and abroad were contacted to see if and how their patients had been affected. Maureen B. Poh-Fitzpatrick, M.D., of Columbia University School of Medicine answered that none of her patients seemed to be adversely affected and that, at most, they were curious as to her impression about any possible credibility of such tales. However, she explained that her patients had a form of porphyria that was not involved with this hypothesis. Her patients thought it was a great deal of silliness, but she qualified this by suggesting that perhaps patients with other forms of porphyria might have been more adversely affected than her particular group.

There are approximately only forty porphyria specialists in the United States. Some of them reported that their patients were able to handle the publicity fairly well, being more amused than angry. However, publicly and in private correspondence, most of the scientific community has not supported the porphyria hypothesis. In a *New York Times* headline in the Letters to the Editor section, "Vampire Label Unfair to Porphyria Sufferers," porphyria specialist Dr. Claus A. Pierach of Abbott Northwestern Hospital in Minneapolis, Minnesota, expressed his concern. He charged that the idea of porphyria patients having something in common with werewolves or vampires was too "far-fetched":

> Dr. David Dolphin's assumption that blood-derived heme might benefit these patients is as wrong as his connotation of harm from garlic. There is no evidence heme is gut-absorbed, and patients may eat garlic with impunity.

He concluded, "It was irresponsible to perpetuate the myth linking porphyria with fairy tales. Our many patients lead normal lives and deserve no such blemish." However, in a later response to my inquiry he wrote that something good might come out of all the "hoopla," bringing more attention to the disease and the porphyria patients closer together.

D. Montgomery Bissell, M.D., a porphyria specialist and researcher at the University of California at San Francisco, summarizes the medical objections to the porphyria hypothesis. He points out that Dolphin's remarks did not address any of the various forms of porphyria, that no patients have a craving for blood, and that blood given by mouth to persons with heme-deficient porphyria (CEP or AIP) is useless. Dr. Bissell declared that even transfused blood would likely have little effect. Instead, what these people need is a chemical called hematin, which is extracted from blood. Finally, he refuted the concept that a sudden loss of a lot of blood could trigger the disease in some-one genetically predisposed. Bissell explained that the heme-deficient porphyrias involve the liver and not the bone marrow, and that blood loss has no effect on liver heme metabolism. For this reason acute attacks of porphyria cannot be induced by blood loss.

Dr. Karl Anderson of New York Medical College in Valhalla, New York, stated that CEP (the rarest form of the disease and the one that comes closest to fitting the scheme) could not have given rise to vampire stories because no one in the Middle Ages knew that its victims had a blood deficiency. He emphasized that these victims do not develop a thirst for blood.

Jerome Marmorstein, M.D., of Santa Barbara, the consultant to a porphyria family, expressed his concern. He saw the linking of a real disease with mythological figures as an act with devas-tating effects on patients. He stated, "One might understand how a myth might have arisen. But this has nothing to do with sci-entific reality. As for the claim that the ingestion of blood might relieve the pain of porphyria attacks, there is no scientific basis for this at all."

Marmorstein continues,

> All this might seem hilariously funny to some, but I seriously wonder if others with this depressing, incurable, and often disabling genetic disease might actually be driven to the act of suicide by this ridic-ulous allegation, especially if it achieves credibility through the most respected scientific organization in America [American Association for the Advancement of Science]. . . . The real issue remains the as-yet-undetermined amount of emotional damage and social iso-lation inflicted on the innocent victims of this incurable disease.

Here was a physician who could clearly see the emotional rami-
fications of associating porphyria with a shadowy, blood-sucking figure.

Outside the United States, Dr. Alcira Batlle de Albertoni,
director of the Center for the Investigation into Porphyrins and
Porphyrias (CIPYP) in Buenos Aires, Argentina, responded that
about 80 percent of her patients were negatively affected. They
did not want to talk about it, while the remaining 20 percent did
not mind it at all. She mentioned that these figures were not
statistical, but rather "personal estimations from spontaneous
reactions."

In Scotland there was limited press coverage; therefore, there
was little concern. Michael R. Moore, M.D., of the Porphyrias
Service in Glasgow, wrote that current awareness in the United
Kingdom of the vampire / porphyria connection was low because
of "limited press coverage." After making fairly extensive subtle
inquiries among his patients to discover if they were aware of an
association between vampires and porphyria, he reported that
the connection was quite unknown to patients, relatives, and the
general public. Because of this he decided not to circulate the
questionnaire for fear of causing alarm in patients who had not
heard of the supposed connection. He discovered that associations between porphyria and vampires or werewolves did not
figure at all in his patients' minds—"one transatlantic import that
we, fortunately, so far, have avoided," he exclaimed with relief.

Dr. I. A. Magnus, at Guy's and St. Thomas's Hospitals of the
University of London, also answered that Dolphin's story had
had little impact on porphyria patients in the United Kingdom.
As far as he knew, they had not suffered ostracism. "On the
contrary," he wrote, "one or two felt quite pleased with themselves at the possibility of being related to Mary Queen of Scots
or George III of England."

What Dr. Magnus was referring to is an earlier hypothesis
which attempted to account for the "madness" of King George
III. This controversial hypothesis suggests that George III and
certain other members of royalty from the houses of Hanover,

Stuart, and Brandenburg-Prussia suffered from a form of porphyria. According to the hypothesis, porphyria was the biological basis of the king's well-known bouts of manic-depressive
behavior, melancholy, and other peculiar ailments of other royal
victims—for example, Mary Queen of Scots, Frederic the Great,
Augustus, Duke of Sussex.

Dr. Magnus suggested that the questionnaire be referred to a
porphyria patient of his who heads the London porphyria support group. This patient remarked that she had heard David
Dolphin on a radio program and that her initial reaction was one
of dismay. After hearing him speak, she said she could identify
with American patients. "My experience has been that the public at large does not understand what porphyria is or what effect
it has on patients and they are only too willing to accept these
very negative stories.

A response from S. Kramer, M.D., head of the Porphyria
Research Unit at the University of Witwatersrand, Johannes-
burg, indicated that the Dolphin theory had received little media
exploitation in South Africa. Dr. Kramer wrote that there had
been an occasional reference to porphyria and werewolf stories
in the Middle Ages, but few patients had taken it seriously because
variegate porphyria (the most common South African form) is
known to be inherited from descendants of a Dutch immigrant.
Kramer, like Dr. Moore in Glasgow, decided not to raise the
question of the vampire / porphyria connection with his patients
for fear of causing either anger or anxiety on their parts.

In Poland, the situation was quite different. Ewa Kostrzewska, M.D., revealed that Polish print and radio journalists
sensationalized the report. "The journalists did not care about
the truth, and real and serious information."

She says that her patients became depressed and demanded
that she contradict the information in the press or on the radio,
giving a true explanation about the illness. She said that some of
the patients had trouble in their work because of unpleasant and
distressing jokes made by colleagues. Children of the patients

were faced with difficulties at school. She expressed concern for the porphyriacs because of the sensitivity of their emotional systems. She felt the situation to be harmful—especially the joking, which damaged the patients.

R. S. Day, a South African electron microscopist, gave a heated response to the earliest press coverage. Responding to publicity that apparently Dr. Kramer had been unaware of, Day chastised a popular South African family magazine which ran an article titled "Draculas Do Indeed Exist." It showed a photo of a vampire drinking blood. It was captioned, "Their lust for human blood is unstoppable. . . . And now an academic says that the Dracula myth can be explained by a rare form of porphyria, a disease which occurs quite often amongst Afrikaners."

Writing in *New Scientist,* Day called the theory "nonsense." He emphatically declared that porphyria patients, relatives, friends, and the public should be given assurance that they are not "predisposed to bloodsucking, sado-masochism, assault or murder, and that garlic will not poison them."

Day sees the biggest danger as being the larger number of undiagnosed patients (90 percent), who, as a result of the publicity, will now be fearful of seeking medical advice. He concluded that the linking of a potentially fatal disease with Bram Stoker's fictional character might even "result in Dracula literally scaring people to death."

In summary, the medical objections to the relationship between vampire beliefs and porphyria symptoms are that the drinking of whole blood cannot satisfy the need for heme, a component of blood, which must be directly absorbed into the bloodstream; acute attacks cannot be induced by blood loss; porphyria patients do not have a thirst for blood; there is no clinical evidence to support the idea that garlic has an adverse effect on porphyria patients and the only form of porphyria which has the symptoms of photosensitivity, hairiness, pointy teeth, *and* a need for additional blood is CEP, the rarest form. Since there have been only sixty cases reported in the world, it is highly unlikely that the rarest form of a disease, which occurs so infrequently (less than 5 percent of carriers have attacks), could have served as the origin of such a widespread myth.

Moreover, the linking of vampires to porphyria seems to be based more on the concept of these vampires as created by Bram Stoker for his famous novel *Dracula* than on recorded accounts, legends, and lore from the past when beliefs about vampires thrived.

Since Dr. Dolphin stated that he was talking about people in the Middle Ages, it is necessary to look to the accounts from the past to see if his associations hold up. For example, he refers to the photosensitivity and subsequent pallor of porphyria patients, who must avoid the sunlight. This may correspond to Stoker's creative writing and white-faced movie versions of vampires, but it does not necessarily pertain to the early folklore about the vampire. As mentioned in an earlier chapter, the bodies of persons accused of being vampires in those times that were exhumed were described as being dark, black, or ruddy in color, and never with pallor.

Other points from folklore which diverge from the hypothesis include Dolphin's citing of pointed teeth as evidence of commonality. Actually, possessing fangs and being long of tooth are other parts of the Stoker book and the movie image and are not found in references from earlier times. As noted earlier, it was the tongue, rather than the teeth, that was thought to be the tool of attack.

In contrast, today fangs have become a hallmark of vampire descriptions. John Vellutini, editor of the *Journal of Vampirology* and a critic of the porphyria hypothesis, states that in contemporary folklore vampire teeth are usually described as shining or gleaming, "terms hardly suggestive of discoloration." Yet tooth discoloration, caused by very high levels of porphyrins, is what happens to porphyria patients with CEP—again, the only form that even comes close to matching Dolphin's ideas.

A further relationship which Dolphin tries to establish is the incidence of the disease with the incidence of vampire folklore. He refers to isolated pockets of small, intermarrying populations. As an example, he cites Transylvania. Transylvania was the geographical place selected by Stoker for his creative exposition and is not known as a center for vampire beliefs. Rather, vampire beliefs have been recorded from all over the world and are not confined to isolated geographical locations. The limited distribution of porphyria does not match the widespread phenomenon of vampire stories and beliefs.

Vellutini proposes another criticism. "The attributing of photosensitivity to the legendary vampire represents personal speculation rather than folklore." He points out that the notion of the vampire restricting its activities to the night is a common and contemporary misconception. He gives several examples from Greek beliefs indicating that vampires appeared in full daylight, even at noon.

Vellutini asks a significant question. "Why is it that the eye-catching porphyria sign of red blood urine has never occurred in any vampire accounts?" He voices a strong argument against the porphyria/vampire connection when he observes that there has never been any recording of red or purple urine found in traditional vampire lore. He charges that if porphyria had been the source of vampire legends, this could hardly have been ignored, particularly in the past, when the color of one's urine was a common diagnostic for illness.

As more evidence to refute the hypothesis, Vellutini refers to the fact that it totally ignores one of the most significant parts of the vampire tradition—the undead state. Finally, he suggests that "no one theory can hope to do justice to vampirism's inherent complexity."

By now it should be clear that porphyria/vampire hypothesis has not been supported by the medical community, which works directly with porphyria patients. The physicians' clinical setting differs greatly from the laboratory environment where chemical analyses are carried out far removed from patients. Thus it is possible to understand one of the reasons that these two perspectives on porphyria are not in agreement. In addition, traditional vampire characterizations from centuries past differ from those Dolphin attempted to correlate with a porphyria association.

In keeping with the best scholarly tradition, Dr. Dolphin placed his ideas in the arena to be challenged and questioned by his peers. Indeed, a few scientists accepted his association. One Dallas patient said that since the publicity, her attending physician was now saying that her attacks were cyclical with the full moon. Another physician, this time a psychiatrist in Arizona, told the granddaughter of a porphyria patient that she also had the "vampire disease." This occurred three years after Dolphin's original presentation. However, this greatly disturbed the child and her entire family.

It is apparent that the Dolphin hypothesis is more tied to the concept of vampires as conceived by Bram Stoker, personified by Count Dracula, and embellished by movie versions, particularly as embodied by Bela Lugosi. Stoker's Count Dracula is fiction. Vampires are a fiction—one we have all absorbed.

What happened to porphyria patients was an astounding example of the consequences of the popularity and pervasiveness of vampire concepts and beliefs in American culture. If this were not so, then the association between porphyria and vampires would have been dismissed by the public and the patients just as it was in England, where patients rejected the idea, preferring instead to link themselves with royalty, an important aspect of British culture and mythology. A former Briton wrote to Dr. Dolphin emphasizing this point.

> I'll bet you never realized that since porphyria is considered a rare disease, we victims can be rather vocal. That's because we usually receive no real understanding and like Mary Queen of Scots, are thought to play sick just to get our way. I know to put the milk in the cup before the hot tea. There is no such thing as an ex-Englishman.

American patients were not so lucky. To have one's physical condition equated with such an emotion-laden symbol was indeed a misfortune. These patients, whose physical symptoms may include emotional imbalances because of the metabolic nature of the disease, were in most cases not equipped to handle the unexpected release of emotions from family, outsiders, and even from themselves. The indelible mark of the vampire became a stigma on their burdensome disease.

Sociologist Erving Goffman defined *stigma* as follows: "A person is reduced in our minds from a whole and unusual person to a tainted, discounted one." Before the Dolphin publicity, patients were involved only with coping with the demands of their disease. Following what seemed to many a cataclysm, American patients were suddenly perceived as less than human—now associated with a monstrous creature and having to pay a tremendous emotional toll.

The relation of stigma to disease is well known and documented. Unlike the yellow fever epidemics of the eighteenth century, the black death of the fourteenth century, and the AIDS epidemic of today, the frightening factor of contagion is not an issue here. Fortunately, because of its rarity and genetic nature, porphyria does not pose a threat to public health. Despite this, though, porphyria patients still became victims of prejudice.

Diseases which become stigmatized are those that are generally treated with repulsion, dread, or fear. In such situations, society labels the patients different or deviant; the stigma is considered nonreversible and permanent.

To illustrate this point, almost a year following the publicity surrounding the Dolphin hypothesis a porphyria patient became disturbed by seeing a four-hour television miniseries called "Deliberate Stranger," a docudrama about serial murderer Ted Bundy. According to this patient, as Bundy was about to be arraigned he said he felt like a vampire. She also reported that the show disclosed that Bundy's female victims were identified by the teethmarks he had left on them.

The patient believed that this television show renewed old prejudices of neighbors who knew of her condition. Her perception was that the vampire stigma was still attached to her from the original publicity, even though there was no mention of the disease, or purported connection with vampirism, in this miniseries. She cited examples of being talked about and being made fun of by local tradesmen. Whether or not this is an accurate interpretation of her neighbors' attitudes and behavior is impossible to say. What is significant is that the patient herself was unable to cast off the association with the vampire. From now on she and other patients will be plagued by the nagging kernal of doubt set off by the vampire / porphyria hypothesis. Given the popular presence of the Dracula / vampire figure in this society, it is surprising that the repercussions to porphyria patients were not even more extreme than they were.

The media reaction to Dr. Dolphin's hypothesis demonstrates that emotional attachment to some beliefs may overpower reason and shows the harmful effect of such beliefs on porphyria patients. In spite of the positive and sympathetic way in which vampire fans, students, and TV audiences perceive the vampire, the patients' negative experiences of emotional pain, isolation, humiliation, and fear reinforced the older, more sinister beliefs—those, no doubt, tied to that common foundation of beliefs in evil supernatural beings.

The stories and allegations about vampires began to recirculate; because this folklore was associated with sex, blood, and death, the resulting fear and uncertainty were almost insurmountable for patients to deal with. The patients least affected were those who were able to utilize humor as a combatting force. Yet, we can't forget the porphyric patient who said, "You have to keep a sense of humor, even though at times when it was so bad, I cried a lot, alone."

Now that the vampire's presence in Americans' consciousness has been revealed, it is possible to comprehend the dynamics that occurred. It makes a powerful statement about the place of the vampire in this country. Small wonder, then, that the porphyria patients received so much attention when their disease was momentarily, and incorrectly, linked with this phenomenon. Dr. Dolphin's hypothesis merely triggered a reflex releasing deeply ingrained associations, information, and emotions from the public and the media.

The All-American Guy

Unlike the lore of Eastern European vampires, the lore of the American vampire does not bind and unite communities. American vampires have adapted to the soil to which they have been transplanted, reflecting the individualism of the American people.

American vampires do exist—in the fantasy world of those who dress up as Halloween celebrants or pretend like lonely Belle with her make-believe vampire lover. They exist in the real world of others who actually imitate their behavior by drinking blood to bring them something positive in return, solace, comfort, sexual arousal, self-importance—elements we all crave. However, they have created a ritual that feeds that need.

Vampires titillate by their erotic behavior; they kindle the making of verbal sexual innuendos in jest. They have an impact on men of science. They arouse passion and fear. They become a common basis of communication for fans, a gold mine of income and creativity.

Writers, filmmakers, and sponsors can count on the vampires' bankability. They bring in big bucks and fit in neatly with the free-enterprise system. That is why the media are so full of them.

In turn the media, particularly television, become the primary channel for indoctrinating youngsters and teaching them how vampires look, behave, and talk. The source for this goes back to Bram Stoker, but its popular manifestation and folklore come from Bela Lugosi's portrayal.

These pop-culture vampires have become a potent part of American culture and beliefs and stories about them are widespread. Vampire tales are thrilling. Regardless of whether they are believed, the information is passed along. This became evident in the student survey I conducted. Even though only 27 percent believed it was possible for vampires to exist, most of the rest knew all about their media-defined characteristics.

People like to talk about vampires but sometimes their beliefs in them can be used against others, as they were in the Philippines. People can use the vampire against themselves as well—witness the unfortunate Panama City event. Or they can inspire certain unstable members of society to commit violence against others, as happened once in Sauk Rapids–St. Cloud, Wisconsin. In addition, their presence in this culture negatively affected the physical and emotional health of porphyria patients.

From their first arrival on these shores vampires have been linked with witches and the devil, and this association has remained. But there is a difference. With the exception of how they affected the emotionally disturbed teenagers referred to in this book, American vampires have become less lethal and more benign than their Old World antecedents. They are more sympathetic characters.

American vampires are appealing because of the humor associated with them. They permit and stimulate laughter. They give a laugh to the first-graders doing their sums; Count Chocula makes breakfast more entertaining; they give a chuckle to the computer users of DRC. Unlike their European, Latin American, African, and Asian counterparts, the fun they inspire in everyday conversations about them is one of their most desirable qualities. Although fans overlooked this aspect of their appeal in their official responses, their letters, asides, and fun-filled conventions and publications strongly reflect this humor. However, fans did corroborate in part what experts have declared—that the sexual, powerful, immortal elements of the vampire are what most strongly draws them to him.

While on the surface it at first seemed incongruous that vampires were so prominent in this technologically advanced society, after carefully examining and analyzing the data, I believe one can see that they seem to exemplify American ideals and values. Sexuality, power, and immortality were listed as the top attractive qualities of the creature by the fans. This is congruent with the interests often attributed to the larger American society.

That American culture places great emphasis on sexuality and sexual prowess is evident. The proliferation of sexual manuals and how-to books as well as the presence of pundits like Dr. Ruth, who publicly gives advice on how to repair faulty sexual relationships, are testament to this preoccupation. From the bombardment of sexual innuendos in television ads ("Nothing comes between me and my Calvin's") to the more blatant expositions becoming prevalent (a career woman telephones her handsome lover still in bed and slyly refers to the great night they spent together) sexuality is promoted as an activity that adults *should* be involved in. Fear of AIDS may be inhibiting some of this activity, but for most the only change has been an emphasis on "safe sex."

Products are sold on the basis of sex. Since the fifties car ads have featured glamorous women, the implication being that if you buy the car, you get the girl. Women's perfumes promise Joy and Passion. The ads for Poison and Opium imply that if the woman uses them she'll get her man. Popular books give guidelines: *How to Make Love All the Time; Super Marital Sex; Sex with Confidence; The G Spot; The Sensuous Man; The Joy of Sex.*

Power, too, is a hallmark of the vampire and lures the fans. Some of those who identified with the vampire by imitating his behavior or calling themselves vampires demonstrate that the power it brought them was pleasing. There is no denying that power is highly valued in our society. For that is what competition is all about—winning and losing. Only the winners gain the power. An informant tells about the corporate event where games were being played and the captain of the losing team cried out, "Second sucks!" Like Hertz, he wanted his team to be number one. He, like most Americans, could not be consoled with the Avis philosophy, "We Try Harder."

The corporate world makes concrete the benefits of power. The higher up the executive, the more desirable his work environment—bigger desk, deluxe carpeting, windows, private bathroom. And the military, of course, demonstrates the power hierarchy through numbers of stripes, bars, and stars.

The importance of power in this culture is explicit in the big winners of the Super Bowl, World Series, presidential elections, Academy Awards, and Miss America contests. Power is embodied in actor Michael Douglas's character Gordon Gekko, who proclaims that greed is good, because *Wall Street*—the film and the financial industry—reflects winning at its most tangible level.

Americans admire powerful people and this culture tells us that we can all become that way. The preoccupation with improving status is an activity Americans pursue with zeal. Power is an equal-opportunity goal. One of the first how-to books related to power, Dale Carnegie's *How to Win Friends and Influence People,* has maintained an almost permanent position on the bookstore shelves since it was first published in 1936, becoming the bible for climbing the "ladder of success." Many have attempted to emulate Carnegie and bookstores are packed with variations on how to gain power: *Dr. Robert Anthony's Advanced Formula for Total Success; Unlimited Power: The Way to Peak Personal Achievement; When Smart People Fail; Dress for Success.*

A perfume for men is called Caesars. "Wear It and Conquer!" the ad asserts. Its female counterpart is Caesars Woman. "Relive the Legend," the banner exclaims. Here you have the perfect product for vampires to endorse—the man who imperiously takes and the woman who waits in fragrant anticipation for him to take her.

A similar message is intimated in the man's perfume Eau Sauvage—wild water. And what will this magically transformed wild man do? He will vanquish his enemies with his power and the woman will be his spoil. In this instance, being wild doesn't conjur up tuxedo and cape images, but the results and the messages mesh.

Another important characteristic that draws fans to the vampire symbol is his immortality. That, too, is a trait that resounds in contemporary American culture. Indeed, we have almost a fetish about preserving youthful appearances and behavior, to postpone aging and death. Why else would Retin-A be considered such a breakthrough? News of its ability to smooth rough skin, fade spots, and reverse wrinkles was given prominent space on TV news shows, in newspapers, and in magazines—"A Facelift Out of a Tube"; "Retin-A: New Hope for Aging Skin." Dermatologists and pharmacists were swamped with requests.

Other methods of striving for immortality are found in the fitness craze that Americans engage in. From aerobics to yoga, t'ai chi to marathon races, from fancy classes at expensive gyms to following along with Jane Fonda on the VCR at home, the goal is to keep the body trim, supple, and young looking. And especially fat free, for thinness represents youthfulness.

Where else in the world is dieting such an obsession? While most countries and some U.S. citizens are preoccupied with the struggle to obtain sufficient food, many Americans are concerned about overeating and how to melt pounds away. Newspaper ads vow miracles, such as losing seventy-one pounds in six weeks. Torture methods abound to make fat people thin and overweight people less heavy: fat-magnet pills; powdered concoctions; liquid diets; fasting; milkshake-type drinks; support groups; prepackaged weighed and measured food parcels; exercise; wrapping to eliminate "cellulite"; sweating; fat farms for adults, for children; health spas.

There is an ever-changing diet philosophy—*The F Plan Diet; Thin Within; Beyond Diet; Act Thin, Stay Thin.* Every year there is a new breakthrough, be it the grapefruit diet, the jockey diet, the rice diet, or the Scarsdale diet. It is a continuous flow of advice that gets outdated and replaced, or recycled.

Ninety-two-year-old George Burns singing "I wish I was eighteen again" epitomizes the American dream of staying "Forever Young." Products like Youth Dew and Eterna 27 and anti-aging creams play with our emotions. To be young implies that one is still sexually vital. The old saying "There may be snow on the roof, but there's still fire in the basement" is just another version of "The old boy's not dead yet!" This is an affirmation that being old is equated with being impotent—in bed as well as at the office. That message is embedded in the joke about the old man who was brought before the judge for raping a young coed. The charge? Assault with a dead weapon.

"You Make Me Feel So Young," a popular song of the past, conveys the sentiment that it is very desirable to be younger than one really is. Americans are not happy about facing the reality of time's effect on their bodies. The common greeting "You haven't changed a bit" is a compliment implying that it is not good to age. The book *How to Have Great Legs at Any Age* reflects Americans' wistful look at the aging process.

A Los Angeles television news feature titled "Nifty After Fifty" conveyed to viewers that the age of fifty—half a century—is ordinarily conceived of as being on the downhill side of life. The newswriters must have decided to counter that popular notion by showing exceptions to it. This was done by featuring people who were successful in spite of their age.

Hair products, too, reveal the concern to prevent natural processes from taking place. For men who are losing their hair products are available to avoid seeing the inevitable in the mirror. Toupees, weaving, transplants, and potions are some of the promised miracles. Women use all varieties of chemicals and treatments to cover up gray hair, and males are not immune. Grecian Formula for Men advertises heavily on television. Ads try to convince a potential buyer that once his hair returns to its previous darker color, women will start looking at him again and his peers will pay more attention in the boardroom to this reanimated young buck.

Is this so far removed from the vampire?

The three major attractions of the vampire are totally compatible with American ideals of power, sex, and immortality. Sometimes it is difficult to separate these three from one another because the idea is that with power you can have sex, and the aging process limits or eliminates both power and sexual abilities and opportunities.

To be a vampire, then, isn't so terrible. With his elegant presence and his sophisticated ways, he need never worry about wrinkles. His only concern is finding the next victim, and that's not so bad because he always emerges victorious. He gets what he wants. He can't help it if he breaks society's rules. His compulsion is out of his control; he's not responsible for any of the unhappiness, fear, or discomfort he might cause others. And he's oh-so-attractive!

Power, sex, and immortality are the qualities of vampires that Americans relate to. They are sentiments that are echoed in all the film and book variations. Students and fans are intrigued by these desired qualities as well. Apparently these vampires satisfy the American public, for it seems they never tire of the tale.

And so it appears that American vampires are perfectly suited to this culture. They reflect those values which many Americans hold dear. They like to succeed. They always get the girl. Their fans never see vampires suffer anxiety about retirement, convalescent homes, and whether or not their social security checks will be enough to cover their needs. Vampires have magically bypassed the struggles that Americans face on a daily basis. Uniting themselves with the vampires, the American public leaves their burdens behind—borne away by this alluring, omniscient presence. American vampires are indeed an appropriate symbol for American life and hold an important and beloved place in this society.

Notes

Complete citations for all works mentioned in this section are found in the Bibliography.

The names of all informants have been changed to ensure their anonymity. Personal field research was gathered through correspondence and by telephone interviews. Other data came from the archives of the Count Dracula Fan Club, generously made accessible by its founder and president, Dr. Jeanne Youngson.

1. Vampirism Today

p. 19 Robert McCully describes the Assyrian bowl with vampire motif in "Vampirism: Historical Perspective and Underlying Process in Relation to a Case of Auto-Vampirism," p. 440.

p. 28 Drinking animal blood is not uncommon among butchers and those who work in slaughterhouses. In a paper titled "And All That Bull!" presented at the 1987 American Folklore Society meeting in Albuquerque, New Mexico, Yolanda Snyder revealed why some of the men in the slaughterhouse do this—for nourishment, "Just like drinking milk!" and for shock value by those who drink it directly from the newly killed animal.

p. 29 Olga Hoyt gives more details of the young man who believed he was Dracula in *Lust for Blood,* p. 203. She also furnishes a complete transcript of the interview between Youngson and the woman who sucked the bloodied cotton swabs, pp. 204–209.

p. 33 Nat Freedland writes about Anton LaVey and the Church of Satan in *The Occult Explosion,* pp. 148–154.

p. 33 Information regarding the Order of the Vampyre is available from either Lilith Aquino or Robertt W. Neilly, Co-Grand Masters. See Appendix 2 for addresses. Lilith and Michael Aquino appeared on the Oprah Winfrey television show, KABC, on February 17, 1988.

p. 35 Reference to psychic vampires is found in "Not All Vampires Suck Blood" in Anton Szandor LaVey's *The Satanic Bible*, pp. 75–80. There is further reference in the "General Information and Admissions Policies" of the Temple of Set, p. 6.

pp. 39–40 The report of the vampire terrorizing Ft. Lauderdale was found in the May 20, 1977, edition of the *Dallas Morning News*, reprinted in the *Fortean Times*, 29, Summer 1979, pp. 40–42. The Seattle vampire was reported in the *Journal of Vampirism*, 1, No. 3, Spring 1978, p. 7.

p. 40 Felix Oinas documents cases of Yugoslavian vampire impersonators and describes other vampire capers in his article "East European Vampires and Dracula," p. 111.

pp. 40–42 A LEXIS / NEXIS computer search turned up the referred-to stories: "Dracula Strikes Again," United Press International, Columbia, Missouri, October 4, 1985; "New-Fangled Attacks Strike Town," Associated Press, Mineral Point, Wisconsin, April 2, 1981; "Man Dressed as Vampire Dies After Stabbing Self Accidentally," Associated Press, Parma Ohio, November 1, 1981.

p. 42 Information regarding the Sauk Rapids–St. Cloud, Minnesota, murder involved with the movie *The Lost Boys* appeared in the *Los Angeles Times*, April 1, 1988, Part VI, p. 2.

2. Blood Is Thicker . . .

p. 47 *The Occult in America* was edited by Howard Kerr and Charles L. Crow. The citation comes from p. 2.

p. 47 Richard Dorson also refers to supernatural beliefs among European immigrants in *American Folklore*, p. 7.

p. 47 References to the Ojibwa and Cherokee beliefs are found in George Stetson, "The Animistic Vampire in New England," p. 12.

p. 48 The example of ghosts comes from *The New Golden Bough* by Sir James George Frazer, p. 262.

p. 48 References to the zombies are found in *The Serpent and the Rainbow* by Wade Davis, p. 18.

p. 49 Harry Senn's work, *Were-Wolf and Vampire in Romania*, cites information about the German publication of vampire books, pp. viii, ix.

p. 49 The Yugoslavian incident relating to Arnola Paole comes from the writing on vampirism by Rupert Furneaux, first appearing in

Legend and Reality, published by Allan Wingate, London, and later reprinted in a 1984 newsletter-journal of the Count Dracula Fan Club, published by Dracula Unlimited, p. 3.

pp. 49–50 Robert McCully concisely summarizes worldwide vampire beliefs in "Vampirism: Historical Perspectives and Underlying Process in Relation to a Case of Auto-Vampirism," p. 440.

p. 50 Senn refers to the vampire's bonding of the Romanian community on pp. xiii, 10.

p. 50 In an interview with vampire scholar Paul Barber, he described details of the physical description of corpses thought of as vampires. This information is found in his book *Vampires, Burial, and Death.*

p. 51 A Javanese native and an American teacher who lived and worked in Indonesia provided the stories on the Indonesian form of vampire.

p. 51 Dozens of articles have been written on the weeping woman in white, *La Llorona.* Here are a few examples: Bacil F. Kirtley, "La Llorona and Related Themes," *Western Folklore,* 19, 1960, pp. 155–168; Frances Toor, *A Treasury of Mexican Folkways,* pp. 531–532; Bess Lomax Hawes, "La Llorona in Juvenile Hall," *Western Folklore,* pp. 153–170.

p. 52 Rabbi Joshua Trachtenberg describes the *estrie* on pp. 38–39 of *Jewish Magic and Superstition.*

p. 52 The Ibibio version of vampirism is found in Daniel Offiong, "Witchcraft Among the Ibibio of Nigeria," p. 155.

p. 52 The Togolese beliefs come from Geoffrey Parrinder, *West African Psychology,* pp. 165–166.

p. 52 The *ligaroo* is referred to in Jane C. Beck, "West Indian Supernatural World," pp. 237–238.

p. 53 William Madsen writes of the *tlaciques* in "Hot and Cold in the Universe of San Francisco Tecospa, Valley of Mexico," p. 129.

p. 53 Report of the Silesian vampire incident, attributed to Henry More, is found in Harry E. Wedeck, *A Treasury of Witchcraft,* p. 179.

p. 53 See Jan L. Perkowski for information about the Kashubs in *Vampires of the Slavs,* pp. 136–139.

p. 54 Gypsy beliefs are detailed in Elwood B. Trigg, *Gypsy Demons and Divinities: The Magic and Religion of the Gypsies,* pp. 143–151.

p. 55 Richard Dorson discusses providences in *America in Legend,* pp. 17–31, and in *American Folklore,* pp. 24–35. He quotes Katharine Briggs on p. 13 of *America in Legend.*

p. 56 Indian fears of the devil and the incident describing the colonist participating in an Indian healing rite are found in Dorson, *American Folklore,* p. 18.

p. 56 Interactions with the devil in daily life and references to the

Increase Mather account of the Frenchman who sold his soul to the devil are contained in Dorson, *American Folklore,* pp. 13, 33.

pp. 56–57 The quote from *The Devil and Daniel Webster* comes from Benét's work, p. 14.

p. 57 The devil's sermon from "Young Goodman Brown" is taken from p. 122 of Hawthorne's work.

p. 58 Cotton Mather's work *The Wonders of the Invisible World* describes the Salem witch trials and reveals his well-known point of view that New England was alive with evil forces.

p. 58 Leo Bonfanti documents the witchcraft law and ways to defeat witches' spells on p. 2 of *Strange Beliefs, Customs, & Superstitions of New England.*

p. 58 Dorson relates Increase Mather's interdictions against anti-witchcraft behavior in *America in Legend,* p. 33. He describes the witches' mode of arrival in America in *American Folklore,* p. 35.

pp. 58–59 For an excellent discussion of witches and witchcraft see Keith Thomas, *Religion and the Decline of Magic,* pp. 435–583. Another good source is *The Witch Figure* by Venetia Newell.

p. 60 Reverend Deodat Lawson's observations can be found in Levin, *What Happened in Salem,* p. 83.

p. 60 Curtin and Stetson discuss concepts regarding the relation of vampires to consumption. Other nineteenth-century examples of vampire phenomena are found in the works of Kinder, Dujardin, Wright, and Skinner.

p. 61 The 1854 report from the *Norwich Courier* was reprinted in "Reporter's 'Stake-Out' Puts Bite on Vampire," *Norwich Bulletin,* October 31, 1976, p. 24.

pp. 62–63 Michael E. Bell's work is found in a 1983 unpublished report to the National Endowment for the Humanities as part of the Rhode Island Folklife Project.

p. 63 Stetson's quotes are found in "The Animistic Vampire in New England," pp. 8–10.

p. 64 C. A. Fraser writes about British consumption-causing vampires in "Scottish Myths from Ontario," and hypothesizes as to the rationale of such an association.

pp. 64–65 The Potts speech is recorded in the May 1920 edition of the *Archives of Neurology and Psychiatry.*

p. 65 For examples of vampire references from the black communities see Mary Alicia Owen's account of Aunt Mymee and the vampires turning into mosquitoes in *Voodoo Tales.*

p. 66 S. M. P. recounts the tale of Old Sue in "Voodooism in Tennessee."

pp. 66–67 The Bell witch legend has been documented by Arthur Palmer Hudson and Pete Kyle McCarter in a 1934 edition of the *Journal of American Folklore*.

p. 68 United Press International reported "GI's Risk Necks in Vampire Watch," February 6, 1981, Kitzingen, West Germany. This was found in a LEXIS / NEXIS computer search.

p. 75 Information about the *aswang* (also spelled *asuang*) comes from Filipino informants and from the monograph *Vampirism in the Philippines: A Brief Description and Survey*, by Halford Jones of Santa Cruz, Marinduque, Philippines, published by the Count Dracula Fan Club, 1985.

p. 76 Major General Lansdale describes his exploits with the *aswang* in *In the Midst of Wars: An American's Mission to Southeast Asia*, pp. 69–73. Information from his widow was obtained through correspondence and telephone interview.

p. 76 Lansdale's CIA activities in the Philippines are also documented in Victor Marchetti and John D. Marks, *The CIA and the Cult of Intelligence*, pp. 24–26. For alternative interpretations of American/Filipino relations see *The Untold Philippine Story* by Hernando J. Abaya and *An American Made Tragedy* by William J. Pomeroy.

General Lansdale used folklore again to influence the people of Vietnam in 1955. Supporting the reelection of President Ngo Dinh Diem, General Lansdale had Diem's ballots printed in red, a color considered by Vietnamese as an omen of good luck. At the same time he saw to it that the opponent's ballot was a shade of green, considered to be the sign of the cuckold. Diem won 98 percent of the vote. *The Pentagon Papers* by Neil Sheehan et. al. itemizes many of Lansdale's Vietnam activities.

pp. 77–78 Tomatsu Shibutani gives many examples of manipulation of rumors in *Improvised News*, Chapter 7. The Genghis Khan and Chesterfield incidents are described on pp. 192–193.

p. 78 Christa Kamenetsky writes on "Folktale and Ideology in the Third Reich" in the *Journal of American Folklore*, pp. 168–178. A more complete analysis of Nazi misuse of folklore will appear in a forthcoming book by James R. Dow and Hannjost Lixfeld, *The Nazification of an Academic Discipline: German Volkskunde of the Third Reich*.

p. 78 M. Dean Havron, Martin Sternin, and Robert J. Teare give a sample of questions used for determining informal communication channels in *The Use of Cultural Data in Psychological Operations Programs in Vietnam*, an unclassified U.S. government document, pp. 73–75.

3. Power of the Media

pp. 79–80 The stealing of the holy wafers was turned up in a LEXIS / NEXIS computer search, "Sacrilegious Theft," Associated Press, Altamont, New York, March 17, 1978.

p. 82 The report of the new Dracula liqueur appeared in the column "New Product Watch" by Martin Friedman published in *Adweek,* November 9, 1987, p. 54.

pp. 83–84 The George Lois reference is taken from an interview in Jonathan Price, *The Best Thing on TV: Commercials,* p. 80.

p. 85 The Numero Uno Pizza ad has been reproduced with permission from Gelet Enterprises, Inc.

p. 91 The Bernheimer review, "California Ballet Offers 'Dracula' in San Diego," appeared in the *Los Angeles Times* on November 2, 1987.

p. 91 The Mountain Bell advertisement was seen in the *Albuquerque Tribune* on October 29, 1987, p. C8. Stor's full-page furniture ad appeared on October 31, 1987, in the *Los Angeles Times,* Part I, p. 14.

p. 92 The 1987 cards referred to were produced by the following companies: Hallmark, Gibson, C. Recchia, Nosecard, American Greetings, and Recycled Paper Products.

pp. 93–94 Objection to Hallmark's production of the Transylvania University T-shirts was reported in the Long Beach, California, *Press-Telegram,* October 30, 1987, p. A2.

p. 94 Caroline E. Mayer writes about the General Mills packaging problem in "Necklace Chokes Count Chocula," which appeared in the *Los Angeles Times,* October 19, 1987. There is more information to be found in the *Jewish Monthly,* December 1987, p. 41.

p. 94 Kelly A. Lally describes Assignment Night in Mississippi in "Living on the Edge: The Folklife of Air Force Pilots in Training," p. 116.

p. 95 For a listing of children's books related to vampires see the Riccardo bibliography, which also documents vampire films, stage productions, fiction, and nonfiction.

p. 96 Reference to the English Dracula ice pop can be found in the Dukes article, p. 47.

p. 96 "Drac-in-a-Box" is manufactured by JAX of Lincolnville, Maine.

pp. 96–97 The "Count Duckula" episode referred to aired in Los Angeles on February 27, 1988.

pp. 97–98 The vampire-related arithmetic problems can be found in Ryono's *Wilma's Word Problems,* pp. 4, 7, 16, 19.

pp. 100–101 Maila Nurmi tells about her show and song parody in

"The One—The Only Vampira" in *Fangoria*. According to the *Los Angeles Times*, October 25, 1987, Calendar, p. 15, Nurmi claims that Elvira and television station KHJ "ripped off" the character she created in the 1950s. Nurmi, now in her mid-sixties, filed a lawsuit against Elvira (Cassandra Peterson) in 1988 claiming that Nurmi's creative trademark, public reputation, and ability to market her portrayal allegedly had been damaged. See the *Los Angeles Times*, "Only in L.A.," September 13, 1988, Part II, p. 2.

p. 101 The rejected writer of the vampire script revealed his disappointment and dismay in confidentiality.

p. 102 *Vampire at Midnight* was produced by Jason Williams and Tom Friedman and previewed at a special screening in Encino, California, November 10, 1987.

p. 102 The Schumacher quote appeared in *American Film*, 12, No. 9, July / August 1987, p. 64.

p. 102–3 The films scheduled for 1988 release were described in the *Los Angeles Times* Calendar section, January 17, 1988, on pp. 9–10, 14, 17, 36, 38.

p. 103 Leonard Klady wrote the review of *My Best Friend Is a Vampire*, *Los Angeles Times*, May 9, 1988, Part VI, p. 3.

p. 103 Pirie's estimates can be found in *The Vampire Cinema*, p. 6.

p. 103 Conrad's cartoon appeared in the *Los Angeles Times*, May 27, 1986, Part II, p. 5.

p. 103 Gary Larson's "The Far Side" cartoon, Universal Press Syndicate, appeared in the *Los Angeles Times* Sunday Comics Section, July 17, 1988.

p. 104 The California State University, Los Angeles, *University Times* published the Troy Taroy AIDS cartoon on January 15, 1987, p. 2.

p. 104 *Red Tide* by Justin Tanner opened on May 21, 1988, for a six-week run at the 2nd Stage Theater in Hollywood.

pp. 104–6 The "Lust in the News" story was reported on "The Ken and Bob Show," February 19, 1987, KABC-AM radio, 7:00–7:15 A.M. segment. The *Weekly World News* story was reprinted in *Journal of Vampirology*, 2, No. 3, p. 23. The original article was dated November 26, 1985. "AIDS-Wary Vampires Pull in Their Fangs!" was written by Margret Pfander. "Fang Gang Vampires Attack Man Watching Dracula Movie on Television" by Irwin Fisher appeared in the *Weekly World News*, August 9, 1988, p. 20. "Bizarre Vampire Marriage" was written by Henry Weber for The *Weekly World News*, August 2, 1988, pp. 24–25.

p. 106 Peter Tosh performs "Vampire" on the Capitol recording *No Nuclear War,* released 1988.

p. 106 The British Gothic fad is detailed in an article by Helen Chappell published in the *Guardian.*

p. 106 Radio Werewolf provided their perspective in an October 1987 interview.

p. 107 Playwright Chris Hardman was interviewed by phone regarding "Dracula in the Desert."

p. 108 See bibliography for exact citations on Jeanne Youngson's *The Count Dracula Chicken Cookbook* and *How to Become a Vampire in Six Easy Lessons* by Madeline X.

p. 108 *Greenberg the Vampire* was written by J. M. DeMatteis with graphics by Mark Badger and published by Marvel Comics, 1986.

p. 109 "O Captain, My Captain" by Katherine V. Forrest is included in a book of her short stories, *Dreams and Swords,* published by Naiad Press, 1987, pp. 107–165.

p. 109 Figures on *The Vampire Lestat* appeared in "Flesh for Fantasy" by Geri Hirshey, *Rolling Stone,* November 20, 1986, pp. 92–93. Figures for *Salem's Lot* appeared in *Publishers Weekly,* 108, No. 7, November 8, 1975, p. 110, and on p. 33 of the Underwood and Miller book.

p. 110 *On the Nightmare* was written by Ernest Jones. James B. Twitchell wrote *The Living Dead.* Paul Barber wrote *Vampires, Burial, and Death.* These are but a few of the sources available. For an extensive vampire bibliography see both Riccardo and Barber.

p. 110 Information about American tourist behavior in Romania can be found in an article by Gillette and another by Urma.

pp. 112–13 Persons and events thought to have influenced Stoker's creation of the Dracula novel have been referred to in the Dukes article, p. 46. In addition, McNally and Florescu's speculation as to why Stoker chose Transylvania is cited in *In Search of Dracula,* p. 162. McNally's observation about the influence of "Superstitions from Transylvania" is found in *Dracula Was a Woman,* p. 98.

p. 113 Lisa Mitchell tells about Lugosi's burial in his cape, p. 79. The Christopher Lee quote comes from the Leonard Wolf book, p. 174.

p. 115 The recollection of Lugosi in front of the mirror comes from an interview with a fellow actor who wishes to remain anonymous.

p. 115 Mitchell's words are found on p. 78 of her *New West* article. The quotation from Lennig is found in his work on p. 217.

p. 116 For a discussion of xerography and the "Paperwork Empire" see Dundes and Pagter.

p. 117 Jerzy N. Kozinski wrote both the book and screenplay version of *Being There,* published in 1970 by Harcourt Brace Jovanovich. The film was released in 1979 by United Artists.

p. 118 The average daily TV viewing time of the American public is presented in Richard Gertner, editor, *Television and Video Almanac,* 32nd edition, New York / London: Quigley Publishing Co., 1987, p. 14A.

p. 118 Information about the California reading test can be found in the work of Mehan and Wood, p. 38.

4. Vamp Followers

p. 120 Patrick Garrison's poem originally appeared in the program for the Manhattan Shadows Convention held in New York City on September 24, 1983.

Appendix 2 contains a listing of societies and independently published journals affiliated with vampire, "Dark Shadows," and Dracula organizations and fan clubs.

p. 122 Puns, jokes, and riddles were taken from the following fan publications: *Journal of Vampirism, Vampire Journal, New Atlantean Journal, Vampire, Count Dracula Fan Club News-Journal.*

p. 123 "Song of the Happy Vampires" appeared in the *Journal of Vampirism,* 2, No. 1, Fall 1978, p. 1.

p. 127 The following cast members appeared in person at the Los Angeles 1987 "Dark Shadows" convention: Julia Duffy, John Karlen, Jerry Lacy, Diana Millay, Lara Parker, Christopher Pennock, Lisa Richards, Robert Rodan, Kathryn Leigh Scott.

p. 133 The 90-page *Vampire Journal* was published Fall / Winter 1986.

p. 135 Charlotte Simsen's article in *Coast* magazine was reprinted in *Vampire Quarterly,* 6, November 1986, p. 36.

p. 136 Vellutini produced "The Use and Abuse of the Dead for Felonious Judicial and Therapeutic Purposes" in *Journal of Vampirology,* 4, No. 1, 1987.

p. 137 "Vampire Liberation" by M. L. Carter appeared in the *Count Dracula Fan Club News-Journal,* Spring 1988, pp. 9–10.

5. The Lure

p. 143 The reference to Twitchell can be found in his article "The Vampire Myth," p. 83.

p. 144 The quotation from Paul King, M.D., was taken from a telephone interview.

p. 145 Fifty-four persons answered the questionnaire placed in fanzines or responded as members of vampire organizations. These fans were primarily from the United States, but there were four from elsewhere—two from Canada and one each from Ireland and Turkey. Frequently their letters arrived in envelopes decorated with vampire motifs, or they were written on stationery with vampire designs, or the writers included drawings, such as bats or fangs, in the body or at the end of the letters.

p. 147 The Ernest Jones description and quote can be found on p. 119 in the 1951 edition of his work.

p. 147 Stephen King's observations are found in *Danse Macabre* on p. 77 and his quotation is from p. 75.

p. 148 Herschel Prins's references are found in "Vampirism—Legendary or Clinical Phenomenon," p. 289.

p. 149 Bob Greene's article "A Red-Blooded American Girl" describes his encounter with the teenager who desired to be drained.

p. 150 Richard L. Vanden Bergh and John F. Kelly discuss biting and sucking of blood as an act of oral sadism in their work "Vampirism" using Havelock Ellis as one of their sources.

p. 150 The work of Lawrence Kayton deals with the relationship of schizophrenic patients to vampire themes. See pp. 310 and 313 of his article.

p. 151 The Ernest Jones references are found on pp. 119–120, 127.

p. 151 Psychiatrist D. James Henderson presents his views on incest in "Exorcism, Possession, and the Dracula Cult," pp. 603–629.

p. 151 Harry Stone, professor of English at California State University, Northridge, is presenting his hypothesis in a book nearing completion, *Night Side of Dickens: Cannibalism, Passion, Necessity*. The ideas referred to here were taken from his David L. Kubal Memorial Lecture, "Dickens and Cannibalism," presented at California State University on January 21, 1988.

p. 152 Stephen King's reference to raping with the mouth is found in his book on p. 75.

p. 154 The correlation between World War I and the popularity of the vampire was made by writer Walter Karp in "Dracula Returns," pp. 40–41.

p. 154 The story about Death being tied up in a tree is known by folklorists as Tale Type 330 and 332. This particular variant was taken from an Appalachian Jack Tale, "Whickety-Whack, Into My Sack," as told by Ray Hicks on a Folk-Legacy recording.

p. 154 Ernest Becker's views are expressed in *Escape from Evil*, p. 123.

p. 157 *My Life as a Dog* was directed by Lasse Hallstrom and written by Lasse Hallstrom, Reider Jonsson, Brasse Brannstrom, and Per Berglund, based on the novel by Reider Jonsson. Produced by Waldemar Bergendahl, it won the Swedish film critics' best picture of the year award in 1985 and twelve-year-old Anton Glanzelius, the star of the film, was voted best actor. In the United States, both the director and his screenplay were nominated for an Oscar at the 1987 Motion Picture Academy Awards.

p. 158 The Shuttle and Redgrove quote comes from *The Wise Wound,* p. 266. A gynecologist in practice for over twenty-five years refutes the author's hypothesis linking menstrual problems with sexual dysfunction. Further Shuttle and Redgrove references are found on pp. 266–267.

p. 158 For the bat / menstruation relationship see Lévi-Strauss, *From Honey to Ashes,* p. 382.

p. 161 Anne Rice's comments are included in "Oh You Beautiful Ghoul, You Master of Macabre!" by Patricia Corrigan, originally published in the *Post Dispatch,* reprinted in *Vampire,* 3, No. 5, February 1987, p. 4, and in the Steve Chapple interview "Anne Rice Unbound," originally published in *Image,* May 18, 1986, reprinted in *Vampire,* 3, No. 3, October 1986, p. 6.

p. 161 John Allen Stevenson writes about the vampire as foreigner in "A Vampire in the Mirror: The Sexuality of Dracula." References are made to pp. 142, 144, 147 of this work.

p. 161 Johnson's quote is found on p. 433 of his article.

p. 163 The insight from the Count Dracula Fan Club member was printed in "Interview with Sue Marra Byham," by Shelley Leigh-Hunt. This was published in the *Count Dracula Fan Club Newsletter Special Edition,* 1987, p. 13.

p. 163 The Winkler and Winkler quote can be found on p. 203 of their article.

p. 166 Alan Dundes's remarks were aired in a discussion of April Fool's Day and humor on "Nightline," an ABC-TV evening show hosted by Ted Koppel, April 1, 1987. Humor specialists Steve Allen and Dr. Harvey Mindess disagreed with Dundes's hard-line Freudian view.

p. 167 Lennig analyzes Lugosi's unique speaking style on p. 22 of his work.

6. Vampire Victims

p. 171 Professor David Dolphin's three-page abstract "Werewolves and Vampires" was distributed at the AAAS meeting, May 30, 1985, Los Angeles, California. There is no longer version of the paper available, nor has Dolphin's essay been published, since chemists do not ordinarily present their work in narrative form.

p. 173 Lee Siegel of Associated Press titled his article "Vampires and Werewolves: Just Folks with a Rare 'Nasty' Disease?" It was filed May 30, 1985.

p. 174 Articles appeared in the *San Francisco Chronicle,* May 31, 1985, and the *Washington Post,* May 31, 1985, Sec. 1, p. 42. The *Newsweek* story by Jean Seligman with Susan Katz appeared June 10, 1985, p. 72. The *Sacramento Bee* write-up by Christine Russell was printed May 31, 1985, Sec. 1, p. 1.

p. 174 The Polish newspapers were *Glos Szczecnski,* June 17, 1985; *Nowosci,* September 27, 1985; *Trybuna Robotnicze,* June 17, 1985.

p. 174 The coverage in the *Senior Weekly Reader* occurred in Edition 6, Vol. 40, Issue 7, October 25, 1985, p. 3, as well as in the *Weekly Reader,* Edition 5, Vol. 64, Issue 7, October 25, 1985, p. 2.

p. 174 The Providence, Rhode Island, *Evening Bulletin* reported "Vampires Still Hair-raising," by C. Eugene Emery, Jr., on May 31, 1985, pp. A1, 2.

p. 175 Porphyria characteristics, symptoms, treatments, and incidence have been taken from an excellent and regularly updated brochure published by the American Porphyria Foundation and from the informational videocassette that they rent out, produced by the Health and Science Network. The mailing address for the American Porphyria Foundation is listed in Appendix 2.

The medical information in this chapter has been verified by both D. Montgomery Bissell, M.D., and Jerome Marmorstein, M.D.

Personal medical anecdotes were taken from phone interviews and written correspondence with patients.

p. 176 There has been one acquired case of AIP reported in the work of Laiwah et al. However, this interpretation has been challenged by Brian C. Shanley in the *Lancet,* May 28, 1983, pp. 1229–1230. The documentation regarding acquired PCT in Turkey is found in the writing of Peters et al.

p. 177 A description of the South African variety of porphyria (VP) is found in "Variegate Porphyria in New England" by Jan Muhlbauer et al., p. 3095.

p. 189, 190 Dr. Marmorstein's views were expressed in person, were quoted in a *Los Angeles Times* article by Ann Japenga, and are found in his writing in the *Medical Tribune.*

p. 185 The "St. Elsewhere" episode, "Loss of Power," first aired in mid-December 1985 and was rerun in 1986. The "Divorce Court" episode, "Jennings vs. Jennings," first aired in November 1986.

The porphyria vampire / werewolf connection was again brought into a televised dramatic format in the fall of 1987 when Fox Broadcasting began airing its promotions for a new and very successful serial, "Werewolf." One version, seen during the broadcast of the Emmy awards, mentioned that the werewolf's condition was caused by porphyria. This ad continued to be shown and, once again, calls of protest were made to the American Porphyria Foundation by patients and relatives of patients.

p. 188 George Clifford's story appeared in the July 7, 1987, edition of the Newport News, Virginia, *Daily Press*. The follow-up regarding Brownell's murderer was detailed by Ron Shawgo, "Mutilation Death Defendant Guilty," January 7, 1988.

p. 189 Dr. Pierach's retort to Dolphin appeared in the *New York Times,* June 13, 1985, p. A34.

p. 189 Dr. Bissell's views were expressed through letters, by phone, and at a patient information meeting held at the University of California, San Francisco Medical Center, on May 17, 1986. All other responses from the scientific community were obtained through personal correspondence.

p. 191 Ida Macalpine and Richard Hunter support the connection between King George and porphyria in their book *George III and the Mad Business.* However, this view has been challenged by Geoffry Dean in "The Porphyrias: The Royal Purple?"

p. 192 Detailed information about the treatment and symptoms of the South African variety of porphyria, variegate porphyria, can be found in the pamphlet *Porphyria and You,* published by the Genetic Services Department of Health and Welfare, Pretoria, Republic of South Africa.

p. 193 Dr. Day's views are found in "Bloodlust, Madness, Murder and the Press," pp. 53–54.

p. 193 John Vellutini's criticism of the Dolphin hypothesis appears in the *Journal of Vampirology,* 2, No. 3, 1985. To obtain information about independently published journals and those distributed by vampire, "Dark Shadows," and Dracula organizations see Appendix 2.

p. 197 Goffman's definition is found on p. 3 of his work.

p. 197 For a discussion of stigmatized health conditions see Joan Ablon.

7. The All-American Guy

p. 204 "A Facelift Out of a Tube" appeared in *U.S. News & World Report,* February 1, 1988, pp. 11–12.

p. 204 *Newsweek* published "Retin-A: New Hope for Aging Skin," written by Terence Monmaney, on February 1, 1988, p. 59.

p. 204 "Wipe Wrinkles Away with an Apple a Day," by Susan Jimison, appeared in *World Weekly News,* May 3, 1988, p. 41.

Acknowledgments

No book can ever be written by one person without input and help from others. This book, in particular, could never have been completed without the generous assistance of the patients who shared painful memories, the physicians who took time to answer my inquiries, the students who participated in the surveys, the editors who placed my questionnaires in their publications, and all those persons who answered the questionnaires with such careful attention. I am indebted to all of them.

In addition, I am deeply grateful to the significant help received from the following persons: Ken Bailey; Paul Barber, Ph.D.; Andrea Berk; D. Montgomery Bissell, M.D.; Jan Brunvand, Ph.D.; SSgt. Otto Bumberger; Amy Caldwell; James Callahan; Rebecca Castillo; Terry Cottrell; Larry Danielson, Ph.D.; Carol Del Signore; Lou DiMarco and the R. M. Palmer Co.; Desiree Dodson and the American Porphyria Foundation; Koleen Dollaghan; David Dolphin, Ph.D.; James R. Dow, Ph.D.; Mark Dresser; Larry Eberle and the ECAD Co.; George O. Enell, Ph.D.; Barbara Fister-Liltz; Rosalie Franche; Sarah Garey; Susan M. Garrett; Josette and Patrick Garrison; Ronald J. Gelet and Gelet Enterprises, Inc.; Peggy Green, D.V.M.; Sheila Good; Hallmark Cards Inc.; Eric Held; Carolyn Hinckley; Charles Keck; Norman Klein, Ph.D.; Ewa Kostrzewska, M.D.; Pat

Lansdale; Jerome Marmorstein, M.D.; Mike Marshall; Philippe Michelot, Ph.D.; Lisa Mitchell; Michael Moore, M.D.; Patrick B. Mullen, Ph.D.; Patrick G. Murphy and the Schlage Lock Co.; Erick C. Offerman; Jon Olson, Ph.D.; Elliott Oring, Ph.D.; Eva Osiatinska; Dorothy Pittel; Morris Polan, University Librarian of the John F. Kennedy Memorial Library at California State University, Los Angeles; Margaret Rader; Martin Riccardo; Sharida Rizzuto; George Rollins; Jane Ross and the JAX Co.; Lee Siegel; Frank Schaffer; Karl Seligman, M.D.; Mickey Shapiro; Leila Sharafi; Rachel Spector, R.N., Ph.D.; Alan Stein; Suzanne Sullivan; Professor Madge Summerbell; Frances Cattermole-Talley, Ph.D., archivist, Archive of the Encyclopedia of American Popular Beliefs and Superstitions; Cheryl Torosian; and Lucia van Ruiten.

Special thanks go to Professor Kay Enell for her provocative and insightful consultations; to Montserrat Fontes for her excellent suggestions, outspoken reactions, and editing expertise; to Janice Garey for her patience in listening and resourcefully responding to my constant mulling over of ideas; and to Jeanne Youngson, Ph.D., who kindly gave me access to the files of the Count Dracula Fan Club and to her personal research as well. The contributions of these friends were invaluable.

Every challenge benefits from a rooting section, and in embarking on this project I, too, was bolstered by the tremendous moral support received from faculty and staff in the English Department at California State University, Los Angeles, and from my colleagues of the California Folklore Society.

Above all, I wish to express my appreciation for the enthusiastic and critical support of Robert A. Georges, Ph.D., former Chair of the UCLA Folklore and Mythology Program, and to Michael Owen Jones, Ph.D., director of the UCLA Center for the Study of Comparative Folklore and Mythology. I will never forget their generosity in hours spent going over this manuscript and their commitment to seeing that this work reached fruition.

These two esteemed folklorists were midwives to the project.

Finally, I would like to express my gratitude to Mary Cunnane, my editor at W. W. Norton, who, akin to the old family doctor, slapped the first breath of life into this book.

Appendix 1
Questionnaires

I. *Questionnaire for Porphyria Patients*
The following was printed in the newsletter of the American Porphyria Foundation, January–March 1986 issue.

A Different Research Effort
HOW WERE YOU AFFECTED BY THE PUBLICIZING
OF PROFESSOR DOLPHIN'S THEORY REGARDING
THE ASSOCIATION BETWEEN PORPHYRIA
AND VAMPIRES?

Professor Norine Dresser, Department of American Studies and English at California State University, Los Angeles, is currently documenting the effect of the Dolphin publicity on the social relationships of porphyria patients and the resultant emotional effects. She is requesting information about such matters as the *specific* ways in which friends, relatives, and acquaintances treated you differently after the media coverage.
Professor Dresser is looking for answers to the following questions:

How did relatives respond? What did they do and say? What was your response? How did this make you feel?

How did friends and acquaintances respond? What did they do and say? What was your response? How did this make you feel?

Did others make jokes at your expense? What did they say? How did this make you feel?

Were you avoided? Describe what happened. How did this make you feel?

How did you feel about your own condition after the publicity?

If you had other experiences in addition to the ones mentioned above, please record them. The more details you include, the more useful this research will be. On the other hand, if some of the above questions do not apply to you, simply ignore.

No names of participants will be used in the report. All those who participate will receive a copy of the summary of findings, providing that addresses are included. However, if preferred, information may also be submitted anonymously.

> Please send responses to:
> Professor Norine Dresser
> Department of English and American Studies
> California State University, Los Angeles
> 5151 State University Drive
> Los Angeles, CA 90032

Thank you for your participation!

II. *Questionnaire for Students*

Four high school teachers representing three different high schools and five college and university instructors from four different institutions circulated these surveys. Subject matter taught in these classes included social studies, Spanish, English, anthropology, and journalism.

The primary advice given to teachers circulating the student questionnaire was that there should be no discussion of the topic beforehand. The following written instructions accompanied each packet of questionnaires.

Dear Colleague,

I would appreciate you presenting this questionnaire in a serious manner, explaining that it is part of some university research. Assure your students that their names will not be required.

Your observations about student reactions will be valuable. Did they get silly and make jokes? Did some of them seem fidgety or anxious about the questions? Did they seem sincere in filling out the forms, or did they make light of it? Any remarks you have will be important input.

Thank you for your assistance in this exploration of current beliefs about vampires and werewolves.

Norine Dresser

Name:
School:
Subject matter taught to participating students:
OBSERVATIONS:

The following questionnaire was circulated to the students. Note that I included questions about werewolves as well, to see if and how students differentiated between these two entities. However, I did not deal with the werewolf data in this book.

1. Do you believe it is possible that vampires exist as real entities? Yes _____ No _____
2. If yes, why? If no, why not?
3. Describe the physical characteristics of a vampire.
4. How are they dressed?
5. How does one become a vampire?
6. Where did they originate?
7. Under what circumstances does a vampire appear?
8. What does a vampire do?
9. How can you protect yourself from a vampire?

10. How do you kill a vampire?
11. Do you believe it is possible that werewolves exist as real entities? Yes _____ No _____
12. If yes, why? If no, why not?
13. Describe the physical characteristics of a werewolf.
14. How are they dressed?
15. How does one become a werewolf?
16. Where did they originate?
17. Under what circumstances does a werewolf appear?
18. What does a werewolf do?
19. How can you protect yourself from a werewolf?
20. How do you kill a werewolf?
21. What is the relationship between werewolves and vampires?
22. How old were you when you first learned about vampires and werewolves?
23. Who told you?
24. Under what circumstances?
25. How old are you?
26. Male _____ Female _____
27. Highest level of education completed?
28. Where were you born? (city/state/country)
29. Where did you grow up? (city/state/country)
30. In what city do you currently reside?
31. Today's date?

III. *Questionnaire for Vampire Fans*

The questionnaire for vampire fans was distributed in several ways. When I first discovered the "Dark Shadows" network, one of the fans offered to share some names and addresses of fellow fans taken from her Rolodex of over 200 entries. We decided to select thirteen names of persons who this fan thought would be interested in answering my questions. The thirteen questionnaires were sent with self-addressed, stamped envelopes included. Through this process I discovered the existence of fanzines and other related vampire publications. After contacting editors, most agreed to reprint my questionnaire in the next issues of their publications. However, the editors of *Parallel Times* requested that I send 300 copies of the questionnaire, which was inserted into their Fall 1986 edition.

Here is the questionnaire which fans answered.

I am conducting research into contemporary beliefs in vampires and vampirism. If you would like to participate in this project, please fill out this form and mail to: Professor Norine Dresser, Department of English, California State University, 5151 State University Drive, Los Angeles, CA 90032. All participants will receive a summary of this survey if name and addresses are included. THANK YOU FOR YOUR PARTICIPATION!

1. Do you believe it is possible that vampires exist as real entities? If yes, why? If no, why not?
2. How old were you when you first learned about vampires?
3. Who told you?
4. Under what circumstances?
5. Where were you residing at the time?
6. What do you believe accounts for the appeal of the vampire? (for both yourself and others)
7. If there are any other observations you would like to make, please do so. You may continue your writing on the reverse side or use additional paper.

Appendix 2
Organizations and
Publications

I. *Porphyria*
   American Porphyria Foundation
   Desiree Dodson, Executive Director
   P.O. Box 11163
   Montgomery, AL 36111
   (205)265-2200
Publishes a quarterly newsletter of information for patients.

II. *"Dark Shadows," Count Dracula, and Vampires*
   (Note: The following organizations require a self-
   addressed, stamped envelope for responses to inquiries.)

   The Bram Stoker Club of the Philosophical Society, Trinity
      College, Dublin
   Joseph Smith, Chairman and Treasurer
   Bram Stoker Club, Philosophical Society
   Graduates Memorial Building
   Trinity College
   Dublin 2, Ireland

$10 annual membership, newsletter. Plans to start a *Bram Stoker Journal*.

Collinsport Call
Jeffrey Arsenault, Editor
P.O. Box 252—Prince Station
New York, NY 10021
A "Dark Shadows" newsletter, $2 per issue, published irregularly.

The Collinsport Record (formerly *Inside Dark Shadows*)
Sharida Rizzuto, Editor
P.O. Box 213
Metrairie, LA 70004
A full-size "Dark Shadows" fanzine. $15 per year or $5 per sample copy.

The Collinwood Journal
Sharida Rizzuto, Editor
P.O. Box 213
Metrairie, LA 70004
A "Dark Shadows" newsletter published three times a year. $15 per year or $5 per sample copy.

Count Dracula Fan Club Newsletter
Dr. Jeanne Youngson, President
29 Washington Square West—Penthouse North
New York, NY 10011
$50 annual membership includes newsletter, news-journals, special bulletins, and Drakpak.

Count Dracula Society
Dr. Donald A. Reed, National President
334 West 54th St.
Los Angeles, CA 90037
(213)752-5811

Honorary membership, $10; Regular Member, $20; Leader Member, $50.

Count Ken Fan Club Newsletter
Publication of the Count Ken Fan Club
Ken Gilbert, President
18 Palmer Street
Salem, MA 01970
Annual membership $2.50 provides monthly newsletter, membership card, and pencil.

The Friends of Dark Shadows
Sharida Rizzuto, Editor
P.O. Box 213
Metrairie, LA 70004
Quarterly newsletter, $15 per year.

Houston Dark Shadows Society
A. P. Riggs
303 Bremond
Houston, TX 77006
$7.50 annual membership provides a T-shirt with the society's logo, a subscription to quarterly newsletter, *Lone Star Shadows,* photograph of Collinwood, laminated Barnabas bookmark, monthly meetings to watch old episodes and conduct writing campaigns for continued syndication.

Inside the Old House
Dale Clark, Editor
11518 Desdemona Drive
Dallas, TX 75228
"Dark Shadows" fan fiction, artwork, poetry, interviews. $3 per 60-page issue.

Journal of Vampirism
Quarterly newsletter of The Vampire Studies Society
Martin V. Riccardo, Editor and Publisher
Organization and publication no longer in existence.

Journal of Vampirology
John L. Vellutini, Supervising Editor
P.O. Box 881631
San Francisco, CA 94188
$10 for five issues. Specializes in vampirism and hemophilism.

The Monocle
Mark Hardy, Editor
392 NW Astoria Ave.
Port Charlotte, FL 33952
$1 per issue, published irregularly. A "Dark Shadows" news-
letter.

Order of the Vampyre
Lilith Aquino, Co-Grand Master
P.O. Box 4507
St. Louis, MO 63108

Robertt W. Neilly, Co-Grand Master
P. O. Box 7137, Station A
Toronto, Ontario MSW IX8, Canada
This is a closed organization open only to members of the
Temple of Set, headed by Michael A. Aquino, Ph.D., who can
be reached at the above St. Louis address. The Order of the
Vampyre produces two newsletters, *The Vampyre Papers* and
Nightwing, available only to members.

Parallel Times
Publication of Alternate Shadows
Patrick L. Garrison, Executive Editor and Publisher

Josette E. Garrison, Editor
P.O. Box 507
Ithaca, NY 14851
$3 per issue, minimum membership of two issues at $6.50.
Four-issue membership available for $12.

Shadowgram
Marcy Robin, Editor
P.O. Box 1766
Temple City, CA 91780
$5 for 5 issues.

Transfusion
Newsletter of the Quincey P. Morris Dracula Society
Charlotte Simsen, Chairman
P.O. Box 381
Ocean Gate, NJ 08740
Annual membership $15 for the first year, $5 subsequent years,
includes quarterly newsletter.

Vampire
Publication of a Special Interest Group of American Mensa,
    Ltd.
Terry Cottrell, Editor
5116 Mill Race Circle
Richmond, VA 23234
$4 for 6 issues yearly, $8 foreign, $.50 sample.

Vampire Information Exchange Newsletter
Eric Held, Editor
P.O. Box 328
Brooklyn, NY 11229-0328
$7 per year within the United States, $9 foreign. Six issues per
year.

The Vampire Journal
Publication of Dracula and Company
Thomas Schellenberger, President
Sharida Rizzuto, Editor and Publisher
P. O. Box 994
Metrairie, LA 70004
$15 membership includes quarterly, three newsletters, and membership card. Single copy of *Vampire Journal* is $5.

Vampire Quarterly
Susan M. Garrett, Editor
142 Sunvalley Drive
Toms River, NJ 08753
$2 per issue or $7 per year.

The Vampire's Journal
P. O. Box 5685
Stockton, CA 95205
$6 for four issues a year, cash only.

Vampyre Society
Allen J. Gittens
38 Westcroft, Chippenham, Wilts.
SN140LY England
Write for information regarding overseas membership and newsletter prices.

The World of Dark Shadows
Kathy Resch, Editor
P. O. Box 1766
Temple City, CA 91780
$3 per issue, published irregularlv

Bibliography

Abaya, Hernando J. *The Untold Philippine Story*. Quezon City, Philippines: Malaya Books, 1967.

Ablon, Joan. "Stigmatized Health Conditions." *Social Science and Medicine,* 15B (1981):5–9.

Barber, Paul. *Vampires, Burial, and Death*. New Haven, CT: Yale University Press, 1988.

Beck, Jane C. "The West Indian Supernatural World: Belief Integration in a Pluralistic Society." *Journal of American Folklore,* 88 (July–September 1975):235–244.

Becker, Ernest. *Escape from Evil*. New York: Free Press, 1975.

Bentley, C. F. "The Monster in the Bedroom: Sexual Symbolism in Bram Stoker's *Dracula*." *Literature and Psychology,* 22 (1972): 27–34.

Bernheimer, Martin. "California Ballet Offers 'Dracula' in San Diego." *Los Angeles Times,* November 2, 1987, Part VI, 1, 7.

Bierman, Joseph. "Dracula: Prolonged Childhood Illness and the Oval Triad." *American Imago,* 29 (Summer 1972):186–198.

Bonfanti, Leo. *Strange Beliefs, Customs, & Superstitions of New England*. Wakefield, MA: Pride Publications, 1980.

Chappell, Helen. "Vault-Face." *Guardian* (London), April 21, 1987, 10.

Clifford, George, III. "Human Remains Found." Newport News, Virginia, *Daily Press,* June 25, 1987, A1, 6.

Clifford, George, III. "Vampire Illness Could Provide Clue in Killing." Newport News, Virginia, *Daily Press,* July 7, 1987, B1–2.

Copper, Basil. *The Vampire in Legend, Fact and Art*. Secaucus, NJ: Citadel Press, 1974.

Curtin, Jeremiah. "European Folk-Lore in the U.S." *Journal of American Folklore,* 2 (1889):56–59.

Davis, Wade. *The Serpent and the Rainbow.* New York: Warner Books, 1985.

Day, R. S. "Bloodlust, Madness, Murder and the Press." *New Scientist,* September 13, 1984, 53–54.

Dean, Geoffrey. "The Porphyrias: The Royal Purple?" *Journal of the Royal College of Physicians* (London) (October 1970), 47–61.

Degh, Linda, and Andrew Vazsonyi. "Legend and Belief." *Genre,* 4, No. 3 (1971):281–304.

DeMatteis, J. M. *Greenberg the Vampire.* New York: Marvel Comics Group, 1986.

DeMatteis, J. M., and Kent Williams. *Blood,* 4 vols. New York: Marvel Entertainment Group, 1987.

Dorson, Richard M. *American Folklore.* Chicago: University of Chicago Press, 1959.

Dorson, Richard M. *America in Legend.* New York: Pantheon Books, 1973.

Dow, James R., and Hannjost Lixfeld. *The Nazification of an Academic Discipline: German Volkskunde of the Third Reich.* Bloomington, IN: Indiana University Press, in press.

Dresser, Norine. "Etats-Unis: une Affaire Qui Marche." *Terre Sauvage* (Levallois-Perret, France) (January 1986), 54.

du Bolay, Juliet. "The Greek Vampire: A Study of Cyclic Symbolism in Marriage and Death." *MAN* (Journal of the Royal Anthropological Institute), 17, No. 2 (1982):219–238.

Dujardin, Richard C. "An Unusual Tradition at an Unusual Church." *Providence Journal-Bulletin* (October 9, 1982), A7.

Dukes, Paul. "Dracula: Fact, Legend and Fiction." *History Today,* 32 (July 1982):44–47.

Dundes, Alan, and Carl R. Pagter. *Urban Folklore from the Paper Work Empire.* Publication of the AFS Memoir Series, ed. Hugh Jansen, 62, 1975.

Forrest, Katherine V. "O Captain, My Captain." *Dreams and Swords.* Tallahassee, FL: Naiad Press, Inc., 1987, 107–165.

Fraser, C. A. "Scottish Myths from Ontario." *Journal of American Folklore,* 63 (1893):185–198.

Frazer, Sir James George. *The New Golden Bough.* New York: Anchor, 1959.

Freedland, Nat. *The Occult Explosion.* New York: G. P. Putnam's Sons, 1972.

Freud, Sigmund. *Jokes and Their Relation to the Unconscious*. New York: W. W. Norton, 1960.

Furneaux, Rupert. "The Vampire." Reprint, New York: *Count Dracula Fan Club Newsletter-Journal*, 1984; originally appeared in *Legend and Reality*, London: Allan Wingate, Ltd., 1959.

Gillette, Robert. "Dracula—Can't Kill a Good Myth." *Los Angeles Times*, October 31, 1985, Sec. 1, 1, 20.

Glut, Donald F. *The Dracula Book*. Metuchen, NJ: Scarecrow Press, 1975.

Goffman, Erving. *Stigma*. Englewood Cliffs, NJ: Prentice-Hall, 1963.

Greeley, Andrew M. *The Sociology of the Paranormal: A Reconnaissance*. Sage Research Papers in the Social Sciences, Vol. 3, Series 90-023 (Studies in Religion and Ethnicity). Beverly Hills: Sage Publications, 1975.

Greene, Bob. "A Red-Blooded American Girl." *Esquire* (May 1981), 22–23.

Griffin, Gail B. " 'Your Girls that You All Love Are Mine': *Dracula* and the Victorian Male Sexual Imagination." *International Journal of Women's Studies*, 3, No. 5 (1980):454–465.

Havron, M. Dean, Martin Sternin, and Robert J. Teare. *The Use of Cultural Data in Psychological Operations Programs in Vietnam*. Arlington, VA: Advanced Research Projects Agency, 1968.

Hawes, Bess Lomax. "La Llorona in Juvenile Hall." *Western Folklore*, 27 (1968):153–170.

Hawkins, Colin, and Jacqui Hawkins. *Vampires*. Morristown, NY: Silver Burdett, 1982.

Hawthorne, Nathaniel. "Young Goodman Brown." *The Complete Writings of Nathaniel Hawthorne*, Vol. 4. Boston: Riverside Press, 1900, 102–124.

Henderson, D. James. "Exorcism, Possession, and the Dracula Cult." *Bulletin of the Menninger Clinic*, 40, No. 6 (November 1976):603–628.

Hoyt, Olga. *Lust for Blood*. New York: Stein and Day, 1984.

Hudson, Arthur Palmer, and Peter Kyle McCarter. "The Bell Witch of Tennessee and Mississippi: A Folk Legend." *Journal of American Folklore*, 47 (1934):45–63.

Hufford, David J. "Ambiguity and the Rhetoric of Belief." *Keystone Folklore Quarterly*, 21 (1976):11–24.

Hufford, David J. *The Terror that Comes in the Night*. Philadelphia: University of Pennsylvania Press, 1982.

Illis, L. "On Porphyria and the Aetiology of Werewolves." *Proceedings of the Royal Society of Medicine,* 57 (January 1964):23–26.

Japenga, Ann. "Vampire Theory Haunts Porphyria Victims." *Los Angeles Times,* August 25, 1985, Sec. VI, 1, 23.

Johnson, R. W. "The Myth of the Twentieth Century," *New Society* (December 9, 1982), 432–433.

Jones, Ernest M. *On the Nightmare.* London: Hogarth Press, 1931; reprint, New York: Liveright Publishing Corporation, 1951.

Jones, Halford E. *Vampirism in the Philippines: A Brief Description and Survey.* New York: Count Dracula Fan Club Research Division, 1985.

Kamenetsky, Christa. "Folktale and Ideology in the Third Reich." *Journal of American Folklore,* 90 (April–June 1977):168–178.

Karp, Walter. "Dracula Returns." *Horizon,* 18 (Autumn 1976):40–41.

Kayton, Lawrence. "The Relation of the Vampire Legend to Schizophrenia." *Journal of Youth and Adolescence,* 1 (1972):303–314.

Kerr, Howard, and Charles L. Crow, eds. *The Occult in America: New Historical Perspectives.* Urbana and Chicago: University of Illnois Press, 1983.

Kinder, Nancy. "The 'Vampires' of Rhode Island." *Yankee* (October 1970), 114–115, 166–167.

King, Stephen. *Danse Macabre.* New York: Everest House, 1981.

Kirtley, Bacil F. "La Llorona and Related Themes." *Western Folklore,* 19 (1960):155–168.

Kittredge, George Lyman. *Witchcraft in Old and New England.* Cambridge, MA: Harvard University Press, 1929.

Laiwah, Albert, A. C. Yeung, George G. Thompson, Mary F. Philip, Martin J. Brodie, W. Garth Rapeport, Graeme J. A. Macphee, Michael R. Moore, and Abraham Goldberg. "Carbamazepine-Induced Non-Hereditary Acute Porphyria." *Lancet* (April 9, 1983), 790–792.

Lally, Kelly A. "Living on the Edge: The Folklife of Air Force Pilots in Training." *Midwestern Folklore,* 13, No. 2 (Fall 1987):107–120.

Lansdale, Edward Geary. *In the Midst of Wars.* New York: Harper and Row, 1972.

LaVey, Anton Szandor. *The Satanic Bible.* New York: Avon, 1969.

Lennig, Arthur. *The Count.* New York: G. P. Putnam's Sons, 1974.

Lévi-Strauss, Claude. *From Honey to Ashes: Introduction to a Science of Mythology,* Vol. 2. Trans. John Weightman and Doreen Weightman. New York: Harper and Row, 1973.

Levin, David. *What Happened in Salem,* 2nd ed. New York: Harcourt, Brace and World, 1960.

Linn, Jennifer. " 'Vampire' Fails to Make Appearance." Panama City, Florida, *News Herald,* March 1, 1988, 1C.

Linn, Jennifer, and Mike Cazalas. "Vampire Rumors Unsettle School." Panama City, Florida, *News Herald,* February 27, 1988, 1B–2B.

Macalpine, Ida, and Richard Hunter. "A Clinical Reassessment of the 'Insanity' of George III and Some of Its Historical Implications." *Institute of Historical Research Bulletin* (University of London), 40 (1967):166–185.

Macalpine, Ida, and Richard Hunter. *George III and the Mad-Business.* New York: Pantheon Books, 1969.

Marchetti, Victor, and John D. Marks. *The CIA and the Cult of Intelligence.* New York: Laurel, 1980.

Marmorstein, Jerome. "Vampires, Werewolves, and Porphyria: Confronting Media Irresponsibility." *Medical Tribune,* 25 (September 1985):45.

Masters, Anthony. *The Natural History of the Vampire.* New York: G. P. Putnam's Sons, 1972.

Mather, Cotton. *The Wonders of the Invisible World.* Boston, 1692. Reprint, Mt. Vernon, NY: Library of the Fantastic and Curious, 1950.

Mayer, Caroline E. "Necklace Chokes Count Chocula." *Los Angeles Times,* October 19, 1987, Part IV, 1, 4.

McCully, Robert S. "Vampirism: Historical Perspective and Underlying Process in Relation to a Case of Auto-Vampirism." *Journal of Nervous and Mental Disease,* 139, No. 5 (November 1964): 440–452.

McNally, Raymond T. *A Clutch of Vampires.* Greenwich, CT: New York Graphic Society, 1974.

McNally, Raymond T. *Dracula Was a Woman.* New York: McGraw-Hill, 1983.

McNally, Raymond, and Radu Florescu. *In Search of Dracula: A True History of Dracula and Vampire Legends.* Greenwich, CT: New York Graphic Society, 1972.

Mehan, Hugh, and Houston Wood. *The Reality of Ethnomethodology.* New York: John Wiley and Sons, 1975.

Mitchell, Lisa. "I Remember Bela." *New West,* 7 (June 1976):76, 78–79.

Muhlbauer, Jan, Madhu A. Pathak, Peter V. Tishler, and Thomas B. Fitzpatrick. "Variegate Porphyria in New England." *Journal of the American Medical Association,* 247, No. 22 (June 11, 1982):3095–3102.

Newell, Venetia, ed. *The Witch Figure.* London and Boston: Routledge and Kegan Paul, 1973.

Nurmi, Maila. "The One—The Only Vampira." *Fangoria,* 30 (October 1983):26–29.

Offiong, Daniel. "Witchcraft Among the Ibibio of Nigeria." *African Studies Review,* 26 (1983):107–174.

Oinas, Felix. "East European Vampires and Dracula." *Journal of Popular Culture,* 16 (1982):108–116.

Owen, Mary Alicia. *Voodoo Tales.* New York: G. P. Putnam's Sons, 1893; reprint, Freeport, NY: Books for Libraries Press, 1971, pp. 209–213.

P., S. M. "Voodooism in Tennessee." *Atlantic Monthly,* 64 (1889):376–380.

Parrinder, Geoffrey. *West African Psychology.* London: Lutterworth Press, 1951.

Perkowski, Jan L. *Vampires of the Slavs.* Cambridge, MA: Slavica Publishers, Inc., 1976.

Peters, Henry A., Ayhan Gocmen, Derek J. Cripps, George T. Bryan, and Ihsan Dogramaci. "Epidemiology of Hexachlorobenzene-Induced Porphyria in Turkey." *Archives of Neurology,* 39 (December 1982):744–749.

Pfander, Margret. "AIDS-Wary Vampires Pull in Their Fangs!" *Weekly World News,* 8, No. 31 (May 12, 1987):29.

Pirie, David. *The Vampire Cinema.* Leicester, England: Galley Press, 1977.

Pomeroy, William J. *An American Made Tragedy: Neo-Colonialism and Dictatorship in the Philippines.* New York: International Publishers Co., 1974.

Porphyria and You. Pretoria, Republic of South Africa: Genetic Services Department of Health and Welfare.

Potts, Charles S. "An Account of the Witch Craze in Salem, with Reference to Some Modern Witch Crazes." *Archives of Neurology and Psychiatry,* 3, No. 5 (May 1920):465–484.

Price, Jonathan. *The Best Thing on TV: Commercials.* New York: Penguin Books, 1978.

Prins, Herschel. "Vampirism—Legendary or Clinical Phenomenon?" *Medicine, Science, Law,* 24, No. 4 (1984):283–293.

Riccardo, Martin V. *Vampires Unearthed: The Complete Multi-Media Vampire and Dracula Bibliography.* New York and London: Garland Publishing Co., 1983.

Ronay, Gabriel. *The Truth about Dracula.* New York: St. Martin's Press, 1972.

Roth, Phyllis A. *Bram Stoker.* Twayne's English Authors Series (TEAS). Boston: Twayne Publishing Co., 1982.

Roth, Phyllis A. "Suddenly Sexual Women in Bram Stoker's *Dracula*." *Literature and Psychology,* 27 (1977):113–121.

Ryono, Susan. *Wilma's Word Problems: Basic Addition and Subtraction.* Los Angeles: Frank Schaffer Publications, 1977.

Senn, Harry A. *The Werewolf and Vampire in Romania.* Boulder, CO: East European Monographs, Columbia University Press, 1982.

Shanley, Brian C. Letter. *Lancet,* May 28, 1983, 1229–1230.

Shawgo, Ron, "Mutilation Death Defendant Guilty." Newport News, Virginia, *Daily Press,* January 7, 1988, A1, 4.

Sheehan, Neil, Hedrick Smith, E. W. Kenworthy, and Fox Butterfield. *The Pentagon Papers.* New York: Bantam, 1971.

Shibutani, Tamotsu. *Improvised News.* Indianapolis: The Bobbs-Merrill Co., 1966.

Shuttle, Penelope, and Peter Redgrove. *The Wise Wound: Eve's Curse and Everywoman.* New York: Richard Marek Publishers, 1978.

Simsen, Charlotte. "In Pursuit of Dracula." *Coast* (October 1986), 20, 22, 25.

Skinner, Charles M. *Myths and Legends of Our Own Land.* Philadelphia and London: J. B. Lippincott Co., 1896; reprint, Detroit: Singing Tree Press Book Tower, 1969.

Sleeves, Fred. "Gay Vampire Catches AIDS." *Sun,* 5, No. 7 (February 1987):7.

Stetson, George R. "The Animistic Vampire in New England." *American Anthropologist,* 9 (1896):1–13.

Stevenson, John Allen. "A Vampire in the Mirror: The Sexuality of *Dracula*." *Publications of the Modern Language Association,* 103, No. 2 (March 1988):139–149.

Stoker, Bram. *Dracula.* New York: New American Library, 1965.

Summers, Montague. *The Vampire: His Kith and Kin.* London: Routledge and Kegan Paul, 1928.

Summers, Montague. *The Vampire in Europe.* London: Routledge and Kegan Paul, 1929; reprint, New Hyde Park, NY: University Books, 1962.

Summers, Montague. *The Werewolf.* New York: University Books, 1966.

Thomas, Keith. *Religion and the Decline of Magic.* New York: Charles Scribner's Sons, 1971.

Toor, Frances. *A Treasury of Mexican Folkways.* New York: Crown, 1947.

Trachtenberg, Joshua. *Jewish Magic and Superstition.* Cleveland and New York: World Publishing Co., 1961.

Trigg, Elwood B. *Gypsy Demons and Divinities: The Magic and Religion of the Gypsies.* Secaucus, New Jersey: Citadel Press, 1973.

Twitchell, James B. *The Living Dead*. Durham, NC: Duke University Press, 1981.

Twitchell, James B. "The Vampire Myth." *American Imago*, 37 (Spring 1980):83–92.

Underwood, Tim, and Chuck Miller. *Fear Itself: The Horror Fiction of Stephen King*. New York: New American Library, 1982.

Urma, Viorel. "Guests Count on Thrills at Hotel Dracula." *Los Angeles Times*, December 20, 1985, Part 8, 7.

Vanden Bergh, Richard L., and John F. Kelly. "Vampirism." *Archives of General Psychiatry*, 11, Part 5 (1964):543–547.

Vellutini, John. "The Epidemiology of Human Vampirism: Porphyria." *Journal of Vampirology*, 2, No. 3 (1985):2–14.

Wedeck, Harry E. *A Treasury of Witchcraft*. New York: Citadel Press, 1966.

Whittinger, John, and Bill Wallace. "Army Says Constitution Lets Satanist Hold Top-Secret Job." *San Francisco Chronicle*, November 3, 1987, A7.

Winkler, Louis, and Carol Winkler. "A Reappraisal of the Vampire." *New York Folklore Quarterly*, 29, No. 3 (September 1973):194–205.

With, Torben K. "A Short History of Porphyrins and the Porphyrias." *International Journal of Biochemistry*, 11 (1980):189–200.

Wolf, Leonard. *A Dream of Dracula*. Boston: Little, Brown and Co., 1972.

Woodward, Ian. *The Werewolf Delusion*. New York and London: Paddington Press, Ltd., 1979.

Wright, Dudley. *Vampires and Vampirism*. New York: Gordon Press, 1973.

X, Madeline. *How to Become a Vampire in Six Easy Lessons*. Chicago: Adams Press, 1985.

Youngson, Jeanne. *The Count Dracula Chicken Cookbook*. New York: Count Dracula Fan Club Limited Edition, 1979.

Index